We Are Catholic

We Are Catholic

Catholic, Catholicity, and Catholicization

Jason Valeriano Hallig

WIPF & STOCK · Eugene, Oregon

WE ARE CATHOLIC
Catholic, Catholicity, and Catholicization

Copyright © 2016 Jason Valeriano Hallig. All rights reserved. Except for brief quotations in critical publications or reviews, no part of this book may be reproduced in any manner without prior written permission from the publisher. Write: Permissions, Wipf and Stock Publishers, 199 W. 8th Ave., Suite 3, Eugene, OR 97401.

Wipf & Stock
An Imprint of Wipf and Stock Publishers
199 W. 8th Ave., Suite 3
Eugene, OR 97401

www.wipfandstock.com

PAPERBACK ISBN: 978-1-4982-8943-6
HARDCOVER ISBN: 978-1-4982-8945-0

Manufactured in the U.S.A.

This book is dedicated
to my wife, Milagros F. Hallig,
to my children, Christine Jason and David Jason,
and
to Drs. Tereso Casino and Cecille Casino,
who demonstrated to me and my family the catholic spirit

Contents

Preface | ix
Abbreviations | xiv

1. Introduction | 1
2. The Catholic Story | 8
3. The Catholic Root | 35
4. The Catholic Faith/Tradition | 57
5. The Catholic Church | 86
6. The Catholic Challenge | 110
7. The Catholic Life and Witness | 128
8. Conclusion | 154

Bibliography | 169

Preface

IN THE CREEDS PRINTED in the hymnal of an evangelical church, the word "catholic" has been intentionally replaced by the word "universal": In the Apostles' Creed it states, "I believe in the Holy Spirit, the holy Church *universal* . . .," and in the Nicene Creed it states, "And I believe in one holy *universal* and apostolic church . . ." I assume that other evangelical churches and evangelical theologians do the same. Understandably, evangelicals do not want to be associated with or mistakenly be identified with a church that bears the name "Catholic." Are the two words—catholic and universal—one and the same? Perhaps in their denotative sense the words carry the same meaning; hence, they can be used interchangeably. However, the word "catholic" is not only a lexical word; it is also a theological word that defines the church of Jesus Christ. The word "catholic" has its theological connotative meaning which the word "universal" does not. While evangelical churches have not rejected this significant historical doctrine of the catholicity of the church (God forbid!), sadly evangelicals have given it a meager attention and an anemic theological discussion, if not with little suspicion, in relation to protestant ecclesiology. Apparently, the subject needs revitalization for evangelicals to recapture the word "catholic" and to appreciate the catholicity of the church. This book is written to help evangelical churches understand the historical, biblical, and theological significance of the word "catholic." I believe that the word "catholic" defines "who we are" and "what we are" as members of the church of Jesus Christ. A proper and fuller understanding of the word "catholic" can help evangelical churches understand the wider and greater body of Christ, and consequently begin to work together knowing the inherent relationship (unity) we have as members of the church of Jesus Christ.

PREFACE

On the other hand, I also want to engage in an informative dialogue with churches that call themselves "Catholic." I have tried as much as I could to be inclusive in my use of the word, but of course, in the context of the Holy Scriptures and the historical and apostolic Christian faith. I know that in such dialogue these perimeters are not objective, but they are neither subjective. Perhaps they are common grounds for all churches that claim to have the same root and relationship with Jesus Christ. It is good to know that the word "catholic" was recognized prior to the divisions—the Eastern Orthodox and the Reformation—within the Christian church. In other words, "catholic" defines the church of Jesus Christ, not a particular church after the divisions. Catholicity is not intended to exclude others in the family and in the faith. In fact, to think of the word "catholic" in an exclusive term is a contradictory in itself. To be catholic is to be inclusive— Jews and Gentiles, Greeks and Romans, male and female, colored and white (I use them for lack of words, I apologize for the use of these politically incorrect descriptions of men and women), rich and poor, and many other labels we place on ourselves.

We Are Catholic is a confession of the church of Jesus Christ vis-à-vis who we are and what we are. Churches will do well to remember that Jesus did not establish a sect within Judaism; neither did he recognize Judaism as the church of God nor instituted a religious organization that would replace Judaism. This confession is a confession of the disciples of Jesus of all nations in the context of the church as the body of Christ—united with Christ and with one another. Moreover, the confession is a missional confession—a commitment to the gospel of Jesus Christ and its proclamation to the world in and through our united witness for Christ.

At the outset, I want to express my gratitude to my family—my parents, to my father who has already gone with the Lord, Juan G. Hallig for his exemplary faith in God and love of the Scriptures; my mother Violeta V. Hallig for her prayers that I would come to know Christ when I was young and her still persistent prayers for me, my family and my ministry; my wife, Milagros F. Hallig, who constantly supported me with her encouragement and understanding believing that God has given me something that I need to share to others so as to be responsible steward; and, my children, Christine Jason and David Jason, who also serve as inspiration in my writing and for teaching me how to be a good father and a loving member of our school of relationship called "home." I also want to appreciate my other siblings who journeyed with me in life and for whom I have set my life as

Preface

an example so they would have something to follow. These are the first men and women in the family of faith who have shaped my understanding of the church in terms of relationships and responsibilities. I have first learnt what it means for me to be "catholic" with them; they have all unselfishly given me the opportunity to be a faithful catholic Christian—loving Christ and my neighbors.

I am also grateful to the International Christian Fellowship Church of the Nazarene (ICF-CON) and other fellowships related to it for the privilege of faith, fellowship, and service. I value the importance of this congregation in my life as a member of the catholic church. I am in a formal sense catholic because of this congregation where I am presently a member as a disciple of Jesus Christ. I thank all of you for letting me journey with you in life and in faith. You have made me strong with your love, prayers, and commitment to serve the Lord together in our own Jerusalem, Judea, and Samaria, and to the ends of the earth. We are not just a congregation, we are a catholic congregation.

I appreciate Philippine International College (PIC) family, my colleagues and co-workers in the Lord for giving me a place of service in preparing young men and women for catholic ministries in the global community. Thanks to Dr. Kwon, Young-han and his wife, Lee, Young-Ok, Rev. Israel Peran, colleagues, faculty and staff, friends and students. You have set yourselves as an academic catholic community for me and the many constituents under our care. The confidence and the trust you have given me have served as inspiration in the process of my writing. Thanks also to my colleagues and students at PIC—Graduate School. Our discussions and dialogues have helped shape some of my thoughts on this book. Thank you for letting me read the first drafts with you.

I also want to thank my personal friends who contributed in one way or another to the writing of this book—to Rev. Arnel L. Piliin, for his friendship and his humble leadership in the Metro Manila District Church of the Nazarene; to all pastors and workers in the district; to Prof. Larnie Sam Tabuena for discussions and dialogues on theology and philosophy in the context of both the church and the society; to missionaries—Dr. Clark Armstrong, Dr. Grant Zweigle, Dr. Mitch Modine, Dr. Darin Land, and others who dialogued with me and read portions of this book and gave their helpful comments; to my former professors—Dr. Dean Flemming, who was my New Testament professor and mentor at AGST, Dr. Roderick Leupp, my theology professor and whose quiet spirit has deepened my

Preface

spiritual journey and whose books have inspired me and broadened my faith in the triune God, and others who had invested in my educational preparation as a minister in the Church of God. My first pastor, Rev. Irvin Recerra, former missionaries, Rev. Peter Burkhart and Mrs. Cheryl McMahan all deserve a special thank for being the servants whom God used to nurture my faith as a disciple believing that God would one day use me in his catholic mission.

To ACTS International Graduate School (AIGS) for giving me the opportunity to further my ministerial preparation through the scholarship I had received. I personally thank my mentors—Dr. Hur, Ju; Kang, Chang-Hee; Chang, Hae-Kyoung; and Won, Jung-Chun. I also want to thank my mission professor Dr. Peter Beyerhaus of Tubingen University for his contribution to my knowledge of the Ecumenical Movement and the issues related to the movement. I never thought that I would be given the opportunity to use the insights I have gained from the many discussions we had in class regarding the issues confronting the movement in particular and the evangelical churches in general.

To Presbyterian churches—Myungsong Church that supported my study at AIGS, Elim Church that gave me the opportunity to serve Filipinos in Korea, Wun-Ju Jael Church that allowed me to minister to the young people in the church, and many other Presbyterian churches that almost adopted me as one of their own. To All Asian Bible and Music College (AABMC) of the Presbyterian Church in the Philippines—thanks to Rev. Koh, Kyoung-jin, faculty and staff, and my many students since I began teaching in 1994. To Yejung Church under the leadership of Rev. Sul, Tong-Ok and Hanbi Mission under Rev. Hwang, Pedro for their generosity in our ministry at Hinirang.

To Asia Graduate School of Theology (AGST) and Asia Theological Association (ATA) through the able leadership of Dr. Teresa Lua, who had given me the opportunity to further expand my thoughts through papers for Asia and the world. In fact, this book was conceived at a conference ATA sponsored in Korea in 2014. It was during an informal conversation during the conference when the need for something that would help our various cultures experience freedom from various discriminations that I began to think along the line of how the church can serve Asia and the world.

Special thanks to Drs. Tereso and Cecille Casino for the support you had given me and my family when I studied in Korea. I appreciate your confidence, investments, and the friendship you extended to us. Your catholic

Preface

spirit has inspired so many young people and pastors whom you have given a place in your heart. Thanks for the testimonies you have shared with us during your travels around the world strengthening the catholic church. Both of you truly possess the catholic spirit. For everything you have done, we are forever grateful. This book is dedicated to you and your kids for the lives you have unselfishly given to the catholic church.

Special mention to friends and families whose supports toward the completion of this project cannot be ignored: Col. Richard V. Steele and family, Rev. Rick Valdeabella, Rev. Ricardo Umayam, Mr. Jijie Mapatac, Ptr. Jun Macas, Missionary Choi, Duck-Il. Rev. R. F. Gandia, Mr. Andy Cubalit, Ms. Anelia Bugaay, Dr. Perla Sunga Intia, and several others who have contributed in one way or another to the project through their generosity.

Above all I want to give all the glory, honor, and praise to God my Savior and my Lord!

Abbreviations

ATA	*Asia Theological Association*
AIGS	*Asian Center for Theological Studies and Mission International Graduate School*
BDAG	*A Greek-English Lexicon of the New Testament and Other Early Christian Literature.* Revised and edited by Frederick William Danker. Chicago and London: The University of Chicago Press, 2000.
BDT	*Baker's Dictionary of Theology.* Edited by Everett F. Harrison. Grand Rapids, Michigan: Baker, 1960.
BSac	*Bibliotheca Sacra*
CD	*Church Dogmatics.* Karl Barth. Edited by G. W. Bromiley and T. F. Torrance. Peabody, Massachusetts: Hendrickson, 2010.
CTC	Critical Theological Commentary
DLNTD	*Dictionary of the Later New Testament and Its Development.* Edited by Ralph P. Martin and Peter H. Davids. Downers Grove, Illinois: InterVarsity, 1992.
DJG	*Dictionary of Jesus and the Gospels.* Edited by Joel B. Green and Scot McKnight. Downers Grove, Illinois: InterVarsity, 1992.
EDNT	*Exegetical Dictionary of the New Testament.* Edited by Horst Balz and Gerhard Schneider. Grand Rapids, Michigan: William B. Eerdmans, 1990.

Abbreviations

EDWM	*Evangelical Dictionary of World Missions.* Edited by A. Scott Moreau. Grand Rapids, Michigan: Baker, 2000.
EvQ	*Evangelical Quarterly*
Ign. Smyrn.	Ignatius, *Ad Smyrna*
ICC	International Critical Commentary
JAET	*Journal of Asian Evangelical Theology*
JAM	*Journal for Asian Mission*
Just Dial.	Justin, *Dialogue*
NICNT	New International Commentary on the New Testament
NIV	*New International Version*
NT	*New Testament*
TNTC	Tyndale New Testament Commentaries
ThT	*Theology Today*
ThI	*Theological Investigation*
OT	*Old Testament*
RSV	*Revised Standard Version*
Works	*Works of John Wesley.* John Wesley. 3rd ed. 14 vols. London: Wesleyan Methodist Book Room, 1872. Reprint, Kansas City: Beacon Hill, 1978.

1

Introduction

Catholic, Catholicity, and Catholicization

As Jesus was walking beside the Sea of Galilee, he saw two brothers, Simon called Peter and his brother Andrew. They were casting a net into the lake, for they were fishermen. "Come follow me," Jesus said, "and I will make you fishers of men." At once they left their nets and followed him. (Matt 4:18-20). Right at the outset of his ministry, Jesus began working on his mission that involved the calling of his disciples. This indicates mission necessity not only because the disciples form an essential element in many aspects of Jesus's ministry to be described in the following chapters of the book of Matthew,[1] but also because of the role the disciples of Jesus would later have in the proclamation of the kingdom of God, which Jesus inaugurated in and through his life and ministry. By the call, Christ demonstrated what the disciples would later do in their own ministries and missions to the world—the calling and making of disciples. Brunner points this when he writes,

> Jesus did not just come, teach here and there, work miracles, die, and then rise. He came and *made disciples*. Jesus' discipling work is important to Matthew's understanding of the gospel. Consequently, right after focusing on Jesus' own presence in his Word, Matthew turns our attention to Jesus' use of his Word in calling the disciples to share his ministry.[2]

1. France, *Gospel*, 103.
2. Bruner, *Matthew*, 142.

He adds,

> In Matthew's Gospel one of Jesus' important services is to create a ministry of workers by which to shape his church to engage the world. Through Jesus' way of making ministers and Christian workers *then* we can learn how to make ministers and Christian workers *now*.[3]

Christ already had the church in sight, and it was the call of the disciples that gave impetus to the life and mission of the church as catholic. The call was not just personal but also missional. They were called not only to follow him, that is, for them to be his disciples, but they were also called to make disciples, that is, to invite others into the kingdom of God. The mission of the disciples would not only be about their own personal salvation or their own walk with Jesus, but it would involve the redemption of the world, a whole course for humanity, for whom Jesus would give himself as a ransom. By calling the disciples and giving them the responsibility of making disciples, Christ has literally given the world in the hands of his disciples—a handful of unlearned men whom he had chosen and yet on their shoulders was placed the most holy but heavy task of making disciples of all nations. And as disciples of Jesus Christ, they carried, on the one hand, the weight of making the world submit to the universal lordship of Jesus Christ; and on the other hand, they had the burden of establishing the universal kingdom of God here on earth as it is heaven. What a privilege; what a task as well. The nature of the call reveals the catholic life and mission of the church—from Christ to the world. Catholicity defines the church—who we are and what we are—we are catholic. This should give us enough reason to consider the subject under consideration and to embrace our identity as "catholic." To understand this catholic calling of the church, our discussion will focus on the three aspects of the call—catholic, catholicity, and catholicization.

Catholic

Jesus's words to his first disciples in Matthew 4:18–20 unravel the twofold call of discipleship—becoming disciples ("Come, follow me,") and making disciples ("and I will make you fishers of men") of all nations, and they indeed define the catholic life of the church. The church is not

---

3. Ibid.

Introduction

about individuals or small groups or even organizations or denominations; it involves them, yes, but the church is greater than they are. Collectively, the church is a community of disciples. What word could better describe the life and mission of the church of Jesus Christ as a collective community of disciples than catholic? Was Ignatius naïve in using the word "catholic" with reference to the church? Or did he prophetically and theologically capture the life and mission of the church as catholic? By associating the word "catholic" with the church, Ignatius gave the church a gift of its identity—a naming of the church, that rightly captures the nature and function of the growing disciples of Jesus Christ in the context of their participation as a community of disciples in God's redemptive plan for the world. Hence, the church is fittingly identified as a catholic community with a call that is likewise catholic. This book is intended to help us understand the catholicity of the church as disciples of Jesus Christ, and by understanding that "we are catholic," we begin to live our lives and fulfill our calling as truly catholic. It is only in and through its catholicity that the church would fulfill its calling as Christ's disciples and fulfill Christ's commission to make disciples of all nations. As such in relation to the church, catholicity, and discipleship are inseparable; one defines the other. The failure of catholicity is a failure of the church; and the failure of the church would mean a tragedy for the world.

In chapters 2 and 3, we will give attention to the historical and biblical understanding of the church as catholic. The church as catholic makes it a unique community—a catholic community. The church is the recipient of God's revelation in history and also the one responsible for the task of its proclamation. As such the catholic identity of the church is a result of its dynamic relationship not only with the Word but also with the world. For this reason, the church cannot be defined on its own apart from its relations. The church is a communion of relationships—a relationship with God, a relationship with the world, and also a relationship within itself. These relationships that define the church are never static but ever dynamic. The relationship of the church with God, on the one hand, is an ever growing relationship. It is a relationship that is grounded on the Word of God. The church as catholic identifies itself with the Word of God: from the promise given to Abraham to its fulfillment in Christ. This is what Ignatius recognized when he said, "Where Jesus Christ is, there is the catholic church." In Christ, the church is truly catholic *a priori*. Chapter 2 traces this relationship of the church with Christ from its early beginning in the life of the early church to its world-wide growth today. The development of the identity of the church as catholic has dynamically grown with the history of the church from the incipient catholic of the early church to other forms of catholic that represented different epochs or vicissitudes in the life and history of the church. The vicissitudes in the history of the catholic church have shown not only the development of the identity of the church as catholic but also the distortions and deviations that had challenged and strengthened the catholic church toward growth and maturity.

On the other hand, the "catholic" concept is a pregnant word not only for its relationship with God but also for its relationship with the world. The church is from the world and is called to serve the world. Hence, it is an inclusive community that invites and welcomes all nations into its unique fellowship. This is seen clearly in the call of Abraham in the Old Testament and its fulfillment in Christ—where in him there is no east or west, south or north, male or female (*cf.* Gal 3:28). Christ fulfilled the promise that was given to Abraham, and the promise came to being in the life and mission of the church as Christ's witness to the world so that the church might become the world in relation to God. God's love for the world is fulfilled in his relationship with the church. The world is redeemed by Christ in and through the church. This is the reason why the church cannot be identified with any nations, like what happened to Israel when it became like the nations with an identity of its own. Sadly, in its history, the church was again tempted to become a nation with structure that identified itself with the Roman Empire. Hence, the Reformation and Revivals in the church of Jesus Christ happened. Chapter 3 focuses on the biblical roots of the catholic church. The church as catholic had its beginning not during the church fathers, but as early as the history of Israel in the Old Testament and its fulfillment in the New Testament. The biblical church from its very beginning was catholic; Israel was supposed to be catholic—a chosen people, a light to the nations. Christ fulfilled the calling of Israel and he called and commissioned his disciples to be the catholic church.

Catholicity

The word "catholic" deals with the identity of the church in the context of its relations and mission; catholicity on the other hand deals with the theological tradition/traditions and marks of the catholic church. It is the living theological legacy of the church of Jesus Christ delivered and passed on from one generation to the next. A church is identified as catholic by its confessions (traditions) and commitments (marks). In and through the history of the church, the confessions and commitments of the church have grown and have become more mature in their expressions. Theological development of the traditions, however, does not mean deviations or cutting off from the biblical theological roots. The Reformation, for example, happened to stop deviations and distortions of the scriptural tradition of the church. Catholicity, however, is a dynamic historical and theological task of the church that gives contemporary and contextual expressions to the scriptural tradition. Hence, catholicity is both tradition (noun) and "traditioning" (verb). This places catholicity within the other three marks of the church—holiness, apostolicity, and unity.

In chapters 4 and 5, we will give consideration to the historical and theological development of the tradition/traditions and marks of the catholic church. The theological tradition of the church is rooted in God's redemptive work in Christ revealed in the Holy Scriptures. By this the catholic tradition is not of human origin; it is given in and through divine revelation that had its fulfillment in the life and ministry of Jesus Christ. God's revelation is fixated in the Holy Scriptures, and so, the Scripture as tradition is fixed. In chapter 4, we will trace the traditions of the catholic church in relation to the fixated tradition of the church. Therefore, we will begin our study with the tradition Christ himself delivered to the church. Christ fulfilled the promise God had given to Abraham—the "tradition" that was given and delivered in the form of a covenant. The tradition Christ handed over or delivered to or passed on to the church was the kingdom of God. The kingdom of God has served as the canon of the traditions of the church. The succeeding historical and theological traditions of the church were measured on the standard of the kingdom of God as the tradition Christ handed over to his disciples and passed on to the church.

The kingdom of God tradition had its historical and theological evolution in the history of the church as Christianity grew to become the predominant religion in the world. There were victories and vicissitudes that had strengthened the life and mission of the church, but at the same time, there were challenges and controversies that shook and shaped the history of the development of the traditions of the church. The phenomenal growth of the church and its mission, the challenges of the heretics and their heretical teachings, the challenge of growing leaderships, the influences of the political and social developments, the rise of various philosophies and educational sciences, and others all contributed to the complex historical and theological development of the traditions of the church.

In chapter 5, our discussion will focus on the historical and theological development of the marks of the catholic church. Catholicity as a dynamic "traditioning" has evolved in its meaning, so that, what has been viewed as the universal connection of the churches of Jesus Christ in various places has developed wider and greater implications in relation to the catholicity of the church. As a result, catholicity is no longer limited to words like universal, general, or total. Catholicity has become a theological concept shaped by the church and its task of "traditioning." The marks presented, however, are not comprehensive and exhaustive; rather they are representative marks.

Catholicization

Catholicization is a methodological approach to the unity and diversity of the church of Jesus Christ. Jesus's prayer in John 17 needs a face indeed. In the same spirit, the apostle Paul also exhorts the believers to keep the unity of the Spirit (Eph 4:3). The church is not responsible for its unity. Unity is a gift of the Holy Spirit. But the keeping of that gift of the Spirit is something that the church will do well to consider. How do we indeed keep the unity of the Spirit? Here I suggest "catholicization" as the way in and through which churches of Jesus Christ can begin working toward the fulfillment of Jesus's prayer in John 17 for the church. Jesus's prayer puts the responsibility of keeping the unity on the shoulder of the church. The Ecumenical Movement began as a response to this prayer. However, much to the success of the movement and the impetus the movement had given to the unity of the church of Jesus Christ, the unity of the church appears to remain elusive. As a result the movement itself has taken a different direction and gone a different way by refocusing on another unity, i.e., religious pluralism.

Shall we give up on the prayer of Jesus and just place it on the eschatological aspect of the kingdom? God forbid. Our desire for unity is something that comes along with the gift of the Spirit itself. Our unity in the Spirit makes us all pray with Jesus—"that all of them may be one. Father, just as you are in me and I am in you. May they also be in us so that the world may believe that you have sent me" (Jn. 17:21). The missing link to our prayer is one that we can find in our own identity as catholic. Catholicity makes us aware of our inherent connections with one another as churches of Jesus

Christ. I believe it is in the same spirit that we can keep and strengthen the unity of the Spirit. I call this as "catholicization"—an approach that focuses on the inward source of our unity, and from there begin to work on the outside. Hence, catholicization is an inside to outside approach (unlike the Ecumenical Movement's of outside to inside approach).

The fragmented spirit that we have unintentionally adapted ourselves to is caused by our weak understanding of the church as catholic. Ignatius' understanding of the catholicity of the church was an excellent starting point where the focus is on Christ rather than on the church. But the historical and theological development shifted the focus on the church and it was used contra heretics. Catholicity had become more of a weapon against the apostates or enemies of the church rather than a Spirit quality that would have kept and strengthened the unity of the church. Sadly, it has taken the church five hundred years since the Reformation to realize that our problem is within ourselves—in our identity as the catholic church. Chapters 6 and 7 deal with "catholicization" in relation to the unity of the church. Catholicization gives us enough reasons to think about and work on our unity. Knowing the given foundations for catholicization we cannot help but live out the unity of the Spirit. Both the ontological and missional aspects of the unity of the church should challenge us enough to act on our unity. We can neither afford to grieve the Holy Spirit, the very source of our unity, nor fail the world, for whom God had sent his only Son in love. The failure of the church would indeed mean a tragedy for the world.

Moreover, catholicity is more of a life than a statement of faith to be confessed to the world. The confession that "we are catholic" is a confession of our being and doing. It does not only affect our witness in and to the world, but also our own life as the church of Jesus Christ. Indeed, we are many as the body has many parts, but we are as well one as the body is. We cannot keep on being fragmented as the body of Christ. It is time for us to live out our unity among ourselves and in the world. Let me begin with the prayer Jesus himself prayed for us,

> "May *they* be brought to complete unity
> to let the world know that you have sent me
> and have loved them as you have loved me."
> (John 17:23b)

2

The Catholic Story
The History of the Catholic Church

JESUS SAID, "As you sent me into the world, I have sent them into the world" (John 17:18). J. H. Bernard notes, "The words carry a reference not only to the original Twelve. . . ."[1] Apparently, the words of Jesus forthrightly point to the future life and mission not only of the disciples themselves, but of the then emerging church which the disciples of Jesus Christ represented.[2] The church was not only called to gather as a community of disciples, but they were also sent into the world to make disciples.[3] Dulles notes this call beautifully in the following words,

> The Church's existence is a continual alternation between two phases. Like systole and diastole in the movement of the heart, like inhalation and exhalation in the process of breathing, assembly and mission succeed each other in the life of the Church. Discipleship would be stunted unless it included both the centripetal phase of worship and the centrifugal phase of mission.[4]

---

1. Bernard, *Gospel*, 575.
2. Ibid.
3. See Dulles, *Models*, 204–26. This model of the church is not only relational but also missional. Dulles writes, "The external mission of the Church can never be separated from its inner life." Ibid., 222.
4. Ibid., 220.

The Catholic Story

Christ himself was the one responsible for the life and mission of the church as a community of disciples.[5] The above prayer of Jesus for his disciples indicates how the disciples would take the responsibility for the mission. He sent the church into the world to announce the good news of the kingdom he himself proclaimed and established in and through his life and death. This is the story of the church—a people called out of (*ek*) the world through the life and ministry of Christ, and commissioned to serve the world through its own life and ministry. The word "*kosmos*" is used here in reference to the world-wide mission of the church to all the nations (*cf.* Acts 1:8), "lost in sin, wholly at odds with anything divine, ruined and depraved."[6] And here flows the story of the church—from Christ to the church, and then to the world.[7]

Christ, the church, and the world altogether define catholicity. Hence, the story of the church is a catholic story; it is a story of this triangulate relationship—Christ, the church, and the world. From its conception to its commission, the church was meant to be catholic (in terms of membership) and to do catholic (in terms of mission). Prior to the sending of the church into the world which formally happened on the Day of the Pentecost (Acts 2), there came first the universal calling of the church as disciples of Christ. The call to discipleship was necessary for the task of discipleship. As Christ represented the Father—being the one sent by the Father himself, so the church represented Jesus—as the one Christ himself sent. As such both the identity and authority of the church are inherently related to its Savior and Lord.

The story of the church is the extended story of Jesus Christ; the mission of the church is also the extension of the mission of Christ. A proper understanding of the church necessitates an understanding of its relationship with Christ. This community of disciples is a unique community that takes its root in the very person of Jesus Christ as the new people of God. In the Old Testament, the people of God were identified with YHWH, the God of Israel; in the New Testament the "people of God" has taken a new identity connected to the person of Jesus Christ—the Son of God. The "new

---

5. Dulles thinks that this is another model of the church. Ibid.

6. BADG, "kosmos," 562, where the authors argue that the "world" as translated is in reference not only to humanity in general but also to its status as hostile to God.

7. See Wright, *Mission of God's People*, 23–32. Indeed, the mission is for the whole world by the whole church with the whole gospel (Christ). This I call as the catholic mission.

people" is rightly called the church of Jesus Christ, which is also known as the church of God (*cf.* 1 Cor 1:2). Jaroslav Pelikan rightly notes,

> The church, therefore, was the inheritor of the promises and prerogatives of the Jews. "Just as Christ is Israel and Jacob, so we who have been quarried out from the bowels of Christ are the true Israelite race," and the "third Israel" spoken of in Isaiah. Likewise, the church had the right to call Abraham its father, to style itself "the chosen people," and to look forward to inheriting the promised land. No title for the church in early Christianity is more comprehensive than the term "people of God," which originally meant "the new Israel" but gradually lost this connotation as the Christian claim to be the only true people of God no longer had to be substantiated.[8]

Its identity as "the new people of God" no longer associates the church with the narrow nationalistic identity of the people of Israel—but one that is catholic.[9] A new epoch in God's work of redemption has come in Christ. This catholicity gives the new people of God the identity of a people from and for all nations. Christ the messiah king is no longer the king of the historical and national Israel; he is rightly the Lord of all nations. Hence, the early confession of the early church: "Jesus is Lord."

With Christ, the story of the church as catholic has begun. This is our story, for we are the church—and *we are catholic*. Catholicity is essential both to the life and mission of the church. What Christ accomplished in and through his life during his earthly life and ministry is now dependent on the church. The church is the community of Jesus's disciples sent into the world through its own life and ministry to proclaim the gospel not only to Jews but to all the nations (*cf.* Acts 1:8). This mission is inseparable from the life of the church. Indeed, "the external mission of the church can never be separated from its inner life."[10] The catholic mark of the church is of utmost importance to the life and mission of the church. Indeed, catholicity makes the church different from the narrow nationalistic identity of Israel. To say that "we are catholic" is to embrace our life and mission as the

---

8. Pelikan, *Christian Tradition*, 26.

9. Wright's theory of the church as the renewed people of God makes the church as a multiethnic community rather than catholic. The church as catholic, though out of nations, is a non-ethnic community. We take our identity in Christ. Israel was supposed to be the means not the goal of God's work of redemption. See Wright, *How God Became King*, 105–25.

10. Dulles, *Models*, 222.

church of Jesus Christ. It is then our responsibility to understand the catholicity of the church. A proper understanding of the catholicity of the church will help strengthen both who we are and what we do as the church of Jesus Christ. We now begin with the catholic story—the story of the church of Jesus Christ—our story.

The Early Church (Incipient Catholic)

With their gospel accounts of the life of Christ, the evangelists hinted their readers that the nature of the church was beyond the geographical and historical boundary of Israel. Jesus himself had prepared and later commissioned his disciples for a mission inclusive of all nations: "Go and make disciples of all nations, baptizing them in the name of the Father, and of the Son, and of the Holy Spirit, and teaching them to obey everything I have commanded you, and lo I am with you always" (Matt 28:19-20). All the four evangelists shared the same mission statement (Mark 16:15; Luke 24:46-49; John 20:21). The community of disciples was sent not only to Israel but to the whole world. This is demonstrated clearly in the life and mission of the early church recorded in the book of Acts.[11] The early church had gone into the world as Jesus commanded them: "But you will receive power when the Holy Spirit comes on you; and you will be my witnesses in Jerusalem, and in all Judea and Samaria, and to the ends of the earth" (Acts 1:8). In Acts a new understanding of the people of God had evolved into a community distinct from Israel. Dunning notes this distinctiveness in Acts,

> The central concern in the communities described in Acts involved their distinctiveness as compared with Israel. As Alex R. G. Deasley says, "In an important measure the remainder of Acts [after Pentecost] recounts a wrestling with the definition of the term Israel, partly without but also partly within the Church." There seems, at first, to be only the awareness that here is a sect of the Jews marked by faith that Jesus of Nazareth was the promised Messiah. But by clearly discernible stages, which Luke marks out, they came to a consciousness that the followers of the Way constituted a significantly different genre of religious community. However, as we have seen, they did not abandon the idea that they were in continuity with Israel of the old covenant. According to J.

---

11. See Marshall, *Acts of the Apostles*, 20. Marshall writes, "Part of the demonstration lies in Luke's claim that what took place in the early church was in accordance with prophecy." Ibid.

N. D. Kelly, this is the presupposition on which the Early Church included the Hebrew scriptures in its canon. If there was a radical discontinuity, as dispensational theology claims, the logical result would have been the rejection of those scriptures.[12]

Theologically, the distinctiveness of the community of the disciples of Jesus was demonstrative of the spirit of "catholicity"—an incipient catholicity under the leadership of the Spirit and the authority of the Holy Scriptures. The question whether the church was a radical discontinuation from Israel was given a clear answer in the spirit of catholicity. The church as catholic was not a rejection of the people of Israel but it is, in fact, a fulfillment of its calling that highlighted the inclusion of the Gentile nations. So that the church is properly understood as an inclusive catholic community—a community of both Jews and Gentiles.

The catholicity of the early church was demonstrated first and foremost by the availability and inclusivity of the Gift—the Holy Spirit. The early church had the conviction and experience that the church was constituted by the Holy Spirit and was the dwelling place of the Spirit.[13] The Spirit was the presence of Christ and the power of God in and through the church. What happened on the Day of the Pentecost among the Jewish believers likewise happened among the Gentile converts. The promised Holy Spirit was not exclusively available to all Jewish believers present on the Day of the Pentecost. While the Day of the Pentecost was unique and highly symbolic of the universality of the gospel and the church, the experience of the Holy Spirit was inclusive and a continuing reality in the life and mission of the church. The book of Acts is replete with subsequent experiences of the Holy Spirit both among the communities of Gentiles and Jews. The guidance and leadership of the Spirit was also available to all of the churches. At Antioch, for example, we have been told how the Spirit had instructed the whole church to set apart Paul and Barnabas for the work of mission among the Gentiles. The Holy Spirit is the Spirit of catholicity.

Moreover, catholicity is demonstrated in how the early church proclaimed the catholic Gospel of Jesus Christ. The Word of God was not exclusively Jewish. The four Gospels were generally written to both communities—Jews and Gentiles; they were no way written exclusively for either of the groups. While they might have been written primarily for Jews or Gentiles, but they all apply to both communities in one way or another.

12. Dunning, *Grace*, 519.
13. Ibid.

The authors of the books of the New Testament reminded readers of the inclusivity of the gospel of Jesus Christ. None of them could claim exclusive right to any of the Gospels or the gospel itself. The rest of the books of the New Testament were also addressed directly or indirectly to the catholic church. Relationships between Jews and Gentiles were given attention so that the church would become a catholic community indeed. The community of the Word is a new community instructed to live in harmony with one another in the spirit of love toward a catholic community. All believers are members of the community as brothers and sisters:

> You are all sons (and daughters) of God through faith in Christ Jesus, for all of you who were baptized into Christ have clothed yourselves with Christ. There is neither Jew nor Greek, slave nor free, male nor female, for you are all one in Christ Jesus. If you belong to Christ, then you are Abraham's seed, and heirs according to the promise (Gal 3:26–29).

Catholicity in the early church was more of a Christian existential reality in Christ through the Spirit and the Word than a theological confession of the church. The early church knew their identity and unity in Christ; they knew they were catholic and they live as catholic through and through. Unlike in the second century and onwards, catholicity was not a problem that challenged the fellowship of all believers and the mission of the church. If they were not catholic, they would have neither survived as disciples of Jesus Christ nor evangelized the whole world for Jesus Christ.

The Church Fathers (Patristic/Creedal Catholic)

Catholicity as a mark of the church came out of the theological development of the tradition of the church (see chapter 4 for a discussion on the Evangelical understanding of "tradition" contra the Roman Catholic tradition). Thus, the "catholic" mark of the church is a theological mark. As the Trinity is to God, so is catholicity to the church. And the church fathers were the ones responsible for the first use of the word "catholic" in relation to the church, and later they developed the concept to become one of the marks of the church of Jesus Christ. What was true to the existential experience of the early church, the church fathers developed it into a theology and became part of the church's confession or tradition.[14] For example,

---

14. Theology was first an objective experience before it became a subjective

the so-called Apostles' Creed that theologically and formally defined the church as "the holy catholic church" was an ecclesiological development highly influenced by the church fathers themselves. A variety of senses or meanings had emerged during this period of the history of the church. These meanings do not necessarily contradict or are independent of each other; they are complimentary in fact and altogether they define the creedal catholic.

Christocentric Meaning (Ignatius)

Though the word "church" in the New Testament is used in reference to a local congregation, it is no way intended to be taken only as such or limited to it. Its relationship with Christ has given it a more inclusive and comprehensive sense. Moreover, the unity of the growing congregations in various places of the Greco-Roman world revealed a greater or grander identity of the churches of Jesus Christ. The churches were not taken as independent

---

confession of the truth. T. A. Noble put it succinctly in the following words, "Christian experience then is not merely the experiencing of theological abstraction called 'salvation' or 'sanctification,' or 'holiness.' Nor is it merely the experiencing of inner subjective events or 'crises,' and certainly not of induced or self-induced crises. It only has objective validity, it is only real, when we experience or encounter the living God. 'My goal is God himself, not joy, nor peace, nor even blessing, but himself, my God.' The Lord God gives himself to be known, to be experienced by us in his Word by his Spirit, to become, if you like, the Divine Objective of our experience. God is the One we experience in 'an experience,' and it is only when we objectively experience God, that there is a genuine event, a genuine 'crisis' with objective validity. Real inner and outer change, real sanctification, certainly requires self-knowledge and self-examination, but it occurs not when our eyes are inward in introspection but when we look outward and upward and our eyes are fixed on Him. Real Christian experience is quite simply falling in love with God. And when we do that, we are never more rational, never more truly human, never more spiritually and intellectually awakened, never more at our best. It is objective experience of the real and living God that results in the subjective inner and outward change we call 'sanctification.' Such experiential knowledge of God must not only be understood in a merely individualistic way. It is true, of course, that the tri-personal God enters into relationship with each of us as persons. WE come to know with Paul, Augustine, Luther, and the Wesleys that Christ died 'for me' (Gal. 2:20): 'Died he for me, who caused his pain? For me? Who him to death pursued? Amazing love! How can it be that Thou, my God, shouldst die for me?' And yet that personal encounter with God must not be understood individualistically, but within the fellowship of the people of God. Historically, the apostles experienced 'God with us' in Jesus. The Incarnate Son, and ever and again as the story of the gospel is proclaimed and the Scriptures are opened and bread and wine are distributed, the people of God experience God's presence in the corporate worship of the church." Noble, *Holy Trinity*, 17.

local congregations or seen as isolated or unrelated to one another. Though many, the churches were seen as one. Such oneness was attributed to their relationship with Jesus Christ. This relationship was experienced in various ways: every believer was baptized in the name of Jesus Christ; the believer's confession was centered on the Lordship of Jesus Christ; each received the Spirit in the name of Jesus Christ; and each believed in God in the name of Jesus Christ.

It was Ignatius (1st-2nd c.) who first used the word "catholic" (Smyrna 8)[15] and rightly identified the church as the "catholic church" when he said, "Where Jesus Christ is, there is the catholic church" (Ignatius ad Smyrn, viii. 2).[16] The word "catholic" may indeed embody the universal connection and unity of the churches of Jesus Christ around the world, but the connection and the unity of the church were primarily anchored in the church's relationship with Jesus Christ—a christocentric meaning. This relationship between the church and Jesus Christ is biblically and theologically unequivocal. The church is catholic first and foremost because of Christ. The emphasis of the word "catholic" is on Christ rather than on the church; Christ defines the catholicity of the church *a priori*.

This is a significant theological recognition of Ignatius. It is definitive of the core or inner catholicity of the church. Catholicity is where the presence of Jesus Christ is. We are not catholic because we fellowship or are gathered together in the name of Jesus Christ; we are catholic because Christ is with us: "For where two or three come together in my name, there *I am with them*" (Matt 18:20). The catholicity of the church is a reality of God being with us. As such, the absence of Christ destroys or dissolves the catholic church; Christ is the canon of the catholicity of the church. Christian fellowship is always and ever graced by the presence of Christ. It is the presence of Christ that gives the church the "*mysterium*" or what Rudolf Otto calls the "wholly other."[17] Christian fellowship is a holy fellowship that allows people to experience that holy awe.

Anthropocentric Meaning (Justin Martyr)

One of the leading apologists of the second century was Justin Martyr (ca. 100–165), who was responsible for defending the Christians in his *First*

15. Cairns, *Christianity Through*, 76.
16. Quoted in Harrison, "Catholic," 112.
17. See Otto, *Idea of the Holy*, 25–30.

Apology before the Emperor Antoninus Pius against false accusations such as atheism and idolatry.[18] Convinced of the truths about Christ and the Christians, Justin had committed himself to defending the Christian faith and its fellowship. He endeavored to convince the Jews of the messiahship of Jesus Christ and the inclusion of the Gentiles to the people of God. He firmly believed that Christ was the fulfillment of the Old Testament prophecies.

Justin used the word "catholic" in reference to the resurrection of all men (Dial. 1xxxi).[19] This defines "catholic" in terms of all men and women whether Jews or Gentiles, Christians or non-Christians. This is clearly an anthropocentric definition of catholicity. It does not, however, refer only to individuals but to all humanity. As such, to Justin, the resurrection of all humanity is a "catholic" resurrection. We can take Justin's use further to mean the one time or altogether resurrection of humanity. This would refer the word "catholic" to corporate humanity. In sum, Justin's idea of catholicity can be summed up in the corporate resurrection of humanity. The spirit of catholicity, therefore, is in the spirit of corporate experience of all men and women.

In the context of the church, catholicity can be referred to the unity and corporate identity of the church—a unity of corporality. The church is catholic not in the individual identity of Christian believers or local independent Christian churches, but in the corporate sense of the church as the body of Christ.

Ecclesiological Meaning (Origen)

Origen was the first systematic theologian of the church in a formal sense. His work *De Principiis* (ca. 185–254) tackled a number of Christian doctrines. Origen was given the credit for being the first to develop and use allegorical system of interpretation, which was later believed to have done so much harm to the interpretation of the Scriptures.

Origen, Eusebius, et al. were among those who categorized the books of the General Epistles as catholic epistles to indicate that they were intended for the whole church rather than a local church.[20] Here the word "catholic" is used in contrast with a local congregation. As such the catholic

18. Cairns, *Christianity Through*, 104.
19. Harrison, "Catholic," 112.
20. Ibid.

church was a reference to all churches of Christ in various places. This gave catholicity a more direct relationship with the church. Thus, this definition is more ecclesiological than Ignatius' and Justin's. This is an important connection because this study is directly related to the church with particular reference to the unity and catholicity of the church.

In a sense, Origen was the first one to attempt to bring the concept of catholicity to the connection and union of all churches. It is a connection that rightly described the reality of the relationship of all churches around the world. By doing so, Origen brought the reality of the connection of churches world-wide to a unifying theological concept that embodied the broader relationship and the wholistic identity of the church of Christ.

Geographical and Statistical Meaning (Augustine)

The above church fathers understood catholic as "universal," that is, in relation to all men and women; albeit similar, Augustine (ca. 354–430) took the concept of universal in reference to the geographical spread and statistical growth of the church in the world. In this sense, the church is catholic because it is widely and numerically spread out in the world. This definition was used in reaction to the heretical teachings of the Donatists, and was also later used against the Reformers. Implicitly, Augustine highlighted catholicity in the language of the mission of the church to the world. I will give more attention to Augustine in the following section. In the meantime, Augustine had given the church structural and theological unity with his various doctrines that empowered the church and its influence in the society in and through its message of salvation. He held the belief that salvation is found in no other institution but the church. "Augustine so emphasized the church as a visible institution with the true creed, sacraments, and ministry that the Roman church considers him the father of Roman ecclesiasticism."[21]

In sum, in and through the various interpretations of the church fathers, catholicity has been given its rightful place in the church's tradition, that is, the church fathers theologically interpreted the life and mission of the church. In fact, it was believed to have come from the apostles themselves, that is, catholicity was a tradition that was faithful to the spirit and teachings of the apostles vis-à-vis the church of Jesus Christ (see the Apostles' Creed, chapter 7). Hence, the undivided church had embraced

21. Cairns, *Christianity Through*, 142.

its catholic identity and later made it one of the official marks or notes of the church: "one, holy, catholic, and apostolic."[22] Partly underlying the development of the catholic mark of the church, however, was the church's doctrinal reaction against false teachings of the heretics (see chapter 4). Catholicity was used as a yardstick to distinguish false and true doctrines. This makes catholicity associated with orthodoxy. Vincent of Lerins wrote: "What has everywhere, always, by all, been believed" (*Commonitorium*, A.D. 434). By this the Church Fathers gave the church the authority to determine not only what is true and what is false, but also the power to declare others heretics on the basis of its catholicity in terms of universality and orthodoxy.[23] The church fathers believed that 'there is no salvation indeed outside the church.

The Roman Church (Roman Catholic)

With the legendary conversion of Constantine to Christianity, there began the movement toward the Roman Church. Constantine granted Christianity freedom and favors allowing Christian churches to freely congregate and worship without fear of persecution. As a result, churches grew rapidly and gained influence and power within the Roman Empire. Constantine's three sons likewise embraced and supported Christianity. Latourette writes,

> In 341 the second of them ordered that pagan sacrifices be abolished in Italy. The third, Constantius, commanded that "superstition cease and the folly of sacrifices be abolished" and removed from the Senate the statue of Victory which had been placed there by Augustus after the battle of Actium. He ordered temples closed. Yet of the pagan rites only sacrifices were forbidden, and processions, sacred feasts, and initiation to the mysteries, still permitted, presumably continued.[24]

Consequently the church had phenomenally grown resulting to more and more territories in the Empire from the East to the West and from the

---

22. In the Roman Catholic, the "marks" of the church are also known as "notes." Barrois, however, sees a distinction in the Roman Catholic Church's understanding of "notes," which are: authority (the church has the exclusive right to teach and govern the faith); infallibility (the church cannot err in matters of faith or morals); and indefectibility (the church will endure until the end of time). Barrois, "Marks," 544.

23. Harrison, "Catholic," 112.

24. Latourette, *History of Christianity*, 93.

South to the North, such as Armenia, Mesopotamia, Central Asia, Persia (or Assyria), Arabia, India, and Ceylon. So that, by the end of the first five centuries, Christianity had become the professed faith of the overwhelming majority of the population of the Roman Empire.[25]

Along the political advances of Christianity was the growing intellectual formulation of its faith. The one that had the greatest influence early on Christianity under the Roman Empire was Augustine. "No other Christian after Paul was to have so wide, deep, and prolonged an influence upon the Christianity of Western Europe and those forms of the faith that stemmed from it as had Augustine."[26] Indeed, Augustine was the father of Roman ecclesiasticism. He wrote a number of books that contributed to the shaping of the Catholic Church and its theology, such as *Confessions*, *Retractationes* or *Revisions*, *De Doctrine Christiana*, *De Trinitate*, and *De Cavitate Dei*. The above writings were so influential not only to the Roman Catholic Church but also to the Protestant churches. Both used Augustine in the construction of their respective theological traditions. Other personalities that contributed to the development of the Roman Catholic Church included Iranaeus (fought against the Gnostics), Tertullian (developed the Trinity), Cyprian (established the primacy of the Bishop of Rome), Jerome (translated the Bible), Ambrose (preacher), Athanasius, and Chrisostom. At par with Augustine's influence with the Roman Catholic Church was Thomas Aquainas, who developed and gave shape and substance to the pre-Reformation Roman Catholic theology and even after the Reformation.

The growing Roman Church had its heretical counterparts and controversies that challenged the unity of the church and perennially hindered it from achieving complete universal oneness. Three major heretical movements had their way inside the church that affected the church from its hierarchy to ordinary laity. They were the Gnostics, Marcionites, and the Montanists. Their influence in the church was both theological and practical. They called the church to a more detailed definition of the gospel and additional tests for admission to the church and continued membership in it. They also had developed their own spirituality based on the teachings of their leaders who claimed direct access to the Holy Spirit. For example, Montanus and his followers claimed to be prophets, mouthpieces of the Holy Spirit. As a result the church found itself in the defensive position.

---

25. Ibid., 97.
26. Ibid.

The positive outcome of the church's response to the heretics was the gradual awareness and development of the catholicity of the church through various theological actions of the church that defined its faith and established its catholic tradition. Kenneth Scott Latourette lists three motives that contributed to the development of the catholic church,

> One was the desire to unite all Christians in conscious fellowship. A second was to preserve, transmit, and spread the Christian Gospel in its purity, that men may enter into the fullness of the life which it reveals and makes possible. The third was to bring all Christians together into a visible "body of Christ."[27]

But in order to achieve what they desired, the church had to confront the heretics and put a stop to their theological and practical influence in the life of the church. And to do this the church had endeavored to concertedly guard the faith:

> (1) by ascertaining lines of bishops who were in direct and uninterrupted succession from the apostles and could therefore be assumed to be transmitters of the apostolic teachings, (2) by determining which writings were by the apostles or clearly contained their teachings and bringing them together in a fixed and authoritative collection, and (3) by formulating as clearly and briefly as possible the teachings of the apostles so that Christians, even the ordinary unlettered ones among them, might know what the Christian faith is, especially on the points in which the Catholic Church differed from Gnostics and Marcionites.[28]

Four "catholic" councils were called by the Emperors and the leaders of the church for the bishops and the theologians of the church to create something that would stop "heretics" and unite the church: (1) The Council of Nicea in 325, (2) The Second Ecumenical Council in 381 that resulted to the Nicene Creed, (3) The Third Ecumenical Council held at Ephesus in 431, and (4) The Fourth Ecumenical Council held at Chalcedon in 451. By them, the catholic church under the influence and authority of the Roman Emperor consolidated itself theologically and politically, and likewise conferred on itself the title "the Roman Catholic Church." This was made official by the edict of the Emperor Valentinian III through the influence of Pope Leo I commanding all to obey the Bishop of Rome on the ground that the latter held the "primacy of St. Peter." Consequently, as Latourette notes,

27. Ibid., 130.
28. Ibid., 131.

In 494 a successor of Leo, Gelasius, declared that the world is ruled by the Emperor and the priests, but that the latter are more important since they will have to give an account even for kings in the day of judgment, and that the Emperor must submit to prelates in divine matters. He also insisted that the Pope was of right preeminent over all priests. He declared that in view of the founding of the Church of Christ upon Peter and of the joint consecration by Peter and Paul of the Church of Rome, the latter "has been placed before the other churches" and hence depended for that position not on any decrees of synods, but upon Christ himself. Moreover, by their presence and martyrdom Peter and Paul, so Gelasius said, had elevated the Roman Church "over all the others in the whole world."[29]

While it appeared that the Roman Catholic Church had successfully established itself as "Catholic," the unity it desired was really superficial. The abuses of the powers of the Roman Church through its councils and that of the Roman Empire through its Emperors had made the many efforts fell short, if not totally useless, in achieving genuine Christian unity. In fact, divisions and deviations both existed within the Roman Church. The Church had in actuality made so many theological and political compromises to keep its structural unity. Hence, the catholicity of the undivided church was more political, structural, and superficial. Latourette rightly concludes,

> The efforts to define the distinctive doctrines of the Christian faith invariably sharpened divisions among Christians. By the close of the fifth century several rival bodies, were in existence, each regarding itself as representative of the true Christianity and most of them calling themselves Catholic and denying that designation to the others.[30]

The Reformation (Reformed Catholic)

On the eve of the Reformation, the Roman Church had gone through a lot of ecclesiastical changes both good and bad. The Roman Church had established itself as the "Catholic Church" with good but self-defined ecclesiastical authority under the tradition of its "Apostolic Succession." The influence of Thomas Aquainas' theology was evident in what the Roman

---

29. Ibid., 187.
30. Ibid., 187–88.

Church confessed and practiced before the division. It was Pope Leo XIII later in 1879 that officially declared Thomas' theological thoughts as the touchstone of Roman Catholic theology.[31] In the fourteenth century and onwards, the authorities of the church held in both hands (the) natural reason and divine revelation as understood by Thomas. And by doing so, the church had literally given itself the power to declare almost anything as dogma under its supreme ecclesiastical self-granted authority, which the church believed as worthy, not only of holy reverence but also of total obedience as one would with the doctrines of the Holy Scriptures. Hence, the practice and proliferation of the doctrine of *indulgentia*.

Although the Roman Church was catholic, it showed itself through its practices that it had been corrupted. What earlier preserved the church from divisions and deviations paused by the heretics poisoned it toward theological distortion and practical corruption. Prior to Martin Luther, the church already had men who began calling the church towards reform, such as John Wycliffe (ca. 1329–1384) and John Hus (ca. 1373–1415). Walker writes,

> Wyclif and Hus have often been styled forerunners of the Reformation. The designation is appropriate if regard is given to their protest against ecclesiastical abuses, their exaltation of the Bible, and their contribution to the sum total of agitation that ultimately resulted in church reform. The fundamental doctrines of the Protestant reformers, however, owed little of their substance to the doctrines of Wyclif and Hus, and they were far more radical in their break with tradition teaching. Nevertheless, insofar as Wyclif and Hus and a great number of "orthodox" thinkers of the late Middle Ages were already confronting the same central issues that the Protestant reformers were to confront, they may be justly called "forerunners" of the Reformation. There remained a basic continuity of "questions," albeit not of "answers."[32]

The Protestant reformers struggled over the church's misuse of its power and abuse of its doctrines, particularly the doctrine of *indulgentia*. Luther and the reformers called on the church to go back to the Scripture and take it as the only source of both theology and practice. They held on the principle of *sola scriptura* as the foundation for the church and its theological traditions. The reformers saw that the church was on the other side

---

31. Walker, et al., *History*, 340.
32. Ibid., 385.

of the truth. The church was guilty of using the Scriptures for the interests of the church rather than for preaching Christ and the gospel of justification by faith. Luther was convinced that the Roman Church was in error. He called on the church to be faithful to the Holy Scriptures.

The Reformation was a call for the church to be *sola scriptura*. It was the Holy Scriptures that defined the church and its theology. The Scriptures served as the *essence* and *existence* of the church. The life and mission of the church are based on the Scripture. The church must be a church *of* and a church *for* the Scripture; not the Scripture *of* and the Scripture *for* the church. To Luther and others the Scriptures were considered as the only authority in the church in matters of faith and practice. The church must submit to the authority of the Holy Scriptures. As such the Reformation offered the church a renewed commitment to the Scriptures as the basis for faith and practice. Orthodoxy was not grounded on the declaration of the church based on the authority of its councils or that of the Pope, but rather on the sole authority of the Scripture. As such to the reformers, the catholicity of the church was not as well grounded on the traditions of the church unless they were faithful interpretations of the Holy Scriptures. Luther was not willing to grant the church any authority apart from the Scripture.

Luther's principle of *sola scriptura* arose from his struggle for the truth. Luther sought earnestly for answers to his dilemma on the idea of the righteousness of God and the justice of God, which had not been satisfactorily answered by his rigid religious experience or devotion even as a monk. Luther wrote on his agony (*anfechthung*),

> Being a monk, I wished to omit nothing of the prayers and often overtaxed myself with my courses and written work. I assembled my hours for entire week and sometimes even two or three. Sometimes I would lock myself up for two or three days at a time, with neither food nor drink, until I had completed my breviary. My head became so heavy that I could not close my eyes to five nights. I was in agony and all confused. As soon as I had improved, I tried to work on my courses, but my head began to swim again. I was so imprisoned in the practice that the Lord had to tear me from this self-torture by violence.[33]

Luther's agony or inner conflict was brought about by his understanding of fear of the justice of God, which Luther understood as active, retributive, punishing, essential righteousness that demands that man keep the

---

33. Luther, cited in Schweibert, *Luther*, 150.

whole law of God.³⁴ Luther found it very disturbing, albeit he personally worked hard to fulfilling the justice of God. Luther testified,

> In the monastery we had enough to eat and to drink, but the heart and conscience suffered pain and martyrdom, and the suffering of the soul are the most painful. I was often frightened by the name of Christ, and when I looked upon Him and the Cross, He seemed to me like unto a flash of lightning. When His name was mentioned, I would rather have heard the devil mentioned, for I believed that I would have to do good works until Christ was rendered gracious to me through them. In the convent I thought neither of money now of the wealth of this world nor women; but my heart trembled and I was agitated thinking how I might render God favorable to it. For I have departed from faith, and I could not make myself believe anything but that I had offended God, when I would have to make favorable again through my good works. But that God would again have His word, which pictures and portrays Christ as our righteousness.³⁵

His struggle or inner conflict had been aggravated by his feeling or belief of being unable to produce a pure love for God.³⁶ Luther developed a strong sense of guilt within himself. He ended up hating God than loving him. He believed that he was not capable of fulfilling the righteous requirements of the righteous God.

In 1512, only a few months after he had received his doctorate, the young Luther was given the opportunity to teach at the University of Wittenberg. He began teaching the Bible beginning from the book of Psalm down to the book of Romans. Unknowingly, this experience led Luther to the answer to his long-time struggle, and gave him what he called the "*turmerlebnis*" (tower experience), or better known as Luther's evangelical breakthrough—an insight into the all-encompassing grace of God and all-sufficient merit of grace. On his exposition of the book of Romans, particularly 1:7, Luther found the answer. It is better at this time to let Luther himself speak for the account of his experience:

> All the while I was absorbed with the passionate desire to get better acquainted with the author of Romans. Not that I did not succeed as I had resolved, in penetrating more deeply into the subject

---

34. Spitz, *Renaissance and the Reformation*, 2:332.
35. E. A., *Dr. Martin Luther's*.
36. Luther sought to love God with all of his heart upon the influence of Occamism. For a discussion on this topic, see Lohue, *Martin Luther's*, 32–34.

in my investigation, but I stumbled over the words (chapter 1:7) concerning "the righteousness of God revealed in the (Scripture) gospel." For the concept of "God's righteousness" was repulsive to me, as I was accustomed to interpret it according to scholastic philosophy, namely, as the "formal or active" righteousness, in which God proves himself righteous in that He punishes the sinner as an unrighteous person . . . until, after days and nights of wrestling with the problem, God finally took pity on me, so that I was able to comprehend the inner connection between the two expressions, "the righteous of God is revealed in the Gospel" and "the just shall live by faith." Then I began to comprehend the "righteousness of God" through which the righteous are saved by God's grace, namely, through faith; that the "righteousness of God" which is revealed through the Gospel was to be understood in a passive sense in which God through mercy justifies man by faith, as it is written, "the just shall live by faith." Now I felt exactly as though I had been born again, and I believed that I had entered Paradise through widely opened doors. I then went through the Holy Scripture as far as I could recall them from memory, and I found in other parts the same sense: the "word of God" is that He works in us, the "strength of God" is that through which He makes us strong, the "wisdom of God" that through which He makes us wise, and so the "power of God," are likewise to be interpreted. As violently as I had formerly hated the expression "righteousness of God," so I was now violently compelled to embrace the new conception of grace and, thus, for me, the expression of the apostle really opened the Gates of Paradise.[37]

This evangelical breakthrough was rooted upon Luther's discovery of scriptural truth, which had long been neglected by the then Roman Church. The Scripture opened Luther's eyes and gave him the tower experience. This circumstance in Luther's life would later be the beginning of his long theological struggle against the Roman Church's doctrines and practices.

In sum, one can infer from Luther's and the Reformation's principle of *sola scriptura* that the catholicity of the church is based on the authority of the Scripture. If catholicity means orthodoxy as was developed by the church fathers, then catholicity must be scripturally-based. No catholicity could be defined or developed outside the authority of the Holy Scriptures.

This emphasis on *sola scriptura* was embraced by yet another genius of the Reformation—John Calvin, who was ranked as the leader of the second

---

37. Luther, *Opera Lutheri*, I, 22–23, in *Luther*, 285–86.

generation of Reformers. The influence of Calvin's theology superseded the man himself not only during the Reformation but more so after. Cairns writes,

> The millions today in Switzerland, Holland, Scotland, the United States, and elsewhere who accept the Reformed faith as their doctrinal basis testify to the importance of the system of theology the John Calvin (1509-64) developed. The term "Calvinism" and the phrase "Reformed faith" have reference to the system of theology developed on the basis of Calvin's system. "Presbyterianism" is the word used to indicate the system of the church government that Calvin developed.[38]

Calvin was more systematic than Luther. Calvin developed a formal system of theology that formally and theologically broke away with the Roman Church. He rejected everything that could not be proved by the Scriptures. Calvin's contribution to the catholicity of the church was both theological and methodological—theologically Calvin held the position that the church was the community of the elect; election, of course, was based on Calvin's understanding of divine sovereignty—God's predetermined disposition toward men and women. Methodologically, Calvin developed a system of theology that developed the Reformed tradition—a tradition within the catholic tradition.

Scholasticism and Rationalism
(Dogmatic and Liberal Catholic)

One of the important consequences of the Reformation was the freedom from what was known as "the Apostolic Succession," which was the cause of many theological distortions and deviations by the thinkers and powers of the then undivided church. The Reformation had indeed freed the church from ecclesiastical manipulations of the interpretations of the Holy Scriptures (that led to a separate Tradition in the Roman Church). The success of the Reformation opened a new epoch in the history of the church. Sadly the Reformation, with the development of a system of orthodox dogma, led to its own intellectualism or more formally called as the Protestant Scholasticism.

---

38. Cairns, *Christianity Through*, 300.

The Catholic Story

On the positive note, the catholicity of the church had taken a new direction among Protestant churches. It moved from the corporate Roman Catholic Church to a series of national Protestant churches in the lands, such as Germany, Switzerland, Scotland, Holand, France, Bohemia, and Hungary. But it did not suggest a broken unity of the church; a new expression of unity emerged—unity in diversity. Cairns writes,

> Although great doctrinal changes were brought about by the Reformation, the student must not think that the new national churches broke completely with all that was handed down by the church from the past. Protestants and Roman Catholics alike accepted the great ecumenical creeds, such as the Apostles' Creed, the Nicene Creed, the Athanasian Creed. They all held the doctrines of the Trinity and (except for the Socinians) the deity and resurrection of Christ, the Bible as a revelation from God, the fall of man, original sin, and the need of a moral life for the Christian. The Protestants had a common area of agreement concerning of faith and life, and the priesthood of believers. In addition, each denomination held to its own particular viewpoint that distinguished it from other Protestants, such as baptism by immersion as the Baptists prescribed and predestination as the Calvinists taught.[39]

Structural unity was replaced by common doctrinal agreements—a theological unity. Among the Protestants, for example, the following doctrines were commonly held: justification by faith, the priesthood of all believers, and the final authority of the Scriptures.

But with the development of "systematic" theology, the church had suffered from dogmatism. What transpired in the seventeenth and eighteenth centuries was more of a dogmatic catholic than a scriptural or biblical catholic. The church was viewed more from the perspective or expression of doctrine than from the relation of faith to the practical life. Orthodoxy had formally defined catholicity.

Dogmatism was later supported and strengthened by the arrival or influence of rationalism in religion. Pure rationalism was a reaction to dogmatism; it led to secularism—the separation between the church and the society, the sacred and the secular. The former was highly supernatural in its approach to life and realities; the latter was highly natural in its approach to life and the world. One was influenced by the doctrine of divine revelation; the other was influenced by the theory of evolution. Some

---

39. Ibid., 349.

theologians, however, married revelation and rationalism resulting to a new breed of dogmatism—liberalism. Biblical scholars, like Frederick D. E. Schleiermacher, George W. F. Hegel, Albrecht Ritschl, Jean Astruc, Karl H. Graf, Julius Wellhausen, Hermann S. Reimarus, Gotthold Lessing, Ferdinand C. Baur, and David F. Strauss adopted historical-critical approach to the Bible.[40] They subjected the study of the Bible to rigid biblical criticism. One of the results of biblical criticism was the search for the historical Jesus and the Christ of faith. Critics held the position that there stood a difference between the Jesus of history and the Christ of faith.[41] They concluded that the latter was the product of the religious awareness of the disciples and their attempt to spiritualized history for their own religious agenda. For example, some theologians, who adopted the critical views of the New Testament, considered that the essence of the gospel was in the ethical teachings of Jesus and that Paul changed the simple ethical religion of Jesus into a redemptive religion. Liberalism had turned the catholic church into a religious organization that promoted its own ethical teachings in and through the books of the Bible. Catholicity was viewed as a religious expression of men and women who adopted Jesus's ethical teachings and later evolved into Paul's redemptive religion.

Ecumenical Movement and Liberation Theology (Ecumenical and Liberation Catholic)

Dogmatism was seen by so many others as a cold orthodoxy lacking the dynamic and living spirit of the church of Christ. "Despite the ecumenism of Calvin, Bucer, and others who longed for the unity of the Protestant churches,"[42] dogmatism sharpened the division that was growing among various denominations within the church of Jesus Christ particularly among Protestant churches. In an attempt to bring the divided church(es) together in the spirit of unity and renewal, a group of Christians mostly Pietists and the Moravians envisioned mission cooperation among Protestant churches, which resulted to joint missionary work in India where the Anglicans worked with the Lutherans. That began the "ecumenical movement" under the leadership of Zindzendorf, who was tagged as an "ecumenical pioneer."

---

40. For a helpful study on these liberal scholars, see Brown, *Jesus in European*.
41. See Shweitzer, *Quest of the Historical Jesus*.
42. Pierson, "Ecumenical," 300.

The ecumenical movement was built on the foundation or aspiration of many Christians for the church of Jesus Christ to be one as Jesus prayed in John 17.[43] The ecumenical aspiration involved the unity of the body in and through ecumenical fellowships, renewal of faith in and through ecumenical creeds, and mission cooperation in and through evangelism and mission. Such is a unity that is visible to the world. It was the visible unity that ecumenical movement was interested in achieving so that the church may live the prayer of Jesus and so that the world may see it. The church had indeed lived and seen the ecumenical spirit and cooperation among Protestant churches in North America and England. These were results of revivals that brought different churches together in the spirit of participation and cooperation towards evangelism and mission. Moreover, the church had seen further missionary movement that stemmed from the revivals—such as the Church Missionary Society and the London Missionary Society.[44]

With the joint efforts of different churches, catholicity has been given a new face in and through the ecumenical movement. The ecumenical movement had exhibited not only a unity in diversity but also a visibility of that unity in and through the spirit of ecumenicity. Through the various ecumenical movements the church had experienced and visibly seen the reality of worshipping and working together as one. Conferences were held with some success. The first was held in Bombay in 1825 that promoted Christian fellowship and exchange ideas. In 1858 and 1862, similar meetings happened where "Anglicans, Presbyterians, Methodists, and Baptists took Communion together."[45]

The meetings led the ecumenical movement to two major streams—the organization of Evangelical Alliance formed in 1846 and the Intercollegiate YMCA that existed on campuses by 1884. These streams came together in the Edinburgh Missionary Conference in 1910 and gave birth

---

43. Kik lists at least six older motivations for ecumenism: (1) the world situation presents a powerful incentive to act with Christian unity; (2) the conquest of the heathen world forms a powerful drive for the Christian church to become united; (3) a frequently mentioned incentive to ecumenism is the prevalent secularism; (4) the growing power and influence of the Roman Catholic Church creates a motive for a united Protestant church that has great popular appeal; (5) a common complaint expresses concern that divided Protestantism cannot speak with one voice and act with united purpose; and (6) the most powerful motive for the establishment of a world-wide church is the conviction that God desires his worshippers to be within the framework of one ecclesiastical structure. Kik, *Ecumenism*, 4–9.

44. Ibid., 301.

45. Ibid.

to the formation of the World Council of Churches (WCC),[46] which was organized in 1948 in Amsterdam and became the major institution that promoted the ecumenical movement.

The ecumenical movement, however, had its own share of dislikes, disgusts, and failures. The influence of liberation theology(ies) on the movement became more and more evident as seminaries and churches of mainline Protestant denominations were influenced by the liberation movement particularly in the third world countries in Asia, Africa, and Latin America where social and economic issues were prevalent. As a result there had been redefinitions of missions and expressions of evangelical theology that caused others to suspect the two movements.[47] Such redefinitions cast a doubt on genuine ecumenism and the possibility of unity. An example of a negative reaction was the Frankfurt Declaration spearheaded by Peter Beyerhaus who fought against liberation-mission and called the churches toward a more biblical position that is true to the evangelical commitment to the gospel of Jesus Christ.[48] He challenged the Evangelicals engaged in the Ecumenical Movement with a mission question: "*Missions—Which Way?: Humanization or Redemption.*" With the strong influence of liberation theology in the World Council of Churches, the ecumenical catholic has drifted to an understanding of the church as God's instrument in bringing world peace and prosperity. Beyerhaus writes,

> The church was understood as part of the world. The only difference between her and the rest of the world is that, because of her knowledge of the saving goal of history, the Church now marches ahead of the rest of humanity as the vanguard in the movement toward this goal.[49]

---

46. This formation was the result of the merger between International Missionary Council (IMC), a subsidiary missionary council under the Students Volunteer Movement (SVM), and the World Council of Churches.

47. However, the more affluent Christian countries had also had their share in the issue. Western liberal theologians had embraced a new understanding of the church and its mission towards the realization of the Kingdom of God here on earth in terms of world peace contra the traditional understanding of salvation as salvation through personal reconciliation with God through faith in Jesus Christ. This issue was addressed by Peter Beyerhaus in his book. Beyerhaus, *Missions*, 17–40. Similarly John Stott rejected sociopolitical liberation, or the humanization of salvation, at Uppsala 1968 and Bangkok 1973. See Johnston, *Battle*, 305.

48. Beyerhaus, *Missions*.

49. Beyerhaus, *Evangelical*, 37.

Evangelical Churches (Evangelical Catholic)

Both dogmatism and pietism, whether conservative or liberal, co-existed under the umbrella name "evangelicals" (though some would not consider liberals as evangelicals; hence for them to be evangelical is to be conservative. This idea of course is no longer true today within the Protestant churches.)[50] Their existence was grounded primarily on a deep conviction for the Holy Scriptures. It was the evangelical churches that embraced an understanding of the church as both one and many. Having affirmed the catholic mark of the church, the Evangelicals have understood catholicity in terms of (the) unity in diversity of the church of Jesus Christ. The catholic spirit among the evangelical churches is sharpened both by the historical and theological understanding that though churches are many, yet they remain as one. This unity is grounded in a common faith and in a common commitment to the gospel of Jesus Christ. While participating in the ecumenical movement, the Evangelicals in general have embraced the idea that there exists an inherent unity among evangelical churches that is based on the Holy Scriptures. The evangelical churches are held together in unity by what they believe based on the Holy Scriptures that truly embody the faith of the Apostles of Jesus Christ. As heirs of the Reformation, evangelicals affirm their strong commitment to the Holy Scriptures as the primary source of both theology and practice. The following are some evangelical characteristics,[51]

---

50. In 1975, the year following the Lausanne Congress on World Evangelization, Professor Peter Beyerhaus of Tubingen distinguished six different evangelical groupings:

The New Evangelicals (including Billy Graham himself), who distance themselves from fundamentalism's science phobia and political conservatism, and strive for the greatest possible collaboration.

The Strict Fundamentalists, who are uncompromising in their separatist attitude.

The Confessing Evangelicals, who attach importance to a confession of faith and a rejection of contemporary doctrinal errors.

The Pentecostals and Charismatics.

The Radical Evangelicals, who acknowledge a sociopolitical commitment and strive to unite evangelistic witness and social action.

The Ecumenical Evangelicals, who are developing a critical participation in the ecumenical movement.

Quoted in Stott, *Evangelical Truth*, 8.

51. Collins lists four enduring emphases of the evangelicals: (1) the normative value of Scripture in the Christian life, (2) the necessity of conversion (whether or not dramatic or even remembered), (3) the cruciality of the atoning work of Christ as the sole mediator between God and humanity, and (4) the imperative of evangelism, of proclaiming the glad tidings of salvation to a lost and hurting world. Collins, *Evangelical Moment*,

1. Bible-based. We believe in the Bible that consists the sixty-six books of the Old and the New Testaments. The Bible as God-breathed (or inspired) is the Word of God to men and women in relation to salvation.

2. Trinitarian. Evangelicals affirm its commitment to the historical and theological understanding of the Christian God, who is Triune—Father, Son, and Holy Spirit.

3. Christ-centered. Evangelicals believe in the person of Christ as both Lord and Savior, and that he—being one hundred percent God and one hundred percent human—alone is the mediator between God and man. And the grace of God in its fullness is received only through him.

4. Justification by faith. At the heart of the evangelical doctrine of salvation is justification by faith. Evangelicals deny any other means to justification except through faith in Christ Jesus. Salvation cannot be secured through any sacraments or societies of the church.

5. The priesthood of all believers. Every believer is a priest. The distinction between the clergy and the laity is unbiblical.[52]

The above theological points are non-negotiable. They are expressions of the evangelical confessions and convictions; they sum up the evangelical truth of the evangelical faith. They hold all evangelical churches together not only in unity but also in diversity.

These evangelical emphases do not invite everybody into a structural unity. Unlike the Roman Church, the Evangelicals do not see the need for a unity of structure. Evangelicals allow diversity of traditions within the evangelical tradition, such as the Reformed tradition, the Wesleyan tradition, the Pentecostal-Charismatic tradition, the Baptist tradition, the Anabaptist tradition, the Orthodox tradition, the Anglican tradition and

---

21. Similarly, J. I. Packer identified six evangelical fundamentals: (1) the supremacy of the Holy Scripture, (2) the majesty of Jesus Christ, (3) the lordship of the Holy Spirit, (4) the necessity of conversion, (5) the priority of evangelism, and (6) the importance of fellowship. Similarly, David Bebbington listed five key ingredients of evangelicalism as conversionism (an emphasis on the "new birth" as a life-changing religious experience), Biblicism (a reliance on the Bible as ultimate religious authority), activism (a concern for sharing the faith), and crucicentrism (a focus on Christ's redeeming work on the cross). See Bebbington, *Evangelicalism*, 2–19, as quoted in Noll, *Scandal of the Evangelical*, 8.

52. Evangelicals today, however, have embraced a more compromising attitude on some social and political issues and have used the Holy Scriptures as the springboard for dialogue and discussions.

a number of independent traditions arising from a combination of two or three evangelical traditions (some would even combine Roman Catholicism with Evangelicalism).[53] This concept of unity in diversity arose from the evangelical understanding of the nature and function of the church of Jesus Christ. The catholicity of the evangelical faith is more of a mosaic fellowship of churches within the church of Jesus Christ united in the Spirit and in the Word. Moreover, the strong emphasis on the gospel and its proclamation to all the nations further define the evangelical catholicity, that is, the church of Jesus Christ exists for the world.

Conclusion

Catholicity is indeed a theological description of the nature and function of the church of Jesus Christ. Its beginning and development show the dynamic and complex revelation and evolution of the truth that defines the church—its life and mission—in and through its triangulate relationship: Christ, the church, and the world. The history of the catholicity of the church is inseparable from the history of the church itself—from conception to the commissioning of the early church, from its theological construction by the church fathers to conflicts with the heretics, from initial consummation under the Roman Church to its corruption by the institutional church, from the call of the Reformation to its compromise in the Ecumenical Movement, and to the challenge it pauses on the Evangelical churches today.

The history of the catholicity of the church also reveals catholicity as both a gift and a task. On the one hand, it is first and foremost a gift of relations anchored in Christ—a relation with the triune God, a relation within the body of Christ, and a relation with the world. On the other hand, it is a task—a task rooted in the divine call, a task of/toward the unity of the church, and a task of mission to the world. Catholicity as a gift and a task puts a balance to its divine and human aspects. The Roman Church has taken catholicity from the perspective of the former—a given divine authority; the Ecumenical Movement has made catholicity a purely ecclesiastical function in the form of a human institution.

Moreover the history of the catholicity of the church shows how it involves both the Spirit and the Word. They serve as the perimeter and power of catholicity. The unity of the church is not a creation of the church; it is

---

53. See Senn, *Protestant Spiritual*.

a gift of God through the Holy Spirit, who is Christ with us. On the other hand, the mission of the church is anchored in the gospel of Jesus Christ revealed in and through the Word. The church and its councils cannot redefine the catholic mission of the church and turn it into a human mission, for example, the humanization emphasis of the Ecumenical Movement. The evangelical and biblical definition of mission in terms of redemption is one that cannot be compromised. Catholicity requires the church to respond in and through faith—submission and obedience. Cooperation must not only be on the level of ecclesiastical cooperation, but cooperation with the Holy Spirit. Unity and mission are both engendered by the church's cooperation with the Holy Spirit in and through the Word. We do well to remember that where the Word is, there is the Spirit of the Lord. The Holy Spirit does not have his own independent work; his ministry is related or connected to the Word that bears witness both to God the Father and Jesus as Lord and Savior.

3

The Catholic Root

The Biblical-Theological Foundation of the Catholic Church

JESUS SAID, "AND I tell you that you are Peter, and on this rock I will build my church, and the gates of Hades will not overcome it" (Matt 16:18). Was Jesus referring to himself or someone else as the rock on which the church would be founded or built? Majority of evangelical scholars take Christ as the rock—Christ the rock of foundation.[1] But in order to understand this relationship between Christ and the church, the life and ministry of Christ has to be taken or seen from the larger perspective of God's redemptive history revealed in the Old Testament and fulfilled in the New Testament. Rightly so, because the story of the church in and through Christ is firmly rooted in God's redemptive history (*heilsgeschichte*) and mission (*Missio Dei*). In this chapter, we will focus our attention on the catholic root or the beginning of the catholic church and its mission in the context of the larger

---

1. See Ladd, *Theology*, 107–10. He argues that there exists a relationship between the Old Testament concept of the people of God and the New Testament concept of the people of God, and their relationship to Jesus and the Church. He writes, "Jesus' announcement of his purpose to build his *ekklēsia* suggests primarily what we have already discovered in our study of discipleship, namely, that the fellowship established by Jesus stands in direct continuity with the Old Testament Israel." The foundation-stone is applied in the New Testament primarily to Christ himself (1 Cor. 3:10ff.; 1 Pet. 2:6–8; etc), but cf. Ephesians 2:20; Revelation 21:14 for the apostles as foundation. Cullmann presents an argument in favor of Peter and that the image is highly significant. See Cullmann, *Peter*.

story of God's redemptive history as recorded in the Bible.[2] The underlying thesis of this chapter states that the stories of the men and women in the Bible serve as the catholic root of the church. This is where the story of the catholic faith all began and partially bloomed or was eventually fulfilled.

The story of the catholic church is a story of faith, that is, it is a religious or spiritual story that is rooted in the God who revealed himself as the holy Creator (in creation) and loving Redeemer (in the covenant), and his revelation demanded a radical response of obedience.[3] The meaning of faith here is both objective and subjective. The objective aspect is centered on God's act of saving men and women from their sins toward righteousness and life. The story of the Bible is set in the context of how men and women lost their footing in God's design for life and the world (see Gen 1–11), and how God reaches out in love to rescue the one he created in his own image. It is a story of God's offer of reconciliation to men and women, and the renewal of the rest of creations towards the establishment of the kingdom of God both here on earth as in heaven, and in the life to come in the language of the new heaven and the new earth. Moreover, the telling of how God reaches out to men and women, and the offer of reconciliation therein is achieved or received in and through faith, i.e., the positive response of men and women to God's work of reconciliation or redemption. This is the subjective aspect of faith.

This story of faith is what is presented or portrayed in the history of Israel as recorded in the Holy Scriptures—both in the Old Testament and the New Testament. The historical line or story plot that runs through the Bible is one that reveals the story of the catholic church deeply embedded in the various stories that make up the whole story of the Bible in the context of God's redemptive history.

The Story of Abraham

The story of faith in the context of God's redemptive history had its actual beginning in the patriarchal history with the call and election of

---

2. Contra Wright's understanding of the Gospel as establishing the kingship of God. See Wright, *How God Became King*.

3. Revelation is rightly defined as the active and passive acts of God intended to make himself and his will known for the purpose of saving men and women from sin and its consequences.

Abraham—the father of the faithful.[4] From this one man came a nation—Israel, and out of that nation came the community of nations—the catholic church. This community of nations is what God envisioned in his work of redemption since its actual beginning. Rightly so because the fall of Adam was not a personal fall but a universal one. Adam was the representative of humanity. The promise given to Abraham, which was God's answer to the fall of Adam, was really meant for all the nations of the earth. God had humanity in his call of Abraham. This is rooted in the universal promise of God to Abraham: "Go forth from your native land and from your father's home to a land that I will show you. I will make you a great nation, bless you, and make great your name, so be a blessing. I will bless those who bless you, and curse him who curses you; and through you shall bless themselves all the communities of the earth" (Gen. 12:1–3). Abraham was called neither for his own sake nor for the sake of a nation after him, but for the sake of the universal communities of the earth—the ultimate goal of Abraham's election and God's covenant with him and his offspring. OT Scholars affirm this truth,

> The choice and blessing of Abraham and the unconditional promises of land and nationhood in vv. 1f, have their ultimate goal v. 3, the great prospect that all communities of earth will gain blessing through him. Here at the beginning of redemptive history is already a word about the end of its course: the salvation promised Abraham ultimately will embrace all mankind."[5]

Hence, Abraham was the father not only of the nation of Israel but also the father of many nations (Gen 17:5; cf. Sarah as a mother of nations, Gen 17:16) or more aptly and theologically the "father of the faithful."[6]

Important in the story of the call and election of Abraham is the element of faith—how Abraham responded in faith and how it was credited

---

4. Torrance, however, thinks, "The church had its earthly beginning in Adam for then it began to subsist in the human society formed by God for immediate communion with himself. But in Adam the whole Church fell through disobedience, and its immediate relation with God was broken and interrupted by the barrier of sin and guilt. It fell not as a divine institution but in its constituent members, and therefore the Church upheld by the eternal will of God took on at once a new form under his saving acts in history." Torrance, "Foundation," 201.

5. LaSor et al., *Old Testament*, 112.

6. Dunning prefers the title "the father of the faithful" to the "father of the nations." The title connotes the theological inclusivity of the nature of the fatherhood of Abraham in relation to the church. Dunning, *Grace*, 512.

to him as righteousness.[7] This is because the story of Abraham was not just a story of grace and election. The story of Abraham is also a story of faith, which demanded from Abraham a radical obedience. This is shown in how Abraham had to abandon his roots—land, kindred, and immediate family—for a most uncertain destination or future of his life and family in response to the word of God (Gen 12:1). The call of Abraham was so radical that all he could do was *to believe and obey*. And by his faith, Abraham received the greatest gift a man could ever receive in his/her life—righteousness, a gift (or grace) of God that would be available to all nations that offers a relationship with God in and through the covenant by the same faith. Abraham had no idea as to where his faith or obedience would lead him, and how it would affect generations after him and his people, and the nations of the earth that would be known as the community of faith centuries after him and his offspring. With the faith of Abraham anchored in God's universal promise, the catholic church was born—many out of one and one out of many, that is, out of one man came many nations and out of the many nations would come the one community—the catholic church, a community of nations. Abraham's faith looked forward to or foreshadowed the faith of the nations of the earth, which would have its realization in the life of the church far beyond Abraham's time and his "ethnic" offspring Israel.

The church, then, was the covenant community in the embryo of God's covenant with Abraham, engendered both by grace and faith. Objectively the covenant was a covenant of grace (God's call and election), but subjectively it was also a covenant of faith (Abraham's response). Hence, it could be properly described as a covenant of grace and faith together. The story of Abraham was not an ordinary story of a nation but a covenant story for all nations—a covenant with the catholic church as its goal. LaSor, Hubbard, and Bush rightly conclude that, "The passage (i.e., the story of the call of Abraham) is also of programmatic significance for understanding the stories of the patriarchs that follow, *and ultimately the story of Jesus and his church*. It reveals that their theme throughout is the progress, vicissitudes, and ultimate victorious fulfillment of those promises which here stand like a rubric at their beginning. The author does not give a biography; he teaches theology, with various themes woven through his stories."[8] As

---

7. See Boadt, *Reading the Old Testament*, 141–44.
8. LaSor et al., *Old Testament*, 112. Italic is mine.

such, the story of Abraham was the beginning of the story of the church whose identity and mission are not ethnocentric but truly catholic.

The Stories of Isaac, Jacob, and Joseph

The story of faith continued historically and theologically in the stories of the patriarchs after Abraham. The promise given to Abraham was reaffirmed to each of the patriarchs thereafter: to Isaac (Gen 26:2–4), to Jacob at Bethel as he left Canaan for fear of his brother Esau, having stolen his birthright (Gen 28:13f.); again to Jacob at Bethel upon his return (Gen 35:11f.); and to Joseph and his sons (Gen 48:1–6). Behind these stories was the overarching redemptive history embedded in the themes of election and covenant.

Like the story of Abraham, the story of Isaac is a story of promise and faith. On the one hand, Isaac was a gift of God to Abraham and Sarah in the context of the promise given them. On the other hand, Isaac was a child of faith and eventually became a man of faith himself. And so in and through Isaac, the story of faith and promise continued. Interestingly and narratively though, Isaac's story was given secondary status in Genesis (but no way that the author considered it less important or less significant). The significance of the story of Isaac is in the fact that he was born as a result of his father's faith and God's promise. Isaac transitioned and connected the stories of Abraham and Jacob, which were both given complete cycles with Ishmael and Esau as secondary characters. The story of Jacob on the other hand portrays the theme of election and promise. It is a story that also denies ethnocentricity in God's redemptive history. Rightly so because the promise given to and the life lived by Isaac and Jacob were not on the basis of purely Abrahamic line but primarily and objectively on the basis of God's election, and consequently and subjectively through the faith of Isaac and Jacob in and through their encounters or interactions with God. This was established by God himself in his covenant with Israel as a nation,

> I also established my covenant with them [the patriarchs], to give them the land of Canaan . . . and I have remembered my covenant . . . I will redeem you with an outstretched arm . . . And I will bring you into the land which I swore to give to Abraham, to Isaac, and to Jacob. (Exod 6:4–8)

The story of Joseph is likewise a transitional story of faith—from a semi-nomadic, patriarchal family to an independent nation, in keeping with the promise. The life of Joseph brings the story of the patriarchs to the time of the promise land and nationhood, advancing God's redemptive plan and fulfilling the Abrahamic blessing or covenant in and through which "all the families of the earth shall find blessing" (Gen 12:3).

In sum, the stories of the patriarchs, beginning with Abraham, portray vividly at its early stage the story of faith—from one man to another, from a family to the twelve tribes, and they all looked forward to their ultimate vision, from a nation to the nations. The emphasis on the universal communities is unequivocally portrayed and communicated in and through God's covenant with the patriarchs. Hence, it is right to conclude that the catholic mark or catholicity of the church had its origin or beginning in the patriarchs.

The Story of Israel as a Nation

From Abraham to the people of Israel, the story of faith was not about men and women as individuals. Thomas F. Torrance believes that,

> It was with the redemption of Israel out of the bondage of Egypt and its establishment before God as a holy people in the ratification of the covenant at Sinai that Israel stood forth as the *Ecclēsia* or Church of God. "I am your God. Walk before me and be perfect. I am holy; therefore be ye holy."[9]

Indeed, the call and the promise of God were preparatory to something greater than the patriarchs or the people of Israel. God's promise would definitely not end in them. God's redemptive history is more about peoples or nations than individuals. This reflects God's original intention that was revealed in creation with his commands to Adam and Eve to "be fruitful and increase in number" so as to "fill the earth and subdue it" (Gen 1:28). And so it is with God's work of redemption—from individuals (the patriarchs) to peoples (Israel and nations). God is interested in creating a people for himself—a kingdom of nations. The story of faith is a story of a people—the people of God. Joseph's journey and settlement in Egypt was the first step in the making of God's people.

---

9. Torrance, "Foundation," 201. This is true in the context of the "church" as the people of God.

The Catholic Root

Out of the foreign land of Egypt and under the oppression of its people, God would multiply and deliver the "children of Israel" who would be the initial recipients of God's promise blessing to Abraham, Isaac, and Jacob, and they, as a people, would carry on a unique identity and mission as the then people of God in and through whom God would bless the nations. This is how the book of Exodus begins its story line of the story of the people of Israel as a nation (Exod 1:7).[10] This early story of Israel was unique, and rightly so, because Israel was a people so unlike the other known people groups or nations of the early Mediterranean world. It was the only people whose origin and future were shaped by their participation in God's call and covenant—a story of faith indeed. This is beautifully captured by Bernard W. Anderson in the following words in relation to its early and humble beginning as a people,

> In their fundamental confession of faith, the Israelite people affirmed that the God whom they worshiped, "heard our voice, and saw our affliction, our toil, and our oppression" and in a never-to-be-forgotten demonstration of grace, "brought us out of Egypt with a mighty hand and an outstretched arm, with greater terror, with signs and wonders" (Deut 26:5–9; see 6:21–25). Israel understood its history as originating in a marvelous liberation from distress and oppression. A dispirited band of slaves, bound together only by their common plight, would never have become a people—a covenant community with a sense of historical vocation—had God not acted on their behalf when they were helpless and hopeless. The verbs of the narrative sweep to a climax: God heard, God saw, God rescued.[11]

No other nations on earth in the ancient world had the same privilege as Israel had. Rightly so because of its unique relationship with God embedded in their story and identity as a people belonging to God. The life and faith of Israel centered on its confession of God's universally intended saving acts:

1. God chose Abraham and his descendants (Acts 13:17; Josh 24:3) and promised them the land of Canaan (Deut 6:23).

---

10. The children of Israel are the sons of Jacob, who are now presented as a people properly described as Israelites, i.e., the people of Israel. Childs notes, "The writer has moved from the tradition of a family to that of the nation. His fusion of the two traditions makes it clear that he understands the exodus as a direct continuation of the history begun in Genesis." Childs, *Book of Exodus*, 2.

11. Anderson, *Understanding*, 53.

2. Israel went down into Egypt (Acts 13:17; Josh 24:4) and fell into slavery (Deut 6:21; 26:5), from which the Lord delivered them (Acts 13:17; Josh 24:5-7; Deut 6:21f.; 26:8).

3. God brought Israel into Canaan as promised (Acts 13:19; Josh 24:11–13; Deut 6:23; 26:9).[12]

God's saving acts in Israel's history was the beginning of the long process and the bigger picture of redemptive history that would find its completion in the blessing of all nations through Jesus Christ and his church. Israel's story is an open-ended story pointing to its greater fulfillment in the Son of Abraham (Matt 1:1), who would draw all people to him (John 12:32), ending the alienation of humanity from God and from one another, and thereby creating a people out of many nations—a catholic people.

The story of Israel as a nation had its ups and downs. There were vicissitudes, victories, vulnerabilities, and volatilities that shaped its history prior to the fulfillment of the covenant given to the patriarchs that unfolded in the story of the coming of its messiah Jesus Christ. Rightly so because redemptive history has taken place in the context of the sinful world to which Israel was not an exemption—the effects of sin and the grace of God together portrayed in the OT served as the influencing factors of Israel's history. The following outlines the major epochs in the history of Israel,

1. The Exodus (Exodus-Deuteronomy)

2. The Conquest and the Settlement in the Land (Joshua)

3. The story of the Judges (Judges and Ruth)

4. The Monarchy (the United Kingdom and the Divided Kingdom) (1 and 2 Samuel; 1 and 2 Kings; 1 and 2 Chronicles, Isaiah, and other books in the Minor Prophets)

5. The Exile (Isaiah, Jeremiah, Lamentations, Ezekiel, Daniel)

6. The Return from Exile and the Rebuilding of the Temple (Ezra-Nehemiah, Esther, and other books in the Minor Prophets)

Each epoch of Israel's history is depicted in terms of how the people of Israel lived its faith, that is, whether the people of Israel were faithful or unfaithful to God and the covenant. God's active participation was not solely on the basis of his election of Israel as a nation, but also on their

12. LaSor et al., *Old Testament*, 55.

active participation in and through faith in the laws God had given them through Moses and entrusted to the priests and prophets. God's participation, however, was to serve not only the people of Israel but the nations with Israel as the light of the world. In and through his active participation, God was leading Israel towards its holy calling or faith vocation as God's instrument in bringing back the nations to him so that the world might be reconciled to its holy Maker.

The prophets were witnesses of this high calling God had given Israel as a chosen nation and consequently of the failure of Israel to live it out. Klaus Koch writes,

> In these writings (the Prophets), "to be chosen" does not imply exclusiveness. The phrase is meant to be understood in a functional sense: Israel has been set aside from the nations so that it may exercise a representative and priestly function on behalf of all human existence. It is quite understandable that his people should at that time had seen itself as the hub of the civilized world, in view of its historical experience, as well as its geopolitical situation on the neck of land joining Asia and Africa. And it was a standpoint borne out by the special character of Israel's religion and cult.[13]

The prophets had called Israel time and time again to its divine purpose and mission to all the nations. But Israel as a nation, with its high 'ethnocentricism' and consequently because of its unfaithfulness to the divine covenant, failed to bring the blessing to all the nations. The story of Israel as a nation would have ended in almost a tragedy (if it were not) had God not renewed the covenant (or better planned a new covenant) in and through the promised Messiah to which the prophets pointed men and women to. The problem of the fall caused by Adam's act of disobedience, and consequently and eventually by the unfaithfulness of Israel to the covenant was given a solution in the faithfulness of Jesus in and through whom all nations have been offered reconciliation to God through faith beginning from Abraham until the last son or daughter of Adam.

Apparently the new covenant is not a discontinuation of God's redemptive history. God had not lost sight of the universal promise he gave to Abraham, Isaac, and Jacob in and through whom all nations would come to be blessed. With the failure of Israel to live by faith and its vocation of faith,

---

13. Koch, *Prophets, vol. 2, Babylonian*, 198–99. See also Koch, *Prophets, vol. 1, Assyrian*. Koch discusses the books of the prophets and their messages in the context of God's history of salvation not only for Israel but for all nations.

however, a new direction has taken place with the covenant that would soon be fulfilled in and through Christ and his church. Both the promise and the election have been given new status—they are no longer exclusively to Israel but inclusively to the church—the new people of God. Hence, the covenant shifted from Israel-centered covenant to church-centered covenant. This direction is actually in line with the universal promise—the bringing of the covenant to communities of the earth. I will give attention to this new direction in the following stories—the story of Jesus and the story of the early church.

The Story of Jesus

The story of Jesus is understandably narrated in the context of the story of Israel. Rightly so, because the promise was in and through Abraham and his offspring. The Evangelists were apt to point the family line of Jesus as coming from Abraham through Israel (see Matt 1:1–12). This is an important connection that ushers or anchors the story of the church to God's redemptive history and its mission in general or its proclamation of the Gospel in particular to all the nations. This portrays that the subjects of the covenant are no longer limited to the people of Israel but now include the communities of the earth. But this should not come as a surprise to us because the saving of all nations was the original intention of God's covenant with Abraham and his offspring.

The story of Jesus is given to us in four narrative accounts—the Gospels. In the past, studies of the life and ministry of Jesus had ignored the unique differences of each of the Gospel accounts in search for or in favor of a more historical Jesus and its presentation, or even a theological Jesus. Newer studies, however, shifted the focus to more independent narrative gospel analysis of each of the Gospels with serious consideration to the uniqueness of each of the Gospels and the contribution they all give to a rich and varied portrayal of Jesus toward a holistic understanding of the life and ministry of Jesus in the light of the catholic church in general and the catholic gospel in particular, and of course, in the context of redemptive history.

Noticeable in the Gospels is the evangelists' presentation of the catholicity of the gospel. This is to say that the gospel in the Gospels is catholic. The life, death, and resurrection of Jesus were not intended to present salvation exclusively for the Jews. The evangelists accented this truth in their Gospel accounts. For example,

> For Luke Christ is not confined to Israel and its people. He portrays the Gospel as truly catholic. The life and ministry of Jesus, though particular, is relived in a wider and different context of its readers with their present faith community that addresses its unique challenges and needs. Similarly, Matthew testifies to the inclusivity of the Gospel. The life and ministry of Jesus is not exclusively Jewish: "Matthew's narrative therefore revolves around the theme of salvation not only for the Jews but also the inclusion of the Gentiles in the future of the kingdom. Such twofold theme is what is developed in the conflict of Matthew's narrative plot." With such inclusivity, no culture or nation has a monopoly of the good news of salvation. The Christian gospel is a gospel for all nations.[14]

The story of Jesus—his life, death, and resurrection—is the story of the gospel intended not only for Israel but for all nations. Using narrative criticism, I will examine how each of the Gospel narratives points to this universal truth of the Gospel, that is, how the evangelists presented the story of Jesus as centering on the universal redemptive plan of God in and through the life and ministry of Jesus that defines the identity and mission of the church in terms of catholic.

Matthew: The Fulfillment of the Promise

Each of the evangelists portrayed the life and ministry of Jesus as the fulfillment of the promise God gave to Abraham, Isaac, and Jacob. Matthew put more emphasis on this fulfillment motif. R. T. France writes,

> The essential key to all Matthew's theology is that in Jesus all God's purposes have come to fulfillment. This of course, true of all New Testament theology, but it is emphasized in a remarkable way in Matthew. Everything is related to Jesus. The Old Testament points forward to him; its law is "fulfilled" in his teaching; he is the true Israel through whom God's plans for his people now go forward; the future no less than the present is to be understood as the working out of the ministry of Jesus. History revolves around him, in that his coming is the turning point at which the age of preparation gives way to the age of fulfillment. Matthew leaves no room for any idea of the fulfillment of God's purposes, whether for

14. Hallig, "Contextualization," 154.

Israel or in any other respect, which is not focused in this theme of *fulfillment in Jesus*. In his coming a new age has dawned; nothing will ever be quite the same again.[15]

Matthew, in fact, began his gospel presentation with the genealogy of Jesus, the Christ (Matt 1:1–17). The point of the genealogy was to show to Matthew's community that the universal promise of God to Abraham, Isaac, and Jacob as it ran in and through the story of Israel has come to its fulfillment in Jesus as the one who would save the people from their sin (Matt 1:21). The salvation of peoples is the ultimate goal of God's redemptive history in and through which all nations would come to and share in the blessing of Abraham. Flemming also emphasizes how Matthew presented the story of Jesus as the turning point of God's redemptive history,

> Matthew reassures his audience on the one hand that in following Jesus the promised Messiah, "they were being completely faithful to their Jewish heritage and would find in Jesus's teaching and example the embodiment of all that God had promised Israel." On the other hand, Matthew's story proclaims that in the life, death and resurrection of Jesus, God has brought about a turning point in the history of salvation, Israel's rejection of its King and the church's mission to the Gentiles (Mt. 24:14; 28:18–20) mean that God is calling non-Jews to be a part of a new people of the kingdom, the future of Matthew's Jewish Christian readers is with the Gentiles.[16]

Matthew's narrative indeed revolves around the theme of the universal salvation inclusive of both Jews and Gentiles. This is the overall plot of the Gospel of Matthew.

For Matthew, therefore, Jesus was the king not only of the Jews but also of the Gentiles. Christ indeed is the messiah-king of all nations. The title "King of the Jews" is an all inclusive messianic title that embraces all peoples of the earth. An irony indeed. This is so because the Jews rejected Christ as their king and savior, opening the way for the kingship of Jesus to be universal—the fulfillment of the promise given to Abraham and his offspring. As a result the subjects of the kingdom are no longer limited to the people of Israel. The kingship of Jesus now includes the nations of the earth. Hence, the title "King of the Jews" could aptly be interpreted as "King of the Nations," or put another way, the "King of the Faithful" inclusive of

15. France, *Gospel*, 38.
16. Flemming, *Contextualization*, 245.

Jews and Gentiles. The Great Commission highlights this truth in terms of the inclusiveness of the gospel and its calling:

> All authority in heaven and on earth has been given to me. Therefore *go and make disciples of all nations*, baptizing them in the name of the Father and of the Son and of the Holy Spirit, and teaching them to obey everything I have commanded you. And surely I am with you always. (Matt 28:18–20)

In Jesus, the kingdom is now made available to all the nations of the earth. R. T. France notes that the kingship of Jesus is a declaration of his universal sovereignty—the climax of the very gospel itself.[17] With the gospel, the promise blessing now comes to reality. Christ, indeed, is the offspring of Abraham in and through whom all nations would come to be blessed.

In Jesus Christ the purposes of God for Israel and the nations come together. That Jesus is the offspring of Abraham is an important theological sign that points to the reality of the universal promise blessing given to Abraham. This reality comes into fullness in the life and ministry of the new community of faith—the church, whose membership is catholic and whose mission is to *make disciples of all nations*.

Mark: The Dawn of the New Age

The Gospel of Mark points readers to the beginning of the Gospel of Jesus Christ—the dawn of the new age. Mark was the first of the four evangelists to have given attention to the non-exclusivity of the fulfillment of the promise of God by announcing the good news primarily to a Gentile community. Such is a radical beginning in and through which the universal promise of God breaks in to usher the covenant to its new people inclusive of both Jews and Gentiles. As such the Gospel is also the beginning of the new people of God—the church whose membership is no longer ethnocentric but catholic and whose mission now includes all nations.

Contrary to the popular Jewish messianic expectation, Mark presented Jesus as the suffering messiah in and through whom all nations would come to faith and share in the blessing of the covenant. This is so because Mark was encouraging his community to endure their own experience of suffering. William Lane notes this beautifully in the following words,

---

17. France, *Gospel*, 45.

When Roman believers received the Gospel of Mark they found that it spoke to the situation of the Christian community in Nero's Rome. Reduced to a catacomb existence, they read of the Lord who was driven deep into the wilderness (Ch. 1:12f.). The detail, recorded only by Mark, that in the wilderness Jesus was with the wild beasts (Ch. 1:13) was filled with special significance for those called to enter the arena where they stood helpless in the presence of wild beasts. In Mark's Gospel they found that nothing they could suffer from Nero was alien to the experience of Jesus. Like them, he had been misrepresented to the people and falsely labeled (Ch. 3:2f., 30). And if they knew the experience of betrayal from within the circle of intimate friends it was sobering to recollect that one of the Twelve had been "Judas Iscariot, who betrayed him" (Ch. 3:19).[18]

Mark anchored the theme of suffering in Isaiah's presentation of the Christ who would come to save the many from sin (Isa 53). Thus, it is right to say that Mark's emphasis on the suffering of Jesus is a commentary to the messianic prophecy of Isaiah intended for all nations (Isa 40–66). The gospel then for Mark is at the outset a catholic gospel intended for all nations (Mark 13:10) rather than for the ethnic Israel. With the gospel of Jesus Christ, the dawn of the new age has come indeed. The covenant has reached a new historical fulfillment with the inclusion of the Gentiles into the people of God. The identity of the people of God is expanded but not in terms of an ethnic expansion of the people of Israel.[19] The new messianic community, though out of Israel, is not ethnically Israel but a new people—the church whose membership and mission is not in terms of Abrahamic line and Israel's ethnic identity as a nation, but in terms of Abrahamic faith and his offspring in and through Jesus Christ.

Mark further highlights the dawn of the new age as related to the new community—the church—with his interest in the Gentile mission. The story of Jesus in Mark revolves around Jesus's ministry in Galilee and its surrounding areas. Scholars believe that the Galilean ministry in Mark is highly symbolic of Mark's interest in the Gentile mission. R. Allan Cole notes this,

> Marxsen and those who follow see a highly symbolic use of the word 'Galilee' in Mark. To them, "Galilee" stands as a symbol for

18. Lane, *Gospel*, 15.

19. See Vanlaningham, "Evaluation," 179–93, where the author argues contra Wright's position that Israel is the church.

the wider Gentile Christian world, just as "Judea" or "Jerusalem" stand for the Jewish world. This links with Marxen's somewhat fanciful view that Mark's Gospel was an exhortation to Jerusalem Christians to flee to Galilee in AD 70, or that it was written to meet the contemporary situation of the church in Galilee, as it was awaiting and expecting Christ' *parousia* or second coming. Galilee therefore stands for Gentile mission, and what we have here is an encouragement of the largely Gentile church of Rome to engage in it.[20]

Mark's gospel is a catholic gospel indeed. The preaching of the gospel to all the nations makes this emphatic: "And the gospel must first be preached to all nations" (Mark 13:10). That the gospel had reached Rome (the center of human civilization at that time) and that Christ was proclaimed to its people there were already indicative of the new age in God's redemptive history—from Jerusalem to Rome, and from Israel to all the nations.

Luke: The Good News for the Poor

Of the synoptic Gospels, Luke is the most catholic Gospel. In his book *A Dynamic Reading of the Holy Spirit in Luke-Acts*, Ju Hur points to how the plot of Luke-Acts depicts a geographical expansion that shows the witness of the church not only to Jews but also to Gentiles,

> The plot depicts a geographical expansion, which is carried out by leading Spirit-inspired characters. Thus, the narrator highlights the geographical setting in developing the plot, e.g. Jesus' witness from Galilee to Jerusalem in the Gospel and his disciples' witness from Jerusalem, through Judea and Samaria, and to Rome in Acts. Jerusalem, thus seems to be the geographical centre of Luke-Acts (or at least of the Gospel). Nevertheless, from the beginning, the gospel of or the witness to Jesus is to be delivered beyond the territory of Israel (Lk. 2:32; Acts 1:8; 2:5–11): the salvific witness is directed not only to Jews, but also to Gentiles (Lk. 2:32; 24:47; Acts 1:8), first through Jesus who is depicted as chosen, baptized/anointed and commissioned by God (Lk. 4:18, 43; 9:48; 10:16; Acts 3:20, 26), and then through Jesus' followers who are similarly chosen, baptized (metaphorically and literally) and commissioned through the risen Jesus by God (Lk. 9:2; 10:1, 3; 22:35; 24:49; Acts 1:5, 8; 2:4; 9:17; 26:17). Most importantly, readers can see at

---

20. Cole, *Gospel*, 95.

almost every critical plot-stage of the mission in Acts (8:29, 39, 10:19; 11:12; 13:2, 4; 16:6, 7; 19:21; 20:22) that the Holy Spirit appears as a reliable mission supporter and/or director who, on the one hand, empowers and guides the witnesses and, on the other, verifies certain groups as God's people. In this regard, the plot is developed through a geographical expansion caused by God's divine agent, that is, the Spirit (including an angel of the Lord), and by God's human agents, that is, Spirit-inspired witnesses, in order to fulfill the plan of God.[21]

Indeed, the concept of salvation in Luke's narrative is not exclusive but inclusive. Jesus is the savior not only of the people of Israel, though in particular he came for them, but also of the whole world (Luke 3:21). Moreover, the meaning of the saving acts of Christ is not limited to Jewish traditional understanding of repentance, forgiveness, and faith. Flemming writes, "Jesus offers liberation from whatever forces create brokenness and exclusion in the human situation, and whatever tries to frustrate God's redemptive purpose."[22] The presentation of Luke's expanded meaning of salvation includes Jesus's healing ministry, Jesus's compassion for the outcast of the society—the poor, the oppressed, the sick, the lepers, the "sinners," the tax collectors, women, children, Samaritans, and Gentiles.[23] Luke's inclusive-salvation is the movement of his narrative plot and characterization in the Third Gospel.

The life and ministry of Jesus centered on his saving activities for the poor. At his inaugural address to his townspeople in Nazareth, Jesus announced before them his mission to proclaim the very gospel to the poor:

> The Spirit of the Lord is on me, because he has anointed me to preach good news to the poor. He has sent me to proclaim freedom for the prisoners and recover of sight for the blind, and to release the oppressed, to proclaim the year of the Lord's favor (Luke 4:18–19).

The gospel to Luke was inseparable from Jesus's activities and associations with the poor. Luke's portrayal of Christ emphasized how Jesus literally ministered to and identified himself with the poor. I highlighted this in the

---

21. Hur, *Dynamic Reading*, 190–91
22. Flemming, *Contextualization*, 254.
23. See BDAG, "sōtēria," 986. The authors believe, "This salvation makes itself known and felt in the present, but it will be completely disclosed in the future." Ibid.

paper I wrote entitled, "The Eating Motif in the Third Gospel, and Luke's Characterization of Jesus as the Son of Man,"

> Luke further presented Jesus as faithful to God and his mission. Jesus clearly said that "the Son of Man came to seek and save the lost" (19:10). He knew his mission and was faithful to it through his association with the lowly ones of the society. When asked by the Pharisees and the teachers of the Law why he ate and drank with tax collectors and sinners, Jesus answered, "It is not the healthy who need a doctor, but the sick. I have not come to call the righteous, but sinners to repentance" (5:31–32). The first person pronoun "I" had the sense of the "Son of Man" as it echoed in their ears, telling them why he came and for whom he came. Eating with sinners was for Jesus an act consistent with his mission, that is, the salvation of sinners. To do otherwise would be to deny the one who sent him. Jesus's faithfulness is highlighted further by Luke's characterization of him as a friend of sinners. Jesus's association with sinners and tax collectors was criticized by the Pharisees and other religious leaders in terms of friendship (7:34). Green notes, "This is the irony of the criticism both John [the Baptist] and Jesus received: They are rejected for behaviors that are actually symptomatic of their faithfulness to the work for which God set them apart." This presentation of Jesus through the words of the Pharisees and religious leaders, with Jesus's confirmatory response, contributes to Luke's characterization of the Son of Man as a faithful savior—a faithful friend of sinners and other outcasts.[24]

The poor in Luke takes the central stage in Jesus's public ministry.[25] Apparently the poor in Luke do not refer to the poor of Israel only but the poor of all nations included. It refers to anyone who sees himself or herself under the mercy and grace of God—the poor, the prisoners, the blind and the oppressed. The poor are those that are wholly dependent on God for life and sustenance.[26] And indeed in and through Jesus the Gospel was preached to the poor (see also Isa 61:1 where the gospel is preached to the poor); hence, Luke's gospel is good news for the poor.

---

24. Hallig, "Eating," 216, with a quote from Green, *Gospel*, 303.

25. See David, "Rich," 701–10.

26. See BDAG, "ptōchos," 896. "At times the reference is not only to the unfavorable circumstances of these people from an economic point of view; the thought is also that since they are oppressed and disillusioned they are in special need of God's help, and may be expected to receive it shortly." Ibid.

John: The Word for the World

The Gospel of John is unique among the four Gospels. The evangelist's presentation of the life and ministry of Jesus is more theological than historical. The words and deeds of Jesus were not only presented but also interpreted; it remains, however, that John did so in the context of proclaiming Christ as did the other evangelists to call people to believe: "These are written that you may believe that Jesus is the Christ, the Son of God, and that by believing you may have life in his name" (John 20:31). To John, however, it is more explicit than implicit as in the synoptic that the gospel of Jesus Christ is not exclusively for the Jews but also for the Gentiles. It is a gospel for the world (cf. John 3:16). With the rejection of Israel, the coming of Christ has been made available to anyone who would believe in him whether Jews or Gentiles: "Yet to all who received him, to those who believed in his name, he gave the right to become children of God" (John 1:12). The concept of the "children of God" now extends clearly and theologically to non-Jews who believed in the Gospel. Such extension is in accord with God's redemptive history—the saving of all mankind: "Look, the Lamb of God, who takes away the sin of the world" (John 1:29b).

Hence, John presented Jesus as the Word for the world: "In the beginning was the Word . . . In him was life, and that life was the light of men . . . The true light that gives light to every man was coming into the world" (John 1:1-9). This is supported by what Jesus said about himself, "I am the light of the world. Whoever follows me will never walk in darkness, but will have the light of life" (John 8:12). The other "I Am" sayings of John presented Christ as inclusively inviting men and women to faith so they would have life in him. And by the personal claims attributed to Jesus about himself and his mission, Christ is presented as the Messiah of the world—the Word for the world. This is most clearly seen in Jesus's dialogue with a Pharisee, named Nicodemus: "For God so loved the *world* that gave his one and only Son, that whoever believes in him shall not perish but have eternal life" (John 3:16). The reference to the world in here is directed to all the nations, men and women who would come to believe regardless of their ethnic identity. This supports the biblical idea of redemptive history as directed towards men and women of all nations. The call of Abraham indeed has the world as its very goal—for God so loved the world. And so in Christ, the promise given to Abraham and his children now comes to its fullness in the life and ministry of Jesus.

The Catholic Root

To John, the story of the life and ministry of Jesus is more than a story of the Jewish carpenter or the king of the Jews. Focusing on the life and ministry of Jesus as a story accentuates the Jewish characteristics of the Gospel. To get out of this mold, John opted to offer a more interpreted story of the life and ministry of Jesus, and by doing so he has effectively communicated a Gospel for the world. John's goal for writing was more than the retelling of the life and ministry of Jesus as did the synoptic gospels. He wrote with a theological purpose that uncovers the identity of Jesus as the Messiah, the Son of God in and through whom people would have *life* (John 20:31).[27] John's characterization of Jesus supports his narrative intent of faith and life. John presented Jesus as the Son of God—a more theological characterization of Jesus. G. Eldon Ladd highlights the centrality of this title when he writes,

> One of the most distinct differences between the synoptic and John is the different role Jesus' sonship to God plays. In the synoptic tradition, Jesus is reticent to speak of his sonship and God's Fatherhood. Pater is used by Jesus of God in Mark four times, Q eight or nine, Matthew some twenty-three times. In the synoptic this form of speech is confined to the latter half of his ministry, and is used by Jesus only when speaking to his disciples. However, Jesus speaks of God as Father 106 times in John, and the usage is not restricted to any period of his ministry or to any group of hearers. He speaks of "my Father" twenty-four times in John, eighteen in Matthew, six in Mark, three in Luke. It is obvious that Jesus' sonship is the central Christological idea in John, and that he writes his Gospel to make explicit what was implicit in the Synoptics. The Gospel is written that people may believe that Jesus is the Messiah, but more than Messiah, he is the Son of God (20:31).[28]

Such theological characterization supports the plot of John as revolving around the sovereign identity of Jesus as the Son of God. R. Alan Culpepper believes that the character of Jesus in the Gospel is static, it does not change.[29] Right at the beginning of the Gospel, the prologue, Jesus was presented in an intimate relationship with the Father—as the pre-incarnate Word who was with God and was God himself (see John 1:1–18). This was held in the middle of the narrative both in words and events, and was

---

27. For a discussion on the meaning of life, which proceed from God and Christ, see BDAG, "zōē," 430.
28. Ladd, *Theology*, 283.
29. Culpepper, *Anatomy*, 103–4.

sustained towards the end of the narrative, informing believers that Jesus was the Son of God. Such theological characterization of Jesus was to present him as the Word for the world whose identity and mission are revelatory of his intimate relationship with God as co-equal and the world as God's co-creator.

The Story of the Early Church

The story of the early church follows directly the story of Jesus. It is actually the valid continuation or extension of the ministry of Jesus in and through the active engagement of the Holy Spirit with the various ministries of the disciples in Jerusalem, Judea, and Samaria, and to the ends of the earth (Acts 1:8). The book of Acts—the sequel of the gospel of Luke—and the letters of Paul (Pauline Letters) and others (General Epistles) that follow have given us the early historical beginnings and developments of the catholic church. They summed up for us the dynamic growth and world-wide expansions of the witness of the church bringing the gospel of Jesus Christ to new territories, conquering men and women of many nations and bringing them before the blessing God promised long before Israel's existence with Abraham—the father of many nations.

After the ascension of Jesus, Luke brings his readers to the historical birth of the catholic church with the coming of the Holy Spirit on the Day of the Pentecost as the disciples, upon the instruction of the resurrected Jesus, were gathered in the upper room praying. Scholars believe that the coming of the Holy Spirit marked the actual historical beginning of the catholic church. The gift of tongues was symbolic of the new reality in God's redemptive history. The Gospel the disciples would soon proclaim to the whole world was here experienced in many languages by men and women who served as the nucleus of the new people of God—the catholic church, a community of nations.

In Acts, Luke outlines the early history of the church in terms of its geographical expansion—Jerusalem, Judea, and Samaria, and the ends of the earth. Using narrative blockings, I offer my own outline of Acts,

1. First Narrative Block: The Witness Initiation (1:1–2:47)

2. Second Narrative Block: The Witness in Jerusalem (3:1–8:1a)

3. Third Narrative Block: The Witness in Judea and Samaria (8:1b–11:18)

4. Fourth Narrative Block: The Witness to the Ends of the Earth (11:19–28:31)[30]

The book of Acts presents to us the catholic witness of the church. But the witness of the church was patterned after the witness of Jesus in and through the power of the Holy Spirit and the suffering of the church. Moreover, the growth and expansion of the church happened in and through the inclusive leadership of the catholic church.[31] For example, both the central churches in Jerusalem and Antioch took responsibility in the mission of the church to all the nations. The leadership of the church was no way exclusive owing it to the new identity of the church as catholic.[32] Later Jerusalem and Antioch centers were joined by other centers such of Ephesus, Corinth, and then Rome in and through which the gospel gained more and more disciples of Jesus Christ, and in the spirit of the covenant, made more children of Abraham.[33]

The early church had also its problems, challenges, and opportunities as it established itself to be the kind of church it should be—catholic. Issues such as unity, polity, theology, and ethics confronted the churches in various places and contexts. Scholars define or describe some of the issues as problems of the emerging early catholicism. The General Epistles, for example, were viewed and studied in the context of early catholicism.

In sum, the early church had reached many nations and had become a community of many nations. The church in Rome foreshadowed the greater life and mission of the early church in what would be known as the catholic church inviting men and women to take part in the blessing God

---

30. Hallig, "Spirit and Suffering," 99.

31. Or better "a diffusion of leadership." See Land, *Diffusion of Ecclesiastical*.

32. Land argues that the innovation of leaders in Acts fostered a diffusion of ecclesiastical authority. By consistently sharing their authority with others, these leaders allowed the diffusion of authority to new individuals rather than the concentration of authority in the hands of the few. Undoubtedly, this selflessness on the part of the church's leaders contributed to the spread of the Gospel throughout the Mediterranean world. By regularly empowering new leaders, the church was able to release its leaders for ministry in new locations without fear of leaving established churches leaderless. Yet one should not suppose that, through such diffusion, ecclesiastical authority became diluted. As we have seen, the leaders in Acts shared their authority without thereby losing it. They were able to do this because their authority was based on deference and mutual honor, not only on legal rights. Thus, the diffusion of ecclesiastical authority resulted in a net increase of authority, which in turn propelled the growth of the church. Ibid., 229–30.

33. See Arnold, "Centers," 144–52. Arnold includes Alexandria of Egypt as important center of the early catholic church.

had given to Abraham, Isaac, and Jacob, and ultimately fulfilled in his one and only begotten Son, Jesus Christ, Abraham's offspring.

Conclusion

The story of the catholic church is a biblical story. It is a story of God's redemptive history—rescuing men and women from sin and restoring them to his image—and the renewal of creations adversely affected by the consequences of the disobedience of Adam. In and through God's redemptive history God intended to create a people for himself—a community not only of one nation but of many nations, who would serve as the kingdom people. It is a story of God's covenant that began with Abraham, Isaac, and Jacob. The covenant tells us that the people of God are far from an ethnocentric community such as Israel; it is a catholic community. Abraham was to be the father of many nations.

The fulfillment of the promise given to Abraham was made realized in and through the story of Jesus and carried on by the church that is truly catholic in life and mission. But the catholic community must not be construed in terms of an ethnic identity or limited to eschatological community. The people of God are a community of nations called to carry on the mission of God here on earth. The biblical story is an open-ended story—a story that will always find its fulfillment in the life and mission of the present catholic church. And on this story, the biblical story, we stand. It is the story of God's redemption in and through Christ—the rock on whom the church—its life and mission—is founded or built—as Torrance puts it—it is "The foundation of the Church."[34]

---

34. Torrance, "Foundation," 199–215.

4

The Catholic Faith/Tradition

Traditions and the Formation of Creeds

In response to the Pharisees and teachers of the law, Jesus said, "Isaiah was right when he prophesied about you hypocrites; as it is written: 'These people honor me with their lips, but their hearts are far from me. They worship me in vain; their teachings are but rules taught by men. You have let go of the commands of God and are holding on to the traditions of men" (Mark 7:6–8). With this, I am almost apprehensive to write something about the tradition or traditions of the church. What if by doing so, the words of Jesus would fall the same way on us, and that with our own traditions the church today is guilty of the same pharisaic hypocrisy and misinterpretations of the word of God so that our teachings are but rules taught by men. Why can't we indeed focus on the plain commands of God and live by them? Sadly revelation is not only plain and simple but also a complex historical and theological recital of God's making known of himself and his will in and through human history, language, and culture.

The work of the church to deliver or to "hand over"[1] (derived from the Greek word *paradosis*) and pass on (from the Latin word *traditio*) its catholic faith had indeed not been easy. It involved the church's faithful narration of the faith-events and their historical and theological interpretations. The long history, and often filled with controversies and struggles, of the formation of the pre-Reformation catholic creeds, for example, already proved the difficulty. But in spite of the challenge, this theological discipline was

---

1. See *Oxford*, 1369 as quoted by H. L. Ellison in "Tradition," 526.

absolutely necessary not only towards the strengthening of the identity and unity of the church but also toward the progress of the witness and mission of the church. And it remains true today. The catholic church today and its Holy Scriptures and their interpretations are the products of the faithful and early works of various Christian traditions. H. L. Ellison writes,

> Where there is evidence that tradition has been carefully preserved, we value its historical testimony, though we subordinate it to the illumination of the Spirit in the interpretation of Scripture. The most striking example of this is the Masoretic Text of the OT. Though this did not take its present definitive form till the sixth to ninth centuries A.D.—the consonantal text is attested by the Qumran discoveries as existing essentially in its present modern scholars are loath to leave it unless the clear sense and divergent traditions of the versions demand it. In the RSV probably 98 percent of the translation remains true to the Masoretic tradition.[2]

Is the catholic faith based on a tradition (singular) or traditions (plural)? The answer to this question depends on several assumptions: Does the Holy Scripture play the role as the only definitive source in the shaping and developing of the Christian Tradition or is the Holy Scripture insufficient as some of the Roman Catholic theologians say?; Is the nature of tradition an organic statement of the catholic faith or a set of ecclesiastical doctrines or precepts?; Do churches receive tradition or construct traditions from the raw material of the Holy Scriptures or others?; Do churches receive various forms of tradition in the same manner? Various councils of the Roman Catholic Church, for example, differ: "whereas Trent, interested in objective content, spoke of traditions in the plural, Vatican II, in *Dei Verbum*, speaks of tradition in the singular."[3]

The catholic faith is based on the church's historical and theological tradition that encompasses various interpretations of the Holy Scriptures from its many members. The various theological traditions within the body of Christ are demonstrative and definitive of the rich and dynamic tradition of the catholic church. It is the "traditions within the tradition" that make the catholic faith so unique, uncompromising, and universal. Though objective in their contents for they have been drawn primarily from the teachings of the Holy Scriptures, the traditions still emphasize their subjective and dynamic characteristics that contribute to the living and catholic

---

2. Ibid., 527.
3. Dulles, *Craft*, 94.

tradition of the church. This makes the spirit of the catholic faith real and active, that is to say that the catholic tradition is identified with the total and on-going life and praxis of the church.[4] And so while tracing the historical and theological development of the tradition of the church in and through its various traditions, it will be demonstrated that the catholic tradition of the church expresses the living faith of the church.[5]

Jesus: The Kingdom of God

The catholic faith originates from God—the revelation that was delivered to the church in and through Jesus Christ by the power and effectual ministry of the Holy Spirit.[6] This means that the tradition of the church is anchored in God's redemptive history revealed in the Old Testament, fulfilled in the New Testament, and delivered to the apostles. At the heart of the Christian tradition is Christ—his person and his preaching.

What defines the life and ministry of Jesus? Or in a more biblical-theological question—what is the unifying center or coherent core of the theology of the New Testament in particular and biblical theology in general that gives witness to the person and preaching of Christ? David Wenham, following the spirit and theology of G. E. Ladd, believes that New Testament theology is all about the divine mission to the world, but that includes the following elements:

1. The *context*: The one creator God, the God of Israel, in his love and in fulfillment of the Scriptures, intervened through Jesus to complete his saving purposes through his people Israel and thus to bring a broken and hostile world back under his rule and to restore it to the love and perfection that God intended.

2. The *center*: Jesus was the Spirit-filled Messiah of Israel and the Son of God. Through his life, teaching, and supremely through his death and resurrection he announced and inaugurated the saving rule of God, inviting others to receive the divine gift.

---

4. Ibid., 95.

5. Distinguishing tradition from traditionalism, Pelikan writes, "Tradition is the living faith of the dead, traditionalism is the dead faith of the living."

6. For a discussion on God and the church, see Torrance, "Foundation," in Ray S. Anderson, ed., *Theological Foundation*.

3. The *community*: Those who receive Jesus and his salvation by faith —baptism and eucharist are expression of such faith—are through and with him the true Israel, children of God, having the Holy Spirit of sonship. They are called to live as a restored community in loving fellowship with God and with each other and to proclaim and live the good news of restoration in the world.

4. The *climax*: The mission of restoration will be complete at the Lord's return to judge the world, when evil will finally be overcome, God's people will be raised and perfected, and the whole of creation will be restored to its intended glory.[7]

In sum, the life and ministry of Jesus demonstrated and delivered to the community of disciples the reality and totality of the Kingdom of God. It is the Kingdom of God that Jesus handed over to his disciples from the Father in and through his redemptive work: "Repent for the Kingdom of God is near" (Matt 4:17, 23; Mark 1:14–15; Luke 4:21). The Kingdom was demonstrated in words and deeds both in the life and ministry of Jesus from his conception and birth, to his public ministries—teaching, preaching, and healing, and to his death, resurrection, and ascension. These are the objective contents of the gospel accounts of the four canonical Gospels that represented the authoritative interpretations of the events of the life and ministry of Jesus centered on the Kingdom of God.[8]

This Kingdom of God tradition was earlier revealed in the Old Testament and later fulfilled in the New Testament. Ladd's diagram illustrating the dynamic Kingdom of God shows this relationship between the Old Testament and the New Testament,[9]

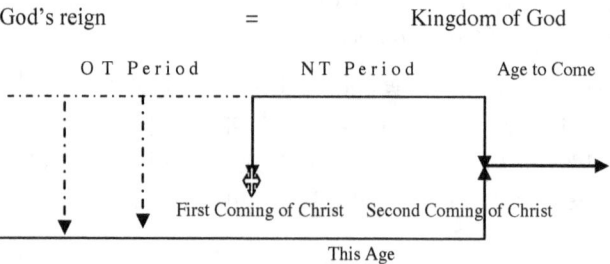

---

7. Wenham, "Unity," quoted in Ladd, *Theology*, 712–13.

8. The emergence of the Gospel traditions occurred in response to the various needs of the early church and the challenges of the heretics particularly the Gnostics.

9. Ladd, *Theology*, 67.

The Catholic Faith/Tradition

Ladd is right to conclude that, "This diagram also suggests that God's Kingdom was active in the Old Testament. In such events as the Exodus and the captivity in Babylon, God was acting in his kingly power to deliver or judge his people. However, in some real sense, God's Kingdom *came* into history in the person and mission of Jesus."[10] It is the same Kingdom of God that Jesus handed over to his community of disciples toward universal expansion. Thomas F. Torrance sums this up beautifully,

> From the very start of his public ministry Jesus came proclaiming the Gospel of the Kingdom of God and saying, "The time is fulfilled, and the Kingdom of God is at hand: repent ye and believe the Gospel," and set about at once calling people to himself in his mission to gather and redeem the people of God. With his advent and presence the transcendent Kingdom of God that had so long been the object of longing and prophecy had arrived and was active among men for their salvation. In the whole historico-redemptive activity of God in Israel the Kingdom of God and the people of God were essentially correlative conceptions, or rather two different aspects, of the one rule of God grounded in creation and made good in redemption. It was to be fulfilled through the saving acts of God in Israel but on fulfillment it would inevitably transcend the boundaries of Israel and take form as the universal kingship of God over all his creation. That Kingdom was to be ushered in with the coming of the Messiah, the anointed King, through whom it would be grounded on earth in the redeeming and raising up of a people who would enter into the Kingdom as its constituent members and be themselves the instrument through which the Kingdom would extend its rule over the ends of the earth. Small though its beginning was, grouped immediately round the person of the Messiah, it would grow and spread until all nations were brought under its rule. "Fear not little flock, for it is your Father's good pleasure to give you the Kingdom."[11]

Christian traditions are all anchored in the Kingdom tradition that Jesus himself delivered through his own life in general and his atoning death in particular. Any traditions that deviate from the Kingdom are not to be considered from God. The Holy Scripture is the objective witness of the Kingdom. In and through the process of the canonization of the books of the Holy Scriptures, the Kingdom tradition has been "inscripturated." And to this both the community of faith and the Holy Spirit actively participated

10. Ibid.
11. Torrance, "Foundation," 206.

to ensure the preservation and continuing proclamation of the Kingdom of God delivered through the Prophets in the Old Testament and through the Apostles in the New Testament. The subjective witness of the Kingdom is the Holy Spirit. The Kingdom tradition is what the Holy Spirit engenders and sustains in the church through his dynamic inspiration and empowerment in and through the Holy Scriptures. Noticeable in the Holy Scriptures are the various traditions of the Kingdom such as,

1. The Mosaic tradition
2. The Davidic tradition
3. The Prophetic tradition/s
4. The Gospel tradition/s
5. The Pauline tradition
6. The Petrine Tradition
7. Other traditions

These traditions make up what is now known as the fixated tradition or the interpreted tradition.[12] Prior to their fixation in the Scripture, they were passed on in different forms, for example, in the New Testament there were at least four: (1) the catechetical instruction, (2) Hymns, (3) Liturgy, and (4) Sacrament. The kingdom tradition is what Jesus came to deliver to men and women of all nations, and handed it over to his disciples. And to this the church is now the witness.

The Early Church: "Jesus is Lord"

One of the early, if not *the* earliest, confessions of the early church was the confession of the Lordship of Jesus Christ: "If you declare with your mouth, 'Jesus is Lord,' and believe in your heart that God raised him from the dead, you will be saved" (Rom 10:9; cf. Jesus is the Christ, John 20:31). By this confession the early church shifted from the Kingdom-centered preaching of Christ to *Christ-centered* preaching of the Kingdom. Christ has become the very content of the Gospel: "For what we preach is not ourselves, but *Jesus Christ as Lord*, and ourselves as your servants for Jesus's sake" (2 Cor 4:5). This is a clear recognition that the early church understood the gospel as more than a message about God or his kingship. The gospel is Jesus

---

12. Dunning, *Grace*, 79–80.

Christ, in whom the fullness of God dwells and in whom we have received the fullness of God's grace and truth. This is to say that the gospel has become inseparable from the person of Christ, and so the Kingdom has also become inseparable from Christ, the King.

The Lordship of Jesus is an important canon of tradition. Traditions take their validity and authority in Jesus Christ as Lord. The Protestants and the evangelicals today have rejected traditions that do not submit to the Lordship of Jesus Christ. The Lordship of Jesus Christ is the ultimate test of the Christian faith. The apostle John strongly declared: ". . . every spirit that does not acknowledge Jesus is not from God" (1 John 4:3). For any tradition to represent the living faith of the triumphant church, it must confess the living Christ as Lord. Otherwise it only represents the beliefs, doctrines or traditions of the dead that belong to the historical archives or the accounts of the past. Both the militant and the triumphant church share a common confession of faith that Jesus is Lord.

The Lordship of Jesus is a post-Resurrection confession that clearly recognized the work of Christ in his state of exaltation (see Acts 2:36). It "embodies as no other the thought that Christ is exalted to God's right hand, glorified, and now intercedes before the Father"[13] on behalf of those who believe in him. Jesus is rightly the Head of the Church because he is the Lord of the Church. It is a Lordship that Jesus wholy and humbly gained for himself as the Messiah of God who submitted to God's will. Philippians 2:1–6 is a perfect summary of this truth,

> Who, being in very nature God,
> Did not consider equality with God
> Something to be used to his own advantage.
> Rather, he made himself nothing
> By taking the very nature of a servant,
> Being made in human likeness.
> And being found in appearance as a man,
> He humbled himself by becoming obedient to death—
> Even death on a cross!
> Therefore, God exalted him to the highest place
> And gave him the name that is above every name,
> That at the name of Jesus every knee shall bow,
> In heaven and on earth and under the earth,

---

13. Ibid., 318.

> And every tongue acknowledge that Jesus Christ is Lord,
> To the glory of God the Father.

The church has no other Lord but Jesus Christ; the world will know no other Lord but Jesus Christ. The Lordship of Christ is undeniable and cannot be compromised: "For even if there are so-called gods, whether in heaven or on earth (as indeed there are many 'gods' and many 'lords'), yet for us there is but one God, the Father, from whom all things came and for whom we live; and there is but one Lord, Jesus Christ, through whom all things came and through whom we live" (1 Cor 8:5–6). It is on this Lordship that the traditions of Christian churches and the tradition of the catholic church stand. By the same confession the church is held together in one spirit; it binds believers world-wide in the unity of the Spirit.

The use of the Greek word "*Kurios*," which literally means "Lord," has a clear reference in the Holy Scriptures to the exalted designation for God himself.[14] It is used in the Old Testament as a substitute for the personal name of YHWH. Hence, to attribute the title to Christ is to recognize not only his exaltation in relation to his Messianic work, but also to his relationship with God. Indeed, "It was the church's primary confession of faith in Jesus (Rom 10:9), and it carried connotations of deity."[15] What the later church would struggle to resolve vis-à-vis Jesus's identity and relationship with the Father through various creeds, the early church had already given the confession its finality in the recognition that Jesus is both Messiah and Lord (Luke 2:11). Both the gospel and the church were anchored in the Lordship of Jesus Christ. The disciples did not doubt Christ's exaltation and his relationship with God. This is seen clearly in John's theological narrative of the life and ministry of Jesus, where in the last two chapters "*Kurios*" is used several times compared to only three times earlier. To Taylor and Ladd, "It is clear that the Evangelist feels it appropriate to speak of 'the Lord' in these contexts, but does not feel at liberty to use the title in connection with the earlier ministry."[16] Moreover, in the writings of Paul and among the Christians world-wide, it is this confession of the Lordship of Jesus Christ that defined their experience of Christ and their initiation into the body of Christ. Ladd strongly supports this,

---

14. See BDAG, "kurios," 576–78.
15. Ladd, *Theology*, 169.
16. Taylor, *Name of Jesus*, 43. Quoted in Ladd, *Theology*, 169.

> The predominant and most characteristic designation for Jesus is Lord (*Kyrios*), not only in Paul's epistles but in the Gentile Christianity at large. People came into the fellowship of the church by believing in the resurrection and confession of the Lordship of Christ (Rom. 10:9). The heart of the Pauline proclamation is the Lordship of Christ (2 Cor. 4:5). The importance of this confession in the Pauline churches is vividly set forth in the words, "No one can say, 'Jesus is LORD' except by the Holy Spirit" (1 Cor. 12:3). Paul obviously cannot mean that it is impossible to utter these words except by the inspiration of the Spirit (see Mt. 7:21). He means rather that a sincere confession of the Christian creed shows that the speaker is motivated by the Holy Spirit. Here is the most obvious mark of the Christian: confession of the Lordship of Christ (1 Cor. 1:2; cf. Acts 9:14, 21; 22:16; 2 Tim. 2:22).[17]

The world has known Jesus more as the Lord than as the Messiah. If the Christian Jews confessed Jesus as the Christ (cf. John 20:31); the Gentile world have made their confession centered on the Lordship of Jesus Christ. What the Scriptures declared about Jesus comes to reality whenever men and women of every nation confess with their mouths that Jesus is Lord. This Lordship of Christ is not only to be recognized by a handful few men and women; the whole universe and all creations in heaven and on earth and under the earth shall know and submit to this Lordship: "That at the name of Jesus every knee shall bow, in heaven and on earth and under the earth, and every tongue acknowledge that Jesus Christ is Lord, to the glory of God the Father" (Phil 2:6; *cf.* Isa 45:23b). The world and everything in it, and history from its beginning to the end shall all come under the power and authority of Jesus Christ as the rightful Lord of creations.

The Apostolic Tradition: "I/We believe..."

The Lordship of Jesus Christ had been proclaimed by the Christians around the world unhindered. Luke rightly described the missionary endeavor of the church world-wide in and through the mission of Paul: "For two whole years Paul stayed there in his own rented house and welcomed all who came to him. Boldly and without hindrance he preached the kingdom of God and taught about the Lord Jesus Christ" (Acts 28:30–31). But of course we know that it happened along with various persecutions not only from the Jews but also from the Roman Empire through its government. Kenneth

17. Ibid., 456.

Scott Latourette describes and explains the experiences of the Christians during the first and second centuries under the Roman tyranny:

> In spite of the apologists, persecution by the Roman government was chronic and persistent. The Christian churches were associations which were not legally authorized, and the Roman authorities, always suspicious of organizations which might prove seditions, regarded them with jaundiced eye. Christians were haled before the courts as transgressors of the laws against treason, sacrilege, membership in a foreign cult, and the practice of magic. Since they would not share in the religious rites associated with the imperial cult, they were viewed as hostile to the state. The antagonism was particularly marked, since Christians, revering Christ as *Kurios*, or Lord of the whole earth, often looked upon the Emperor, for whom the same claim was made, as Anti-Christ, while the imperial authorities were hostile to them as those who gave allegiance to a rival of the Emperor. Correspondence which has survived between the Emperor Trojan (reigned A.D. 98–117) and Pliny the Younger, who was serving as imperial legate in Bithynia, in the later Asia Minor, appears to indicate that Christianity was officially proscribed, that if Christians recanted they were to be spared, but that if they persisted in their faith they were to be executed.[18]

Again it was the Lordship of Jesus Christ that made them bold and at the same time 'hostile' to the Empire. But they did not waiver in their confession. Walker and others say that "in the face of persecution, imprisonment, death, believers understood that they were being called, by unwavering confession of their Lord, to share the suffering by which Christ had overcome the forces of evil abroad in the world."[19]

In and through their boldness in preaching the Lordship of Christ and their unwavering faith in and through their witness for Christ involving various sacrifices, the church had phenomenally grown within the super power of the Roman Empire. By the early fourth century, Christianity had been widely recognized as the most powerful religion alongside the Empire with the support of Constantine. "Whence came these qualities which won for Christianity its astounding victory?"[20] Latourette boldly attributes the answer to the person of Christ. He says,

---

18. Latorette, *History*, 84. See also Walker, et al., *History*, 50–53.
19. Walker, *History*, 52.
20. Latourette listed at least 11 qualities that attributed to the phenomenal growth of

Careful and honest investigation can give but one answer, Jesus. It was faith in Jesus and his resurrection which gave birth to the Christian fellowship and which continued to be its inspiration and its common tie. It was the love displayed in Christ which was, ideally and to a marked extent in practice the bond which held Christianity together ...[21]

The victory of Christianity led to its organization as a world religion and the development of its theology through the formulations of creeds that addressed various controversies brought by the heresies in the church. The church had, in fact as early as the second century, created its own baptismal formula to safe guard the faith of the church. Candidates for baptism were asked three questions as they stood in the water, to each of which they replied "I believe"; and with these three affirmations and the washings which accompanied them, the candidates were understood to be baptized "in the name of the Father and of the Son and of the Holy Spirit."[22] The well known formula of Hippolytus attested to this,

"Do you believe in God the Father Almighty?"

"I believe."

"Do you believe in Jesus Christ, the Son of God, who was born of the Holy Spirit and the Virgin Mary, who was crucified under Pontius Pilate and died, and rose the third day living from the dead, and ascended into heaven, and sat down at the right hand of the Father, and will come to judge the living and the dead?"

"I believe."

"Do you believe in the Holy Spirit, and the Holy Church, and the resurrection of the flesh?"

"I believe."

This and other early Christian formulas were signs of the emerging catholic church. "Such creeds were used as a basis and outline for prebaptismal instruction and are the direct ancestors of the so-called Apostles' Creed as well as the creed commonly referred to as the 'Nicene.'"[23] This "I believe" was not just an expression of their personal faith in Christ but a declaration of their oneness with the body of Christ and its faith. Thus by faith believers have become members of the community of the Kingdom.

Christianity. See, Latourette, *History*, 104–7.

21. Ibid., 107.

22. Walker, *History*, 72.

23. Ibid., 73.

The Apostles' Creed

(Third–Fourth centuries A.D.)

I believe in God the Father Almighty, Maker of heaven and earth.
And in Jesus Christ his only Son our Lord; who was conceived by the Holy Spirit,
born of the virgin Mary; suffered under Pontius Pilate, was crucified,
dead, and buried; He descended into hell, the third day he rose from the dead;
he ascended into heaven; and sitteth at the right hand of God the Father Almighty;
from thence he shall come to judge the quick and the dead. I believe in the Holy Spirit; the holy catholic Church; the communion saints; the forgiveness of sins; the resurrection of the body; and the life everlasting. Amen.

The Nicene Creed

(A.D. 325; revised at Constantinopole A.D. 381)

I believe in one God the Father Almighty; Maker of heaven and earth,
and of all things visible and invisible.
And in one Lord Jesus Christ, the only-begotten Son of God,
begotten of the Father before the worlds, God of God, Light of Light,
very God of very God, begotten, not made, being one substance with
the Father; by whom all things were made; who, for us men and for
our salvation, came down from heaven, and was incarnate by the Holy Spirit
of the Virgin Mary, and was made man; and was crucified also for us
under Pontius Pilate; he suffered and was buried; and the third day he rose again,
according to the Scriptures; and ascended into heaven, and sitteth on the
right hand of the Father; and he shall come again, with glory, to judge both
the quick and the dead; whose kingdom shall have no end.
And in the Holy Spirit, the Lord and Giver of Life; who proceedeth
from the Father and the Son; who with the Father and the Son
together is worshiped and glorified; who spake by the Prophets.
And on Holy Catholic and Apostolic Church. I acknowledge one Baptism
for the remission of sins; and I look for the resurrection of the dead,
and the life of the world to come. Amen.

The Catholic Faith/Tradition

Both creeds were extensions of the "I believe" of the earlier prebaptismal confessions which were believed to be a summary of what the apostles believed and delivered to the churches world-wide. The Nicene Creed, however, arose out of a doctrinal controversy regarding the divinity of Jesus Christ in particular and the Trinity in general. The controversy was engendered by three basic Trinitarian deviations: Sabellianism (Modalism), Subordinationism, and Tritheism. Each posed a challenge to what the early church believed about God the Father and Jesus Christ the Son. Behind the deviations was the influence of paganism and Gnosticism. By the creeds, the church was able to preserve the unity of God and the divinity of Jesus Christ, which in turn preserved the life and unity of the church. It was the life and unity of the church that eventually and consequently transformed the confessions of the church into greater confessions that concerned the body of Christ as a whole—the creeds with the plural personal pronoun "we" as the subject.[24]

The succeeding creeds of the undivided church became an ecclesiastical-theological necessity that established the Christian faith, not in terms of a personal confession "I believe," but in terms of a catholic confession "We believe": "And the Catholic Faith is this, that *we* worship one God in Trinity, and Trinity in unity." Hence, the Christian faith was no longer a personal faith but a catholic faith. Prior, however, to the crystallization of the Christian faith with its various doctrines based on the theological teachings of the Scripture, was the controversy and conflict that developed within the church brought by the private and eccentric interpretations of the Scripture. To which the church responded with the catholic confession of what it believes based on the raw material the Scripture provided. The development, of course, of the more developed and mature confessions of the Christian faith was gradual and progressive. It was an organic evolution of interpretations that led to the development of the theological traditions of the church that expressed the biblical doctrines in the context of the catholic church. This ecclesiastical-theological necessity created the catholic tradition of the church that would reject or at least avoid interpretations

---

24. See Retzinger, *Principles of Catholic*, 23. Retzinger says, "The 'I' of the credo-formula is a collective 'I,' the 'I' of the believing church to which the individual belongs as it believes." Ibid.

that do not truly embody biblical faith or represents the Kingdom.[25] This was the intention of the two following catholic confessions:

The Chalcedonian Definition

(A.D. 451)

We, then, following the holy Fathers, all with one consent, teach men to confess one and the same Son, our Lord Jesus Christ, the same perfect in Godhead and also perfect in manhood; truly God and truly man, of a reasonable soul and body; consubstantial with the Father according to the Godhead, and consubstantial with us according to the Manhood; in all things like unto us, without sin; begotten before all ages of the Father according to the Godhead, and in these latter days, for us and for our salvation, born of the Virgin Mary, the Mother of God, according to the Manhood; one and the same Christ, Son, Lord, Only-begotten, to be acknowledge in two natures, inconfusedly, unchangeably, indivisibly, inseparably; the distinction of natures being by no means taken away by the union, but rather the property of each nature being preserved, and concurring in one Person and one Subsistence, not parted or divided into two persons, but one and the same Son, and only begotten, God the Word, the Lord Jesus Christ, as the prophets from the beginning have declared concerning him, and the Lord Jesus Christ himself has taught us, and the Creed of the holy Fathers has handed down to us.

The Athanasian Creed

(fourth–fifth centuries A. D.)

1. Whoever will be saved: before all things it is necessary that he hold the Catholic Faith;
2. Which Faith except every one do keep whole and undefiled: without doubt he shall perish everlastingly.
3. And the Catholic Faith is this: That we worship one God in Trinity, and Trinity in Unity;

---

25. Dunning, *Grace*, 80.

4. Neither confounding the Persons: nor dividing the Substance.

5. For there is one Person of the Father: another of the Son: and another of the Holy Spirit.

6. But the Godhead of the Father, of the Son, and of the Holy Spirit, is all one: the Glory equal, the Majesty coeternal.

7. Such as the Father is: such is the Son: and such is the Holy Spirit.

8. The Father uncreated: the Son uncreated: and the Holy Spirit uncreated.

9. The Father incomprehensible: the Son incomprehensible: and the Holy Spirit incomprehensible.

10. The Father eternal: the Son eternal: and the Holy Spirit eternal.

11. And yet they are not three eternals: but one eternal.

12. And also there are not three uncreated: nor three incomprehensible, but one uncreated: and one incomprehensible.

13. So likewise the Father is Almighty: the Son Almighty: and the Holy Spirit Almighty.

14. And yet they are not three Almighties: but one Almighty.

15. So the Father is God: the Son is God; and the Holy Spirit is God.

16. And yet there are not three Gods: but one God.

17. So likewise the Father is Lord: the Son Lord: and the Holy Spirit Lord.

18. And yet not three Lords: but one Lord.

19. For like as we are compelled by the Christian verity: to acknowledge every Person by himself to be God and Lord.

20. So are we forbidden by the Catholic Religion: to say, There are three Gods, or three Lords.

21. The Father is made of none: neither created, not begotten.

22. The Son is of the Father alone: not made, nor created: but begotten.

23. The Holy Spirit is of the Father and of the Son: neither made, nor created, nor begotten: but proceeding.

24. So there is one Father, not three Fathers: one Son, not three Sons; one Holy Spirit, not three Holy Spirits.

25. And in this Trinity none is before, or after another: none is greater, or less than another.
26. But the whole three Persons are coeternal, and coequal.
27. So that in all things, as aforesaid: the unity in Trinity, and the Trinity in Unity, is to be worshipped.
28. He therefore that will be saved, must thus think of the Trinity.
29. Furthermore it is necessary to everlasting salvation: that he also believe rightly the Incarnation of our Lord Jesus Christ.
30. For the right Faith is, that we believe and confess: that our Lord Jesus Christ, the Son of God, is God and Man.
31. God, of the Substance of the Father; begotten before the worlds: and Man, of the Substance of his Mother, born in the world.
32. Perfect God: and perfect Man, of a reasonable soul and human flesh subsisting.
33. Equal to the Father, as touching his Godhead: and inferior to the Father as touching his Manhood.
34. Who although he be God and Man; yet he is not two, but one Christ.
35. One; not by conversion of the Godhead into flesh: but by taking of the Manhood into God.
36. One altogether; not by confusion of Substance: but by unity of Person
37. For as the reasonable soul and flesh is one man; so God and Man is one Christ.
38. Who suffered for our salvation: descended into hell: rose again the third day from the dead.
39. He ascended into heaven, he sitteth on the right hand of the Father God Almighty.
40. From whence he shall come to judge the quick and the dead.
41. At whose coming all men shall rise again with their bodies;
42. And shall give account for their own works.
43. And they that have done good shall go into life everlasting: and they that have done evil, into everlasting fire.

The Catholic Faith/Tradition

44. This is the Catholic Faith: which except a man believe faithfully, he can not be saved.

By these creeds the church strengthened its catholic identity through its catholic faith. Hence, as Pelikan writes, "Catholicity was a mark of both the true church and of the true doctrine, for these were inseparable."[26] This is the spirit of the early catholic confession in affirmation of the authority of the catholic tradition as defined by Vincent of Lerins "everywhere, always, by all" (*ubique, semper, ab omnibus*) (Vinc. Ler. Comm. 2.3). The creeds, of course, did not suggest that the catholic faith is one of an intellectual assent, which was far from the intention of the fathers and the councils. Embedded in the Creed is the understanding that with such a catholic faith, those who are saved worship the Holy Trinity: "That we worship one God in Trinity, and Trinity in Unity." And by that the catholic faith is the living tradition of the church that guards its faith and guides its life.

In sum, the strength of these creeds is two-fold: they have protected the church from certain heretical teachings and they have strengthened its catholicity—the catholic church, the catholic faith, and the catholic tradition. As a corollary, the creeds have given birth to a significant task of the church in relation to the Holy Scriptures—the task of interpretations toward catholic theology. The Holy Scriptures need interpretations and a systematic arrangement of various biblical teachings towards a clear but sound definition or redefinition of the historical, biblical, and theological faith of the Christian church. This task is embodied in the works of biblical and systematic theologies.

The Reformation: "Justification by Faith"

The development of the creeds sadly led the church to its own abuse of the catholic tradition. Further conflicts with heretics paved the way for the distortion of the use of ecclesiastical tradition, which had been taken beyond its normative function under the authority of the Holy Scriptures. For example, "against the Gnostic appeal to a secret tradition the fathers had appealed to the universal voice of the church"[27] under the jurisdiction or authority of the bishops of the church. As a result, certain practices in the church arose that could neither be defended on the interpretive principle

---

26. Pelikan, *Christian Tradition*, 33.
27. Dunning, *Grace*, 81.

nor by the authority of the Scripture. The church had defined the apostolic tradition as to mean the authority of apostolic succession granted or extended to the church in and through its leaders or ecclesiastical offices such as the office of the Pope. It was believed that, "The apostolic succession guaranteed the validity of the second—now separate—source of doctrine."[28] Consequently the Holy Scripture was viewed as insufficient. For example, before the Reformation, there were three prevailing positions,[29]

1. Tradition was required for the correct interpretation of the Scripture.
2. Revelation was partly contained in the canonical Scriptures and partly in apostolic traditions/succession.
3. The Holy Spirit abides constantly with the Catholic Church, giving new inspiration or illumination.

These three provided the authority for the popes and the councils to interpret arbitrarily the Scriptures and to add to it new doctrines that were not explicit in the Scriptures. On the eve of the Reformation, the church had gone through a lot of changes both politically and theologically as a result of the authority of the Pope based on the principle or tradition of "apostolic succession" that consequently led to Luther's "Ninety-five theses." Walker and others give us a vivid description of the controversy that led to the Reformation,

> In Late 1517, Luther felt compelled to speak up against a crying abuse. Pope Leo X (1513–1521) had earlier issued a dispensation permitting Albrecht of Brandenburg (1490–1545) to hold at the same time the archbishopric of Mainz, the archbishopric of Magdeburg, and the administration of the bishopric of Halberstadt. This dispensation from church regulations against "pluralism" (multiple offices) cost Albrecht a great sum, which he borrowed from the Augsburg banking house of Fugger. To repay this loan, Albrecht was also permitted to share half the proceeds in his district from the sale of indulgences that the papacy had been issuing, since 1506, for building that new basilica of St. Peter which is still one of the ornaments of Rome. A commissioner for this collection was Johann Tetzel (1470–1519), a Dominican monk of eloquence, who, intent on the largest possible returns, painted the benefits of indulgences in the crassest terms. Luther himself had no knowledge of the financial transaction between Albrecht and the Pope.

28. Ibid.
29. Dulles, *Craft*, 87–88.

The Catholic Faith/Tradition

His objections to the proceedings were pastoral and theological: indulgences create false sense of security and are this destructive of true Christianity, which proclaims the cross of Christ and of the Christian, not release from deserved punishment. As Tetzel approached electoral Saxony—he was not allowed to enter, though many members of the Wittenberg congregation crossed the border to buy letters of indulgence—Luther preached against the abuse of indulgences and prepared his memorable "Ninety-five Thesis," copies of which he sent on October 31, 1517, to Archbishop Albrecht of Mainz and Bishop Jerome of Brandenburg, in whose jurisdiction Wittenberg lay. Whether Luther on that day also posted his theses on the door of the castle church in Wittenberg, which served as the university bulletin board, is a matter of controversy among historians, though it seems most likely that he did.[30]

Luther and the Reformers were fighting for theological corrections of the doctrines of the church that were incoherent with the teachings of the Holy Scriptures. They were convinced that the church had gone too far in its exercise of the "apostolic succession" resulting to theological deviations and wrong church practices such as the selling of indulgence for the benefit of the church and its bishops. Luther cried for what would be the Protestant principle and the basis of Protestant tradition—"*sola scriptura.*" They believed that the church is under the sole authority of the Scripture; the church is bound to follow and preach what the Scripture explicitly teaches. They further maintained "the possibility that the church fathers, the councils, and the creeds have fallen into error, as firmly as the Roman church maintains just the opposite with its doctrine of papal infallibility."[31]

The Reformation gave birth to the Protestant theological tradition that would serve as interpretive of Protestant theology. Out of the theological struggles with the church on forgiveness and salvation created by the selling and granting of *indulgentia* came Luther's theological principle of "*justification by faith.*" To Luther, salvation is a free gift of God to all repentant sinners; hence, it is grace. And this salvation is received only through faith and not by works of buying *indulgentia*. Sinners are justified by faith through the grace of God in Christ Jesus. To Luther, justification by grace through faith is the clear teaching of the Holy Scriptures. The church failed to embrace justification by grace through faith because of its adoption of the philosophy of Thomas Aquainas. Cairns in his synthesis of the

---

30. Walker, *History*, 425–26.
31. Dunning, *Grace*, 81.

interpretation of the Reformation rightly observes that the theology of the undivided church behind its offer of *indulgentia* was highly influenced by Thomas Aquainas' thought on man's will and the church authority to dispense grace on behalf of God,

> It emphasized his teaching that man's will was not totally corrupted. By faith and the use of the means of grace in the sacraments dispensed by the hierarchy, man could achieve salvation. Augustine believed that man's will was so totally depraved that he could do nothing toward his salvation. God would extend grace to man to energize his will so that he could by faith take the salvation that Christ proffered him.[32]

However, it should be noted that the Reformation was not motivated by Augustine's theology. The Reformers resorted instead to the teachings of the Scriptures and called upon the church to closely examine the Scripture. Cairns notes this about the Reformers,

> It was the Scripture that brought home the profound truth to them. The theological cause of the Reformation was the desire of the Reformers to go back to the classic source of the Christian faith, the Bible, in order to counter the claims of Tomistic theology that salvation was a matter of grace obtained through the sacraments dispensed by the hierarchy.[33]

It was the principle of *sola scriptura* that prompted the Reformers indeed to counter the teachings of the church on salvation and its practice of *indulgentia* which for them was a clear theological error—a misinterpretation of the truth of the Scripture on salvation and grace. Theology and Scripture go together in the shaping or molding of the tradition and practice of the church. The church is not in the position to divorce theology and practice from the authority of the Scripture. There is an inherent relationship that exists between the two which the church had to recognize and respect as the steward of the gospel or the kingdom of God. However, due to its romantic relationship with the principle of apostolic succession and Thomas Aquainas' naturalistic theology influenced by Aristotle, the undivided church had developed another source of authority for doing theology that was divorced from the authority of the Scripture. But Luther, out of his personal and evangelical breakthrough, challenged the church to go back to

---

32. Cairns, *Christianity Through*, 275.
33. Ibid.

the source and to reform its ways of doing theology and ministry that were based solely on the Holy Scriptures.

Consequently, justification by faith became the Reformation cry of the Protestants or Reformers and it developed into a hermeneutical-theological principle based on the Holy Scriptures that would shape a new, or better, renewed understanding of the life of the church and its theology and practice that was truly in the spirit of the apostles and the early church father's teachings such as Augustine's. John Calvin, for example, accepted Luther's idea of justification by faith and his principle of *Sola Scriptura*. While he helped in the spread of the Reformation in Germany and France, John Calvin devoted himself to the study of the Scripture and the writing of his *Institutes*, which would become the authoritative expression of the Reformed theology.[34] John Calvin's theology was primarily a result of his rigorous study of the Scriptures and the early church fathers that were faithful to the Scripture like Augustine. Cairns writes,

> Although Calvin's theology has an emphasis similar to that of Augustine, Calvin owes his system to his study of the Scriptures rather than to Augustine. Like other Reformers, he went from the Bible to Augustine to seek the support of that prince of the Fathers rather than going from Augustine to the Bible and the doctrines of the Reformations.[35]

In sum, the Reformation made justification by faith as the measuring stick for ecclesiastical theology and practice. It became the center of biblical and theological studies and the benchmark of practical ministries as well as missions. Sadly, the Reformation led to a split in the church—the Roman Catholic Church and the Protestant churches. Which of them, then, is the catholic church? While the Roman Catholic has taken its basis on the "Apostolic Succession," the Protestant church based its catholicity on the Holy Scriptures. However, both the spirit of "apostolic succession" and the Holy Scriptures are definitive of the catholic church. The two are not only complimentary but they are also inseparable. A doctrine that represents *sola scriptura* is one that is apostolic; an apostolic church must reflect a

---

34. Reformed Theology is based on the "five-points" of Calvinism represented by the simple mnemonic device—the word *tulip*: (1) Total Depravity, (2) Unconditional Election, (3) Limited Atonement, (4) Irresistible Grace, and (5) Perseverance of the Saints. In response to Arminianism, the same was affirmed by the Belgic Confession and the Heidelberg Cathechism which became the doctrinal basis of the Dutch Reformed church. See Walker et al., *History*, 542. See also Calvin, *Institutes*.

35. Cairns, *Christianity Through*, 303.

true spirit of *sola scriptura*.[36] The lack of one does not represent the catholic church indeed.

Pietism: "The Call to Holiness"

The Reformation movement created the following traditions within the Protestant circle—the Lutheran, the Anabaptist, the Reformed, and the Anglican. The succeeding development in the church was influenced by the arrival of a new era—the rise of secularization, modern science, and philosophy. Consequently, the church had gone through rapid transformation, which was aided by a great variety of causes, such as the steady secularization of culture, the domination of the church in both the state and the society, the rise of the professional, mercantile, and laboring classes to constantly increasing educational and political influence, and of course, the rise of modern science and philosophy that paved the way for the development of historical and scientific methods of examining and interpreting thoughts and institutions.[37]

The rise and popularity of science and philosophy led the church to develop a system of orthodox dogma brought about by the Protestants, and particularly the Reformed theology's love affair with philosophy in their interpretations of the Holy Scriptures and in the construction of their own theological traditions. Cairns notes such formidable development,

> This system brought about a new scholasticism, particularly among the Lutherans in Germany, who became more interested in dogma than in the expression of doctrine in practical life. This cold intellectual expression of Christianity, coupled with the severe religious wars between 1560 and 1648 and the rise of rationalistic philosophy and empirical science, led to rationalism and formalism in religion between 1660 and 1730 in England, Europe, and later, America. The distaste for cold orthodoxy among the rationalistic philosophers and scientists, the rise of natural religion, and the insistence that the church is a group of believers

---

36. For a discussion on a Roman Catholic *sola scriptura*, see Rahner, who perceives a Catholic *sola scriptura* in the spirit of a harmony between Catholic "tradition" and Scripture. Rahner, "Scripture," 98–112. See also his article Rahner, "Scripture," 1549–54. Avery Dulles, however, warns of the danger of "dualism between Scripture and tradition," which he says, "was repudiated by the Fourth World Conference on Faith and Order at Montreal in 1963 and by Vatican II in its *Dei Verbum*." Dulles, "Craft," 186.

37. Walker et al., *History*, 568.

The Catholic Faith/Tradition

covenanting together with God and one another led to the rise of toleration and denominationalism.[38]

As a result the church had fallen into a more philosophical, or more aptly, dogmatic Christianity. Religious fanaticism was replaced by religious intellectualism. The gains of the Reformation, with its emphasis on the primacy of the Scripture, slowly faded and yielded to scholasticism. The church moved from symbols to systems, from the Holy Scriptures to systematic (dogmatic) theologies, and from indulgence (*indulgentia*) to intelligence (*intelligentia*). The church's advances on theology have given the church doctrines with sound, solid, and strong theological structures. But on the other hand, there was an unintentional negligence (an unwanted consequence perhaps) on the practical and spiritual expressions of faith, both communally and personally, that left a spiritual vacuum in the life and mission of the church.

The emphasis on pure doctrines and sacraments disconnected the church from the practical and pious expressions of the Christian faith. The vital relationship between God and the believer, which the Reformers sought after and taught their followers, had been replaced largely by a faith which consisted in the acceptance of a dogmatic whole. As a result the church had its theological gravitational pull towards the clergymen who were primarily responsible for the construction of the theology of the church. Most men and women in the pew became passive believers of dogmas handed to them by their ministers. Consequently, the church had become very ritualistic in its exercise of faith and worship, which turned the church and its tradition into a dead orthodoxy. To combat such tendency, Pietism was developed to vindicate a dynamic and active church that would give its people an important role in the building-up of the Christian life and mission. Philipp Jacob Spener, Willem Teelinck, Gisbert Voet, and Jacob von Lodensteyn were among the early leaders of Pietism in Europe. The core beliefs of the Pietists centered on inner spirituality, subjective expression of faith, and individual return to Bible study and prayer. They called on church members to gather within the various congregations of circles—an *ecclesiolae in ecclesia* (a church within the church)—for Bible reading and for mutual watch and helpfulness. Christianity is believed to be far more a life than an intellectual knowledge.[39]

---

38. Cairns, *Christianity Through*, 375.
39. Walker, et al., *History*, 588.

The goal of various spiritual or Christian disciplines was the deep and personal experience of holiness in the context of a dynamic relationship with God through Bible study and prayer. Pietism had been institutionalized through the constitution and reconstitution of the *Unitas Fratrum*, or, as they came to be known, the "Moravian Brethren," under the leadership of Count Nikolaus Ludwig von Zinzendorf.[40] Though Zinzendorf wanted to keep the idea *ecclēsiolae in ecclēsia*, events led to the organization of the Moravian as a separated church or another theological tradition within the Protestant circle, with emphasis on personal devotion to Christ. Moreover, "the Moravians' willingness to go anywhere in the service of Christ gave a missionary thrust to the movement which it has never lost."[41]

The Pietists' call to holiness was given its prime time and eventually developed into another strong tradition within Protestantism through the lives and ministries of the Wesley brothers—Charles Wesley and John Wesley. Historians have placed the Wesley brothers within the Evangelical Revival in Great Britain that had its own life and influence.[42] For example, Cairns believes that, "Methodism was to Anglicanism what Pietism was to Lutheranism."[43] Nevertheless, both were of the same vein of spiritual family that called the church to a spiritual revival with their emphasis on the Christian life in terms of holiness and mission. Charles Wesley and John Wesley were responsible for establishing the "Holy Clubs," whose members were nicknamed as "Methodists" by students for their methodical Bible study and prayer habits and regular attempts at social service in jails and homes of the poor.

John Wesley embraced Luther's justification by faith but also put emphasis on the necessity of holiness or sanctification. He believed that salvation must lead to one's personal and deeper experience of holiness. Wesley's understanding of holiness is rooted in his doctrine of prevenient grace that prepares men and women for the experience of Christian holiness through the sanctifying work of the Holy Spirit. Wesley writes,

> For allowing that all the souls of men are dead in sin by nature, this excuses none, seeing there is no man that is in a state of mere

---

40. Ibid., 592.

41. Ibid., 594.

42. Cairns notes that "the Methodist revival was the third religious awakening in England after the sixteenth-century Reformation and the seventeenth-century Puritanism." Cairns, *Christianity Through*, 384.

43. Ibid.

> nature; there is no man, unless he has quenched the Spirit, that is wholly void of the grace of God. No man living is entirely destitute of what is vulgarly called natural conscience. But this is not natural: It is more properly termed *preventing* grace.[44]

Hence, he believed that it is possible for Christians to live a perfect life here on earth, which he meant as freedom from sin. Aware of the danger of perfectionism, which Wesley never wanted to equate holiness with, John Wesley preferred the term Christian Perfection, or in a more particular and popular expression among his followers, perfect love. John Wesley's message of holiness and with the development of Wesleyan theology in the nineteenth-century holiness movement completed the holiness tradition.[45] The goal of the movement was to "Christianize Christianity" with the clear call to holiness.

The call to holiness is an aspect of the catholic tradition that has indeed enriched the Christian faith with a rekindled passion not only for the Holy Scriptures and its interpretations but also its relation to the life and mission of the church vis-à-vis the believers and the society. Hence, it is right to conclude that the Christian tradition is not just apostolic and catholic but also holy.

Contemporary Theology: "Back to the Word"

At the turn of the twentieth-century, the church would have the state as its rival due to rapid secularization and political liberalism in many countries. The shifts of political powers around the world from Christian democracy to anti-religious totalitarianism posed a great challenge to the church that was struggling to keep its unity in diversity. Added to the external issue or the tension between the church and the state were the internal theological challenges brought by theological liberalism influenced by rationalism and liberation theology influenced by communism.

---

44. Works 6:512.

45. See, Dieter, *Holiness Revival*. The author writes, "The story of the holiness movement is not, consequently, a story of unique twists of unorthodox patterns of theology or Christian life; it is rather an account of a movement at the center of an accelerating current of some of the steadily flowing streams of Christian tradition. The quest eventually resulted in bringing thousands of new converts into the Christian faith and churches, but its main thrust was to reform the church itself."

We Are Catholic

The Christian faith with its catholic tradition confronted various theological ideas that were apparently influenced by various philosophical thoughts and methods. Theories were developed that questioned and challenged the apostolic and catholic confessions of faith based on new sources or foundations of knowledge or "truths." Claims such as "there is no God," "God is dead," "Jesus is just but a historical person," "the Bible is a human book," "Jesus is a myth," and many others were put forward to challenge the Christian faith; they sought to establish new norms for "truths."[46] Some attacked the church and its faith on the socio-political relevance of the gospel it preaches. There were those who confronted the church on socio-economic issues, such as its place in the economic development and human progress based on Darwin's evolution theory. Unprepared to deal with new theological thoughts based on radical historical and scientific methods or perhaps overwhelmed by the challenges, the church suffered loss after loss. Seminaries and churches were taken over by the radical shapers of radical theological thoughts. For example,

> . . . radical humanistic, relativistic, and secular theologies, such as the death-of-God theology, the secular theology of Cox and Robinson, Marxist-tinged theologies of hope by Moltmann and radical liberation, and black and feminist theologies. Sociological salvation through people in time rather than by the eternal God through Christ seems to be the vogue.[47]

Christian orthodoxy and catholic theology appeared to be losing grounds to theological liberalism of the twentieth-century. Apparently the Protestant principle of *sola scriptura* and the Roman Catholic "apostolic succession" or tradition had both suffered serious blows. As a result "mainline churches declined in members and missionaries, but the evangelical churches increased greatly in members and missionaries in the field."[48]

It was the Swiss theologian Karl Barth who initiated and led the church, at the theological level, to a renewal of faith and eventually led to the revival of Biblical Theology through his neo-orthodox theology. While he was not traditionally orthodox (hence the label neo-orthodox), Barth's contribution was in his effort to bring theology back to its original source—the Holy Scriptures. Barth was known for his Word-theology: he redefined the Word of God in terms of an experience or an "encounter" rather than a

---

46. See Brown, "Historical," 326–41.
47. Cairns, *Christianity Through*, 460.
48. Ibid.

theological exposition. The Bible is not the Word of God; it is only a witness to the Word of God.[49] It becomes the Word of God as believers encounter it in and through the preaching of the Holy Scriptures and by personal obedience to it. While conservative and catholic theologians did not accept Barth's proposition, they welcomed the fact that the Holy Scripture regained its rightful place in the church and its faith. The Bible again has become the center of theological works and reflections—back to the Word. Theologians after Barth had used the Scriptures as their primary source to doing theology, although in the context of existential philosophy. The most prominent of them was Rudolf Bultmann, who popularized the hermeneutical methodology of "demythologizing" on the idea that the kernels of revelation was behind the myths of the gospel stories.[50]

Karl Barth had rekindled the spirit of *sola scriptura* and had given breath to the beleaguered catholic faith and its catholic theology/tradition. Again the Scriptures were allowed to speak not only to the church but also to the society in and through its recovered theological voice engendered by the renewed, dynamic, and faithful interpretations of the church. This is an important role that the church has in relation to the society. The Christian traditions based on the Scriptures serve both the church and the society. Barth called this "*evangelical theology,*"

> The qualifying attribute "evangelical" recalls both the New Testament and at the same time the Reformation of the sixteenth century. Therefore, it may be taken as a dual affirmation: the theology to be considered here is the one which, nourished by the hidden sources of the documents of Israel's history, first achieved unambiguous expression in the writings of the New Testament evangelists, apostles, and prophets; it is also, moreover, the theology newly discovered and accepted by the Reformation of the sixteenth century. The expression "evangelical," however, cannot and should not be intended and understood in a confessional, that is, in a denominational and exclusive sense. This is forbidden first of all by the elementary fact that "evangelical" refers primarily and decisively to the Bible, which is in some way respected by all confessions. Not all so called "Protestant" theology is evangelical theology; moreover, there is also evangelical theology in the Roman Catholic and Eastern orthodox worlds, as well as in the many later variations, including deteriorations, of the Reformation

---

49. See Barth, *CD,* 457–537.
50. For a short discussion of demythologizing see, Harvey, *Handbook,* 67–68.

departure. What the word "evangelical" will objectively designate is that theology which treats of the *God of the Gospel*. "Evangelical" signifies the "catholic," ecumenical (not to say "conciliar") *continuity and unity* of this theology. Such theology intends to apprehend, to understand, and to speak of the God of the Gospel, in the midst of the variety of all other theologies (without any value-judgment being implied) in distinction from them. This is the God who reveals himself in the Gospel, who himself speaks to men and acts among and upon them. Wherever he becomes the object of human science, both its source and its norm, there is *evangelical theology*.[51]

Unguided by the Scriptures, traditions only become human teachings—a pharisaic form of hypocrisy—that competes with the sovereign authority of God and his words. Was Karl Barth the savior of Christian theology/faith or was the Spirit behind Barth's emphasis on the Scriptures and Christ as the center of theology? Only history and of course God can judge him and his work. However, the church's indebtedness to and appreciation of Barth's theology were shown in Barth's monumental spirit in the works of contemporary theologians and preachers.[52]

Conclusion: The Church Tradition Today

The tradition of the church today does not represent the dead faith of the triumphant past; rather it is the living faith of the catholic church, both triumphant and militant, anchored in the faithful historical and theological interpretations of the Holy Scriptures and expressed in various and dynamic ways in the life of the church today. It is sustained and nourished by the dynamic life and mission of the church in the world in and through interactions with various cultural contexts and historical circumstances of men and women; hence, the tradition is living and dynamic.

The Word and the Spirit remain to be the grounds of the catholic tradition in general and the various traditions within the catholic church today. The word of God is, as it was, and will always be, the objective ground of the catholic tradition or traditions. The fixated tradition still needs interpretations as it continues to be the norm for the Christian faith and practice. While the interpretive task of the church is active and dynamic, it is limited

---

51. Barth, "Place," 23–24.
52. See, McKim, *How Karl Barth*.

only within the perimeters of the Holy Scriptures. Traditions are the means through which the meaning of the Scriptures are properly and profoundly understood, and devotionally and deeply penetrated. They set the canon for catholic interpretations and applications of scriptural truths. Thus, both the Scriptures and the traditions are mutually dependent toward the salvation of men and women and the establishment of the kingdom of God on earth as it is in heaven. The subjective ground of the catholic tradition is the Holy Spirit. It is the Holy Spirit that illumines the truths of the Scripture and it is the same Spirit that inspires interpreters toward the knowledge of truth. Without the Holy Spirit the divine redemptive intention in God's revelation is inaccessible and would remain beyond human comprehension and experience. The plain word of God does not create conviction; the Holy Spirit does. Without the Holy Spirit, the Scriptures is open to misinterpretations and definitely to misapplications; hence the heresies. Any forms of "traditioning" outside the Word and without the Holy Spirit can only lead to distorted church traditions. But such danger should not stop us from "traditioning"; after all, the Word of God is always in need of fresh and vital interpretations that answer the questions of the present generation. This task is also called the "pilgrim" or ongoing interpretations of the Word of God.[53]

Tradition and traditions are both communal in nature and purpose. They serve the community of faith not only in terms of the local church, but also in the terms of the catholic church. Denominational and doctrinal "distinctives" become part of the catholic tradition when they enriched the life and mission of the catholic church. The church will never be united under a single denominational tradition. A church that thinks so is either ignorant of the unity in diversity of the catholic church, or arrogant of its own self-defined unity that calls everybody to a cult of uniformity. The ecumenical movement today has to focus on the catholic spirit of the church with respect to the catholic tradition and traditions within the body of Christ. Ecumenism must be balanced by the catholicity of the church and work toward the catholic mission in proclaiming the gospel of Jesus Christ both in words and deeds. In other words, ecumenicity and catholicity must go together.

---

53. Richardson, *Reading Karl Barth*, 224.

5

The Catholic Church

The Marks of the Catholic Church

"Watch out for false prophets. They come to you in sheep's clothing, but inwardly they are ferocious wolves. By their fruit you will recognize them," (Matt 7:15–16a) said Jesus to his disciples on his famous "Sermon on the Mount." The need to distinguish true prophets from false prophets has been there since biblical times, whether in the Old Testament or in the New Testament. In fact, the evolution of false prophets and false Jesuses has resulted to false churches today. As a result, the church is faced with questions like: What makes a church a church? What is necessary to have a church? Might a group of people who claim to be Christians become so unlike what a church should be that they should no longer be called a church?[1] The Nicene Creed had cemented the four major marks of the church—"one, holy, catholic, and apostolic"—to define the church of Jesus Christ. And by them the church was able to protect and preserve its life, unity, theology, and ministry.

But the dynamic life and growth of the church today, and the perennial, unyielding, and growing challenges of heresies (they be individuals or groups, not excluding the differences in Christian churches) lead us further to the need for us to qualify the four general and historical marks of the church. What does it mean for the church today, for example, to be "one, holy, catholic, and apostolic"? Unlike in the early centuries of the church where the marks of the church were sufficient to defend the church

---

1. See Grudem, *Systematic Theology*, 864.

and to put the heretics at bay, each mark has become today the subject of much controversy and has been weakened not only by its limited definition and scope but also by its inability to address present situations and needs. This is so because the marks of the church have been historically and theologically at the center of the problem that led to the division of the church. Consequently, both parties have interpreted and used the marks differently. For example, the Roman Church used the marks against the Protestants. And since the Reformation there has been no consensus of meanings. Hence, the Roman Church and the Protestants have suffered from mutual criticisms and theological confusions on the definitions and functions of the marks. My interest in this book is the catholicity of the church in the context not only of my evangelical identity but more so in the context of my being a member of the catholic church—the church of Jesus Christ. I find the traditional definition of catholicity not only limited but also insufficient to embody the historical and theological evolution of the catholicity of the church, which when taken into consideration can meet the contemporary needs and challenges of the church today. While the focus is on the catholic mark of the church, in some sense our discussion will also and further qualify the other three marks of the church.

The word "catholic" was introduced, or rather recognized, as part of the confession of the church by Ignatius and other church fathers. The reason for doing so was primarily to combat early heresies in the church. Catholicity and the other three "marks" were meant to distinguish the true church from the emerging counterfeit claims of groups who called themselves Christian churches. The original concept of the catholicity of the church, however, was limited to the universality of the church as to mean the unlimited territorial frontier. Later Christians further believed that it was the all-inclusive identity of the church which makes the church catholic. Both saw catholicity as an external mark of the church. H. Ray Dunning argues that catholicity is likewise an inner reality. Apparently, the mark is not static but an evolving one to serve an evolving church in an evolving context. If it is so, as I want to argue here, we should not limit catholicity to its original conception or definition. There is a need to clarify and expand the qualities or marks of the catholicity of the church. Consequently then, we are compelled to ask, "What are the 'marks' of the catholic church?"

This chapter focuses on the expanded marks of the catholic church other than what has been primarily and traditionally understood. To think of the catholic church in terms of a geographical territory or an inclusive universality is to limit the catholic meaning of the church. Catholicity is more than geography or people inclusivity. The following are the expanded characteristics or marks of the catholic church.

Catholic as Universal

The word catholic originates from the Greek word *katholikos*, which literally means "throughout the whole," "general," and "universal." Although it is not used in the New Testament to describe the church, the idea or concept is not totally absent.[2] The Bible uses the word "church" mostly in reference to local congregations or house churches (Rom 16:3–5; 1 Cor 16:19; Col 4:15; Phlm 2), but it is also used of the church universal (1 Cor 10:32; 12:28; 15:9; Gal 1:13; Eph 1:22; 3:10, 21; 5:23–32; Col 1:18, 24).[3] The early church fathers used the word "catholic" to refer to what was commonly used among the various churches, whether beliefs or practices, such as the case of the General Epistles. And those that were considered catholic were given normative significance in the life of the church and had become part of the church's traditions shared and observed by various churches as early as the second-century.

The historical and theological evolution of the meaning of the word "catholic," vis-à-vis the church as universal, has led to three interrelated aspects or shades of its meaning, namely a "wholistic" identity, a spirit of interdependence, and an inclusive fellowship. The first aspect focuses on the identity of the church as a whole. The various churches in different places were not seen as independent local groups, but as groups belonging to the one catholic church in terms of the whole under the lordship of Jesus Christ. The image of the church as the body of Christ accentuates the wholistic identity of the church. Hans Küng defines the catholicity of the church as consisting the notion of "entirety," based on identity and resulting to universality.[4] No local church exists on its own. Every church is a part of the whole—the catholic church. This universal identity of the church is anchored in its relationship with Christ as the Lord or Head of the Church. Avery Dulles rightly calls it as the "catholicity of Christ," which he finds three aspects: first, the incarnation as "a mystery of divine plenitude"—God's fullness in and through him; second, Christ's fullness as the

---

2. Clowney, *Church*, 91.
3. Ibid., 111–12.
4. See Küng, *Church*, 303.

head of creation; and third, Christ's headship over the church.[5] As Ignatius said, "Wherever Christ is, there is the catholic church." (Ign. *Smyrn*. viii 2).

Moreover, the idea of the catholic church expresses the spirit of interdependence among the churches world-wide. Paul, for example, encouraged and cultivated interdependence among churches by collecting mission money from other churches to help the church in Jerusalem (1 Cor 16:1–3). As a result, the early church, though was made of a number of churches in various places, never perceived itself as isolated or independent churches detached or disconnected from one another. As the body is made of many parts and each belongs to the body, so is the church (1 Cor 12:12–13). There existed the spirit of interdependence among the early churches. This interdependence can be properly called as the catholicity of the Christian fellowship, which was expressed in the early church in various ways. Another tangible expression in the early church was the shared leadership in the church demonstrated in the council at Jerusalem (Acts 15), where the apostles took responsibility of churches outside Jerusalem by recognizing elders, not only to ensure orthodoxy but also to exercise various ministries of churches for the strengthening of the world-wide churches of Jesus Christ.[6]

Finally, the word catholic as universal must indeed not be limited to the presence of Christians worldwide or formally known as the geographical presence of the church,[7] but it must also focus on the inclusivity of the church, i.e., the church is open to all people regardless of ethnic identities, social statuses, political affiliations, cultural orientations, and many others (1 John 1:12). It is an open society. This inclusivity of the church is anchored in the universality of salvation in Christ.[8] The church is inclusive because Christ himself is inclusive; hence, as Christ is inclusive in his ministry so must the church in its ministry. The church then must not discriminate

---

5. Dulles, *Catholicity*, 34–47.

6. Clowney laments, "Catholicity is sometimes denied in more plausible ways. Advocates of the church growth movement have observed that churches grow faster is they restrict their evangelistic efforts to a homogenous population [. . .] Churches that begin with a strategy of evangelistic approach to a targeted population may end as a sect, defined not by the gospel but by society." Clowney, *Church*, 97.

7. Post-Reformation Roman Catholic theologians in response to the Reformation and using Augustine's argument against the Donatists redefined catholicity as the geographical spread of the Catholic Church and later added numerical preponderance.

8. Protestant theology holds the position that it is by grace through faith contra Roman Catholic theology that provides the possibility of human efforts or works added to God's grace in Christ. For a discussion on this issue see, Clowney, *Church*, 96.

anyone. This means that though the church is God's elect community, it does not select the people who would become its members. The qualifications for membership in the church are intended to help believers understand and live according to the standards of the Christian life and faith. By this the inclusivity of the church is not cheap. It is open but it is not cheap. This inclusivity must not be construed as a privilege without responsibilities. It is grace to be received with conditions or qualifications.

In sum, to be catholic is to be universal. Any spirit of sectarianism is a contradiction to the catholic nature and mission of the church. This universal sense is the basic and fundamental meaning of the word catholic. The church is universal because it is catholic. As such the church as catholic biblically and theologically aligns itself with the universal covenant of God—a covenant for all nations.

Catholic as One

Theologians are right to point out that the catholicity of the church is another aspect of the unity of the church. To be catholic is to be one. This is perfectly demonstrated in the words of the apostle Paul who exhorted believers to live in unity,

> Make every effort to keep the unity of the Spirit through the bond of peace. There is *one* body and *one* Spirit, just as you were called to *one* hope when you were called; *one* Lord, *one* faith, *one* baptism; *one* God and Father of all who is over all" (Eph 4:3–6).

Christians world-wide have all been initiated into the body of Christ, in and through one and the same experience: one body, one Spirit, one hope, one Lord, one faith, one baptism, and one God. There is no variance in all these. They are the same in the east, in the west, in the south, and in the north. The unity of the church is primarily a relational unity anchored in the Holy Trinity—the Spirit, the Lord and the Father. It is a unity that is widely diffused into the body of Christ in and through the effectual ministry of the Holy Spirit with the active participation of Christians in obedience to the call to unity. Dunning notes this truth, "The *koinonia* aspect of the Church is made a reality by the indwelling Spirit of Christ, by whom all acknowledge that Jesus is Lord (cf. 2 Cor 13:14; Phil 2:1; 1 Cor 1:9)."[9]

---

9. Dunning, *Grace*, 531.

The Catholic Church

On the other hand, the unity of the church as one body is functional. Unity is not static but a dynamic characteristic of the life of the church in and through the Word and the Spirit. The church is commanded to keep its unity notwithstanding the internal and external challenges. Jesus and the apostles were not naïve to the reality that the unity of the church would be challenged and that disunity would eventually happen from time to time. Few instances for example were as severe as at Corinth, but even in this case, Paul did not discount the churchly standing of the Corinthian congregation. He recognized their situation as unacceptable and called for renewal and repentance and correction in the light of the ideal.[10] Such attitude is rooted in the spirit of optimism and faith anchored in the church's confession of the Lordship of Jesus and its submission to the Spirit. Indeed, both the Word and the Spirit had kept the church and its unity. It was not the various ecclesiastical cases of factions or divisions that defined the unity or disunity of the church but rather its continuing commitment to Christ and the Spirit. We then can conclude with Dunning that the objective ground of the unity of the church is in its Lord and the subjective ground of the unity of the church is the work of the Spirit.[11]

Another aspect of the unity of the church is its connection and commitment to witness and mission. Jesus made it very clear in his prayer: "May they be brought to complete unity to let the world know . . ." (John 17:23b). It is in and through the unity of the church that the world can find hope, and experience the spirit of unity. The world is divided. There is a growing and widening division that men and women experience world-wide. People have seen and lived in divisions of all sorts—cultural divisions, racial divisions, social divisions, gender divisions, marital/family divisions, political divisions, religious divisions, and many others. Christ came and united humanity in him. His life and death were intended to reconcile not only people to God, but also people to people. The words of Paul to the Galatians echoes the catholic church as one in Christ,

> So in Christ Jesus you are all children of God through faith, for all of you who were baptized into Christ have clothed yourselves with Christ. There is neither Jew nor Gentile, neither slave nor free, nor is there male nor female, for you are all one in Christ Jesus." (Gal 3:26–28)

---

10. Ibid.

11. Ibid., 530–31. The personal pronoun "her" is replaced with "its" for purpose of language inclusivity or to be more politically correct.

By faith, nations have become one under the lordship of Christ in and through the catholic church. This is our responsibility. We cannot allow the presence of division in our churches to hinder us from fulfilling our calling. We must press on until we truly become "one, holy, catholic, and apostolic church."

Catholic as Many

Unable to or rather unconvinced that one can categorize the church in a single model, Avery Dulles admits that the church is a mystery: "Theologically the term 'church' refers to the mystery of Christ as realized in the community of those who believe in him and are assembled in his name."[12] The mystery of the church deepens and widens in the historical and theological evolution of the catholic church. Perspectives on the church vary, such as the church is visible and invisible, local and universal, and institute and organism. We may add yet another perspective—that the church is one and many. We have discussed the former above. Our focus on this section is on the diversity of the church. To think of the church or the catholic church as one and many does not violate the principle of contradiction. Both exist in the *mysterium* of the church. Avery Dulles proposes six models of the church,

1. The Church as Institution
2. The Church as Mystical Communion
3. The Church as Sacrament
4. The Church as Herald
5. The Church as Servant
6. The Church as Community of Disciples[13]

---

12. Dulles, *Models*, 123. He writes, "The term mystery, applied to the Church, signifies many things. It implies that the Church is not fully intelligible to the finite mind of man, and that the reason for this lack of intelligibility is not the poverty but the richness of the Church itself. Like other supernatural mysteries, the Church is known by a kind of connaturality (as Thomas Aquinas and classical theologians called it). We cannot fully objectify the Church because we are involved in it; we know it through a kind of intersubjectivity. Furthermore, the Church pertains to the mystery of Christ; Christ is carrying out in the Church his plan of redemption. He is dynamically at work in the Church through his Spirit." Ibid., 17–18.

13. Dulles, *Models*.

Dulles is right that it would be impossible for a church to possess all the five or six for they are contradictory to each other; though some are complimentary. He says, "They suggest different priorities and even lead to mutually antithetical assertions. Taken in isolation, each of the ecclesiological types could lead to serious imbalances and distortions."[14] What is recognized in these models is the diversity of the church without the exclusion or isolation of any; each is a member of the catholic church. The church is therefore many but one—a communion of churches.[15]

The image of the church as the body of Christ also demonstrates the diversity of the church: one body, many parts. The diversity of gifts and functions within the body of Christ places the catholic church under its theological maxim vis-à-vis the church—unity in diversity and diversity in unity. Reformation scholars believed that when the church was bent toward defining the unity of the church in terms of uniformity resulting to laxity of faith and practice, the Spirit of Christ in and through the Reformation brought the catholic church to the spirit of diversity to protect and preserve its unity. Thus, ironically the Reformation shielded the catholic church from false visible unity anchored in the institutionally created ecclesiastical offices under the authority of the Pope instead of a unity anchored in the authority of the Word and the Spirit. Roman Catholic theologian Avery Dulles laments,

> Furthermore, the tendency of Catholics to rely upon this type of apologetic for their own security in their faith had deleterious spiritual effects. The Church became to some extent a victim of its own rhetoric. In seeking manifest unity, the Church sometimes fell into a cult of uniformity. This period of institutional religion was the age of the monolithic Church, which aspired to a single universal language (Latin), a single theological system (Neo-Scholasticism), a single system of worship (the Roman rite), and a single system of government (the Code of Canon Law). Instead of encouraging new and diversified forms of thought, life, and worship, Catholics of this period tended to pride themselves on their exact conformity to Roman prescriptions.[16]

True catholicity embraces diversity within its realm of influence under the authority of both the Word and the Spirit. As such diversity functions

---

14. Ibid., 194.
15. See Jenson, "Church," 1–9.
16. Ibid., 129.

within our unity of life and purpose, that is, one lives for the other. Diversity is not a plurality of independent and isolated churches; it is a diversity of churches in relation to one another where the dynamic catholicity of divine love reigns supreme. In divine love there is no competition, envy, or selfish ambition. Divine love treats everybody not just as a part of the church but an important part of the church. As Paul said, "It always protects, always trusts, always hopes, always perseveres" (1 Cor 13:7). In the catholic church, people will always find equal value and equal protection in that kind of love.

Moreover, the beauty and growth of the catholic church are reflected in and through its diversity. Diversity engenders the mystery of the church, making it attractive to the world. Such mystery in diversity is like a magnetic force that draws people to Christ and to the church. It is a powerful witness of our catholicity—a unity in diversity. In and through the diversity of the church, the world sees and experiences life and dynamism—an organic beauty of the many. In unity we live, in diversity we grow; but it is in unity in diversity that we bear fruits in and for the kingdom of God.

Catholic as Orthodox

Catholicity arose from the many struggles of the church against heretics. In order to protect and preserve the church from their influence toward survival, a catholic standard for both theology and practice had to be made, otherwise heretics would influence churches world-wide and eventually would cause the churches to weaken if not disintegrate. The cry for the standard had led the churches to put emphasis on their catholic identity on the basis of a defined catholic faith and practice. In sum, catholicity had been interpreted as orthodoxy. Hans Küng points out, "The great turning point came with Constantine, or more precisely with Theodosius, for under the religious edict of 380 the '*ecclēsia catholica*' became the only lawful national religion . . . Paganism and heresy became political crimes, 'catholicity' became orthodoxy, defended by the law."[17]

To be catholic then is to be mindful of what we believe as a church universal. The church is not just a sociological organization, but it is a theological community. The life and mission of the church are based on its theology. The lack of sound biblical theology can lead to deviance in the church. Heresies were born out of lack of reference to sound theology

---

17. Küng, *Church*, 298.

or catholic theology. Catholic theology is a biblical and historical theology in the spirit of the apostles—hence, apostolic. In this sense, catholicity is apostolicity. It was not just a theology agreed upon by any council of bishops or theological leaders or synods. They neither determined nor defined catholic theology. They were doing catholic theology in the context of both the militant and the triumphant church. The basis for catholic theology was not only the plain teachings of the Bible but also the faithful interpretations of the church in and through the traditions of the apostles, the early church fathers, the contemporary issues of the church, and its various cultural contexts.

The historical and theological creedal statements of the church universal gave shape to orthodoxy. Of the four influential creeds, the most used and popular creed is the Apostles' Creed:

> I believe in God the Father Almighty, Maker of heaven and earth. And in Jesus Christ his only Son our Lord; who was conceived by the Holy Spirit, born of the virgin Mary; suffered under Pontius Pilate, was crucified, dead, and buried; He descended into hell, the third day he rose from the dead; he ascended into heaven; and sitteth at the right hand of God the Father Almighty; from thence he shall come to judge the quick and the dead. I believe in the Holy Spirit; the holy catholic Church; the communion saints; the forgiveness of sins; the resurrection of the body; and the life everlasting. Amen.

During the ATA theological consultation I attended and participated in Korea in 2014, Yuan-Wei Liao noted the following statement of Ferguson summing up the development of orthodoxy in the catholic church,

> In reviewing the historical development of establishing orthodox doctrine of Trinity and Christology, Ferguson has given us a succinct description of the foci and the relationship of the first four councils. The Council of the Nicaea (325) emphasized the oneness of God by asserting that Jesus Christ is *homoousios* with the Father while the Council of Constantinopole (381) emphasized the threeness of God by arguing that Father, Son, and the Holy Spirit are three distinct yet mutual-indwelling persons. The Council of Ephesus (431) emphasized the oneness of Jesus Christ by maintaining Mary as *theotokos* while the Council of Chalcedon (451) emphasized the twoness of Jesus Christ by explicating how the

divine and human "natures" (*physes*) were united in the Son's one and the same person.[18]

These and the other creedal statements that follow helped define and give shape to catholic theology. Pelikan writes,

> The criteria of *catholicity* required that a doctrine, to be recognized as the teaching of the church rather than a private theory of a man or of a school, be genuinely catholic, that is, be the confession of "all the churches . . . one great horde of people from Palestine to Chalcedon with one voice reechoing the praises of Christ." In one dogmatic conflict after another, this argument had been used with lesser or greater appropriateness, to refute heresy.[19]

Creedal statements do not suggest that catholic theology is a final theology. Catholic theology has not yet arrived and probably will never arrive at its destination. It is still a theology in a journey, but the journey that already has a given theological map available for us to navigate better. It is a guide but not the way. Catholic theology points us to the Way, the Truth, and the Life (John 14:6). For it is only Christ who can bring us all home to the Father in his Kingdom both here and now, and there and then. And to that aspect we now turn.

Catholic as Christocentric

At the heart of catholicity is not the church, but Christ. Griffith Thomas is very particular in his theological statement about Christianity when he says,

> Christianity is the only religion in the world which rests on the Person of its Founder. A man can be a faithful Mohammedan without in the least concerning himself with the person of Mohammed. So also a man can be a true and faithful Buddhist without knowing anything whatever about Buddha. It is quite different with Christianity. Christianity is so inextricably bound up with Christ that our

---

18. Liao, "Significance," 29. See also Ferguson, *Church History*, 255; Pelikan, *Christian Tradition*, 172–357.

19. Pelikan, *Christian Tradition*, 333. The italic is mine. The word "catholicity" better communicates the catholic spirit of any confession or teaching of the church than the word "universality."

view of the Person of Christ involves and determines our view of Christianity.[20]

Dunning's emphasis is on the same spirit and it is worth repeating it here: "It is inappropriate to say that Christ founded the Church or that He was part of the Church; He was the Church."[21] The church is catholic because of Christ, that is, Christ is its catholicity. There is no church who can singly claim catholicity (for example, the old Roman Catholic Church) for Christ is not exclusively for a church or any particular country such as Israel. It is in Christ that we are in the church; it is also in him that a church is catholic. If "universal" is the basic and fundamental lexical meaning of catholic, the theological meaning of catholic yields for us the relationship of the church with Christ. Catholicity is not an inherent quality of the church; it is derived from its relationship with Christ. Paul puts it succinctly, "There is neither Jew nor Greek, there is neither slave nor free, there is neither male nor female; for you are all one in Christ Jesus" (Gal 3:28).

All models or images of the church are given meaning and reality only in Christ.[22] Any images or models void of Christ is not worthy of association with the catholic church and more so with God and the Spirit. Christ himself made it clear and strong that no one goes to the Father except through him; and the same is true with the Spirit. The fullness of the Spirit is only possible in and through Christ. Indeed, in Christ the fullness of God—the Spirit and the Father—dwells. To be in Christ is to be in God the Father and in God the Spirit. In Christ through his incarnation we find "the mystery of divine plenitude" indeed. He is the Lord of the church not only because he gave himself for the church but also because in him we have the fullness of divine truth and grace.

The catholicity of Christ nullifies all mediatorial means to God and his grace. The sacrificial system in the Old Testament under the old covenant is nullified by the arrival of the final and permanent covenant of God in Christ. It is also the reason why Protestants or Evangelicals as we are known today deny the Roman Catholic doctrine of grace through Mary granting her a "co-mediatrix" role in the bestowal of divine grace. This same catholicity in Christ also denies the notion that God has rejected the Jews (see Rom 11). When the new covenant was handed over to the church, it does not mean that the Jews have lost their part in the Kingdom of God. The church

---

20. Thomas, *Christianity*, 7.
21. Dunning, *Grace*, 530.
22. See Minear, *Images*. Also Dulles, *Models*.

is inclusive of both Jews and Gentiles. Paul was in fact optimistic that all Jews would one day come to repentance and salvation available in Christ (Rom 11:25–32). Anti-Semitism is anti-catholicity; Semitic-exclusivism is likewise anti-catholicity. Catholicity rejects all forms of ethnocentrism, whether social or religious. The church is always and will always be the church of Christ universal.

The catholicity of the church in Christ grants its members not only the status of being justified by grace through faith, but also the access into the sanctifying work of the Holy Spirit so that they join the company of those who have been made holy in Christ.[23] The call to holiness is part and parcel of the life of the catholic church. The apostle Paul described the Corinthians as "those who are sanctified in Christ Jesus and called to be holy" (1 Cor 1:2). Sanctification in and through the Holy Spirit is impossible outside Christ. In Christ believers in the context of the catholic community have been made holy. Holiness is a communal quality of the church.[24] The mark of holiness is a catholic mark. The Holy Spirit does not sanctify believers for their individuality sake; they are made holy so they qualify to become members of the holy catholic church. The work of the Holy Spirit puts into effect the very reason for which Christ died: "And so Jesus also suffered outside the city gate to make the people holy through his own blood" (Heb 13:12).

Catholic as Pentecostal

Paul's command for the believers "to keep the unity of the Spirit" suggests strongly the subjective role of the Holy Spirit in the life of the church as "one, holy, catholic, and apostolic." Jesus promised to send to his disciples the Holy Spirit who would be with them and empower them for life and service (John 14:16–18; Acts 1:8). Indeed, at the Pentecost the Holy Spirit was given not only as a gift from Jesus but also from the Father (Acts 1:4–5) to the church. The Pentecost was the day the church was historically born, and had its official status as the re*new*ed people of God inclusive of both Jews and Gentiles. The Spirit was the seal that marked the church as belonging to Christ and heirs of God's redemption: "And you also were included in Christ when you heard the word of truth, the gospel of salvation. Having believed, you were marked in him with a seal, the promised Holy Spirit,

---

23. For a discussion on Christian holiness and the Holy Trinity, see the excellent work of Noble, *Holy Trinity*, 180–98.

24. See Adewuya, *Holiness and Community*. Also, Kunene, *Communal Holiness*.

who is a deposit guaranteeing our inheritance until the redemption of those who are God's possession—to the praise of his glory" (Eph 1:13–14).

The significance of the Pentecost must be seen in the role it played in God's history of salvation in Jesus Christ through the church represented by the disciples present on that day. The Pentecost revealed the nature and mission of the church as catholic. The Spirit opened a new horizon for the covenant given to Abraham and fulfilled in his offspring, Jesus Christ—it is a horizon that includes men and women of all nations. The Pentecost was not an ordinary event in Jerusalem that day; it marked the finality of Christ's work and the beginning of the catholic life and mission of the church. T. A. Noble captures this truth,

> Pentecost must therefore be seen as primarily a once-for-all unrepeatable event. It is the final event in the series of the mighty acts of God in Jesus. It that sense it is as unique and unrepeatable as the incarnation, the crucifixion, the resurrection, and the ascension. And what it means is that now that the work of Christ has been completed on the cross, it is possible for the first time for men and women to receive the benefits of his atonement. True, men and women received the forgiveness of God before then, but only provisionally in the light of the sacrificial death that was still to come. Even the word of forgiveness spoken by Jesus to individuals during his life on earth was provisional in the sense that the one "full, perfect, and sufficient sacrifice, oblation and satisfaction, for the sins of the whole world" had not yet been completed. But now it had been completed on the cross, the perfect and finished work of atonement. Therefore at Pentecost, now that the atonement was complete, the ascended Christ was able to pour out his Spirit upon "all flesh," all humankind. That universal "pouring out" of the Spirit was what was to condition and energize the mission of the church to the ends of the earth. It was not, of course, that all human beings received the Spirit of the Day of Pentecost in the same way as the apostles. They, as the foundation stones of the church, built on the cornerstone (Eph 2:20), now for the first time each received the Spirit, who was now to remain on each of them as he had remained upon Jesus during his earthly life. And in receiving the Spirit "in" them, they received the full salvation won on the cross—forgiveness, his intimate relationship with the Father ("Abba!"), and the resurrection life of Jesus.[25]

---

25. Noble, *Holy Trinity*, 190.

The Pentecost was the beginning of the more direct and active role of the Spirit in and through the life and mission of the church. On behalf of both the Father and the Son, the Spirit now leads the church. The whole book of Acts demonstrates the various ministries of the Spirit in and through the church, which include the following: he gives life, he gives power for service, he purifies, he reveals, he guides and directs, he gives assurance, he teaches and illumines, he unifies, he strengthens, he rebukes, and many others.[26] The church is rightly the "means of grace" in and through which the Spirit works. This is what the spirit of what Irenaeus said, "Where the church is, there is the Spirit of God; and where the Spirit of God is, there is the church, and every kind of grace." (Iren. Haer. 3.24)[27]

This Pentecostal mark of the catholic church simply means that the church is under the authority, power, and leadership of the Holy Spirit. The Spirit is the Lord of the Church; the Church is the servant of the Spirit. This cooperative work between the Spirit and the church has its Christological and missional aspects. The Christological aspect of the work of the Spirit in the church is grounded on the promise of Jesus to the church that he would neither abandon them nor leave them. The Spirit is Christ in the church. Moreover, the Spirit is the Effector of the grace of God in Christ Jesus. This is the missional aspect of the work of the Spirit in the mission of the church. God's work of salvation in Christ and through the church is effected in and through the Holy Spirit. The authority of the church is in its submission to the authority of the Spirit. The church cannot act on its own authority without the Spirit. Hans Küng rightly reminded the Roman Catholic Church, and the same reminder applies to Protestant churches and others that take their authority in their being "institutions," that the church does not already exist as an organized, hierarchical institution that the Spirit enters and empowers; rather, the church is created by the Spirit, the author of life and consequently the Lord of the church, who grants the gift of faith and forgiveness.[28] When the church is not in the Spirit, then the church does not have any authority whatsoever. The famous dictum that "there is no salvation outside the church" is only true in Christ and *in the Spirit*.

---

26. See Grudem, *Sytematic Theology*, 634–53.
27. As quoted by Pelikan, *Christian Tradition*, 156.
28. Küng, *Church*, 176.

Catholic as Evangelical

The word "evangelical" is derived from the Greek word *euangelion*, which literally means "gospel" or "good news." The word "evangelical" vis-à-vis the church describes primarily the commitment of the church to the gospel of Jesus Christ and its preaching. This commitment was almost personified by Paul in and through his life and mission as a servant of the gospel of Jesus Christ. His words to the Romans succinctly summarizes this commitment,

> First, I thank my God through Jesus Christ for all of you, because your faith is being reported to all over the world. God, whom I serve with my whole heart in preaching the gospel of his Son, is my witness how constantly I remember you in my prayers at all times; and I pray that now at last by God's will the way may be opened for me to come to you. I long to see you so that I may impart to you some spiritual gift to make you strong—that is, that you and I may be mutually encouraged by each other's faith. I do not want you to be unaware, brothers that I planned many times to come to you (but have been prevented from doing so until now) in order that I might have a harvest among you, just as I have had among the other Gentiles. I am obligated both to Greeks and non-Greeks, both to the wise and the foolish. That is why I am so eager to preach the gospel to you who are at Rome. I am not ashamed of the gospel, because it is the power of God for salvation of everyone who believes: first for the Jew, then for the Gentile. For in the gospel a righteousness from God is reveal, a righteousness that is by faith from first to last, just as it is written: "The righteous shall live by faith" (Rom 1:8–17).

The centrality of the gospel and its proclamation are at the heart of the work and mission of the church universal. The church is a community of the gospel. Both its life and mission are shaped by the gospel. Everything that the church does revolves around the gospel of Jesus Christ—its creeds, its sacraments, its message, it various ministries, and many others.

But what is the "gospel" on which the church is based? N. T. Wright challenges the traditional and evangelical understanding of the gospel. He proposes that the gospel is centered not on justification by grace through faith but rather on the Kingdom of God.[29] While I don't think it is right and healthy for the church to totally reject N. T. Wright's thesis, it remains that at the heart of the gospel is "justification by grace through faith."

29. See Wright, *How God Became King*. For discussion on the issue, see Piper, *Future of Justification*.

The evangelists themselves proclaimed the message of the gospel that is centered on sin and forgiveness through Jesus Christ in general and his death in particular. This we cannot surrender to Wright's thesis. Rejection of the gospel of justification is a rejection of the biblical, theological, and historical understanding of the gospel. Justification by faith is the basic and fundamental meaning of the gospel on which the catholicity of the church is also based. This is the gospel that Paul wanted to preach to those who were in Rome—the gospel of Justification.[30] The same gospel unites the catholic church today in and through various historical and theological confessions.[31]

The church's commitment to the gospel is also a commitment to the Word of God and its proclamation. This is demonstrated in Dulles' model of the church as a *herald* where the gospel and the Word of God are inseparable to which the church is ontologically and functionally related.[32] This is a catholic commitment that engenders not only life and love but also communion and commitment. Dulles beautifully captures this truth,

> The Constitution on Divine Revelation begins on a markedly kerygmatic note, with the phrase "hearing the word of God with reverence and proclaiming it confidently," but it immediately goes on to quote from the first letter of John, "We announce to you the eternal life which was with the Father, and has appeared to us. What we have seen and have heard we announce to you, in order that you may have fellowship with us . . ." Thus the word mediates not only what was heard but what appeared and was seen, and the goal of preaching is not mere profession of faith in the message, but rather a communion of life and love.[33]

The word of God is neither the property of the church nor its authority is under the magisterium of the church. "The magisterium of the church," says Dulles "is, to be sure, not over the word of God but under it."[34] The evangelical calling of the church is not only to submit to the authority of the

---

30. See Morris, *Romans*.

31. See also Oberman, *Reformation*, 164–66, where it is argued that the Christian faith is evangelical.

32. See Dulles, *Models*, 76–88.

33. Ibid., 86–87.

34. Ibid., 87. Magisterium is a Roman Catholic doctrine of the authority of the church in and through the office of the Pope and the cardinals.

word of God but also to faithfully proclaim its message of the good news of salvation to all the nations.

Catholic as Triumphant

The apostle Paul comforted and reminded the believers about those who have died in Christ with the following words,

> Brothers and sisters, we do not want you to be uninformed about those who sleep in death, so that you do not grieve like the rest of mankind, who have no hope. For we believe that Jesus died and rose again, and so we believe that God will bring with Jesus those who have fallen asleep in him. According to the Lord's word, we tell you that we who are still alive, who are left until the coming of the Lord, will certainly not precede those who have fallen asleep. For the Lord himself will come down from heaven, with a loud command, with the voice of the archangel and with the trumpet call of God, and the dead in Christ will rise first. After that, we are still alive and are left will caught up with them in the clouds to meet the Lord in the air. And so we will be with the Lord forever. Therefore encourage one another with these words (1 Thess 4:13–18).

The phrase "in Christ" obviously includes those who have died in the faith. The church does not only refer to those who are still living but also to those who have fallen asleep in the Lord. Together we are the church, that is to say, that "the church is constituted by the believers on earth and of those who have died in the Lord and are presently in His company."[35] This is what we call the triumphant church.[36]

As the triumphant church, the catholic church knows no division of time and space. The generations of believers, not only in the New Testament but also in the Old Testament, are all members of the catholic church. The catholic church spans believers from beginning to the end. It is inclusive not only of those who presently believe and those who will still believe in the gospel of Jesus Christ, but it absolutely includes those who have gone before us, and are now serving as the witnesses: "Therefore, since we are surrounded by such a great cloud of witnesses . . ." (Heb 12:1). As such, the

---

35. Smith, "Ecclesiology," 599.

36. Theologians normally differentiate the "triumphant" church from the "militant" church. I don't see any distinction. I use "triumphant" in reference to both.

catholic church refers to the ageless community of believers or fellowship of the saints. In his model of the church as Mystical Communion, Dulles rightly says,

> Many of the Church Fathers, including Augustine, develop the image of the Body of Christ with particular stress on the mystical and invisible communion that binds together all those who are enlivened by the grace of Christ. Augustine speaks of a Church that includes not only the earthly but the heavenly: The angels and the blessed are members of the heavenly part of the Church. Christ as head makes up one totality together with all his members. The Body is not essentially visible, since it includes angels and separated souls. Still less is it societal, since it in includes all men who are animated by the spirit of God. All the just from Abel on are in the Body of Christ, in the *Ecclesia ab Abel*. Augustine already has the idea of the Holy Spirit as soul of the body.[37]

The triumphant church is a present and active reality in the world today. The life and mission of the church are not separated from those who have gone before us. Catholic theology, for example, does not disregard the wisdom of the past in the construction of our contemporary catholic theology. The church anchors its theological works in the wisdom of the fathers that had established the traditions of the present church. There is a theological link that exists between the two. And they are hardly inseparable. To do so is to cease to be catholic. Smith puts emphasis on how the church is made up of two realities. He writes "one reality is waging war against all evil while the other is already in heaven with the assurance over evil."[38] He adds, "Hence the church militant is supported by the church triumphant . . ."[39] The two are indeed inseparable realities in the life and mission of the church.

The triumphant church communicates the victory of the church. Such is an undeniable fact not only in the past but even in the present. Paul's doxology emphasizes this truth, "Thanks be to God, who always leads us in His triumph in Christ" (2 Cor 2:14). This victory, though ours now in Christ, will eventually and finally be ours on the resurrection day: "When the perishable has been clothed with the imperishable, and the mortal with

---

37. Dulles, *Models*, 50–51. The inclusion of "angels" into the Body of Christ is one that does not receive strong approval from the Evangelical circles.
38. Smith, "Ecclesiology," 599.
39. Ibid.

immortality, then the saying that is written will come true: "Death has been swallowed up in victory, 'Where, O death, is your victory? Where, O death, is you sting?' The sting of death is sin, and the power of sin is the law. But thanks be to God! He gives us the victory through our Lord Jesus Christ" (1 Cor 15:54–57). Christ's victory is our victory; his triumph is our triumph.

Catholic as Missional

A church is not catholic if it is not missional. The mission of the church to all nations defines yet another of its catholicity: "Then Jesus came to his disciples and said to them, 'All authority in heaven and on earth has been given to me. Therefore go and make disciples of all nations, baptizing them in the name of the Father and of the Son and of the Holy Spirit, and teaching them to obey everything I have commanded you. And surely I am with you always, to the very end of the age'" (Matt 28:18b–20). This is the Great Commission to the catholic church Jesus left behind. The church was given the task to continue and extend Jesus's finished mission in and through their mission to the world—a catholic mission indeed.

The nature of the church as the "called out ones," derived from the Greek word *ekklēsia*, indicates that the church is a missional community.[40] The mission of the church is nowhere demonstrated more actively, progressively, and perfectly than in the book of Acts. In Acts, the mission was under the leadership and empowerment of the Holy Spirit, notwithstanding the willingness of the church to suffer for Christ's sake. Luke provided us the geographical expansion of the mission of the church—from Jerusalem, to Judea and Samaria, and to the ends of the earth (Acts 1:8). This geographical expansion clearly and succinctly demonstrated the mission of the church as catholic.[41]

At the heart of the mission of the church is the *Missio Dei* (God's mission) in Christ, that is, the salvation of men and women (Mark 2:9, 17, 10:45; Matt 9:13, 18:11, 26:28; Luke 5:32, 7:48, 19:10; John 10:11–18; Acts 5:31). And to this Paul also testified to Timothy: "... who want all men [and women] to be saved and to come to a knowledge of the truth. For there is one God and one mediator between God and men [and women], the man

---

40. For a thorough discussion on the historical and theological meaning of "ekklēsia" see, Roloff, "ekklēsia," 410–15.

41. For a discussion on the mission of the church and the role of the Holy Spirit, see Hur, *A dynamic Reading*.

Christ Jesus, who gave himself as a ransom for all men [and women]—the testimony given in its proper time. And for this purpose I was appointed a herald and an apostle—I am telling the truth; I am not lying—and a teacher of the true faith to the Gentiles" (1 Tim 2:4–7). This mission is deeply imbedded in the life of the church. Dunning rightly says,

> We may at this point tentatively define the Church as that community of people called into being by God for the purpose of carrying out His redemptive mission in the world. In the light of the fuller implications of the images of the Church in the New Testament with their Old Testament background, we may speak of the Church as the saved and saving community.[42]

As the God who called the church is a missionary God, so is the church—a missionary church. It exists not only for God and itself but also for the others—the world: "For God so loved the world that he gave his only Son, that whosoever believes in him shall not perish but have everlasting life" (John 3:16). At the heart of God's redemption is the world. Karl Barth rightly emphasizes that the church is a community for the world: "It is not idly, but as it performs, that the community exists for the world."[43] As such the world is the mission of the church—a catholic mission. This makes catholicity not only ontological but also missional or functional.

Catholic as Kingdom-Mindset

The relationship of the church and the Kingdom has been the subject of many theological discussions and mission dialogues. Questions have been many, such as, is the church the Kingdom of God here on earth? Is the church the servant of the Kingdom? Is the gospel the Kingdom of God? Etc. What then is the relationship between the church and the Kingdom? Having defined the Kingdom as primarily the dynamic reign or kingly rule of God, Ladd proposes five axioms of the church and the Kingdom relationship:

---

42. Dunning, *Grace*, 516.

43. Karl Barth, *Community*, 503. Barth further offers three characteristics of the church in relation to the world that serve as the marks of the true community: (1) the fellowship in which it is given to men (and women) to know the world as it is; (2) the society in which it is given to men (and women) to know and practice their solidarity with the world with the world; (3) the society in which it is given to men (and women) to be under obligation to the world. Ibid., 503–15.

1. The Church is not the Kingdom
2. The Kingdom creates the Church
3. The Church witnesses to the Kingdom
4. The Church is the instrument of the Kingdom
5. The Church is the custodian of the Kingdom[44]

N. T. Wright's proposal advances the relationship by equating the Kingdom of God with the gospel of Jesus Christ.[45] To Wright, the church exists to establish the kingship of God in the world through its mission in the world. This is a call for the church to have a Kingdom-mindset, that is, the church is called to live not only in the world but also for the world by establishing and advancing the Kingdom of God on earth as it is in heaven.

Wright's criticism against the church for its too much emphasis on justification by grace through faith at the expense of the kingdom of God is fair and just; it is worthy of revisiting. Admittedly the gospel of justification by grace through faith has indeed resulted to an imbalance in the church's understanding of the catholic gospel. While it is totally unacceptable for the church to abandon justification by grace through faith, it is high time that we give the Kingdom of God its rightful place as part and parcel of the gospel. After all, isn't the Kingdom of God the very message Christ preached: "Repent, for the Kingdom of God is near" (Matt 4:17). At the heart of the life, death, and resurrection of Jesus is the Kingdom of God. He came not only to save the people from their sins, but also to bring them into the Kingdom. The two are inseparable. Ladd rightly observes this truth,

> Jesus' message of the Kingdom proclaimed the God not only will finally act, but that God was now again acting redemptively in history. In fact, God had entered into history in a way and to a degree not known by the prophets. The fulfillment of the Old Testament promises was taking place; the messianic salvation was present; the Kingdom of God had come near. God was visiting his people. In Jesus, God has taken the initiative to seek out the sinner, to bring the lost into the blessing of his reign. He was, in short, the seeking God.[46]

---

44. Ladd, *Theology*, 109–17.
45. See Wright, *How God Became King*.
46. Ladd, *Theology*, 80.

The Kingdom can only and properly be understood in the context of God's redemptive history. In fact, Christ's coming was already the inauguration of the Kingdom of God, and his death and resurrection truly established the Kingdom of God, and the church is called to announce and advance the Kingdom to and in the world. This call is the Kingdom-mindset which defines further the functional catholicity of the church.

This Kingdom-mindset indeed puts an end to the church's centuries-half-baked gospel and it would offer the world the full gospel of Jesus Christ. What has been for centuries a peripheral to the gospel now comes to become part and parcel of the gospel. Thus, the catholic gospel is not an either/or but a both/end one, that is, the gospel is both justification by grace through faith and the Kingdom of God. The gospel then is a two-fold work of God in the context of God's redemptive history. On the one hand is what remains as the basic and fundamental meaning of the gospel—Justification by faith; on the other hand is the goal of the gospel—the Kingdom of God.

Moreover, the Kingdom-mindset has its goal the eschatological fulfillment of God's redemptive history—the renewal of all things in creation for the restored humanity in Christ. This is the catholic eschatology that universalizes the truth of the Kingdom as belonging to all nations.[47] The eschatological kingdom is the final event in human history that we have known and the beginning of the yet unknown Kingdom-life under the kingship of God the Father, the Son, and the Holy Spirit.

Catholicity rejects both ethnocentrism or a mindset of the same, and denominationalism or denominational-mindset; it embraces a higher community of faith—the community of the Kingdom. This Kingdom community is the catholic community. In the Kingdom, the church is universal, one, many, orthodox, Christo-centric, Pentecostal, evangelical, triumphant, and missional. The Kingdom encompasses the other nine marks of the catholic church.

---

47. Ladd notes this truth as well: "One of the most distinctive facts that set Jesus' teaching apart from Judaism was the universalizing of the concept. Both in the Old Testament and in Judaism, the Kingdom was always picture in terms of Israel. In the Old Testament, sometimes the Gentiles would be conquered by Israel (Amos 9:12; Mic. 5:9; Isa. 45:14-16; 60:12, 14), sometimes they are seen as converted (Zeph. 3:9, 20; 2:2-4; Zech. 8:20–23). But the Kingdom is always Israel's. Late Judaism had become quite particularistic, and the establishing of God's Kingdom means the sovereignty of Israel over her political and national enemies: 'Then thou, O Israel, shalt be happy, and thou shalt mount upon the necks and wings of the eagle . . . and thou shalt look from on high and shalt see thy enemies in Gehenna, and though shalt recognize them and rejoice' (Ass. Mos. 10:8–10)." Ladd, *Theology*, 62.

Conclusion

The catholic mark of the church is one that has defined the inherent relationship among the various communities of faith and the mission they have as members of the church of Jesus Christ. While it has been intended to keep the church from heresies and heretics alike, catholicity has enriched the life and mission of the church both inside and outside its realm of influence. It has brought churches of different major traditions and small denominations together towards the realization of Jesus's prayer for unity. This of course has yet to be strengthened within the greater Christendom. There remains a catholic challenge—the putting of flesh and blood to our unity as a people of the Spirit. I will give attention to this in the next chapter.

Meanwhile, from the Reformation to counter-Reformations, both from the Roman Catholic and Protestant camps, and also to the many Revivals and Renewals that happened in the church among denominations and independent churches leading to unprecedented qualitative and quantitative growth world-wide, the history of the church has brought a richer evolution of its catholic mark. The traditional understanding of catholicity has developed within the dynamic life and mission of the church—from geography and statistics to inclusiveness and acceptance of others, leading to joint participations in theological constructions and missional outreaches. The above elucidation of the expanded marks of the catholic church proves that the church has truly gone far in its catholicity.

In sum, to say that we are catholic is to recognize four maxims derived from the above marks of the catholic church: (1) the church's inherent relationship with the Holy Trinity who created it and its catholicity in and through Christ and by the effectual ministry of the Holy Spirit, (2) the fellowship of the church is not only defined by the communion of believers in various local churches but also the communion of churches world-wide, (3) the beliefs of the church are rooted in the Word of God and its faithful interpretations of the church, (4) the church is not only a saved community but a saving community.

6

The Catholic Challenge

Catholicization—Towards a Theological Praxis of the Unity of the Church of Jesus Christ[1]

JESUS PRAYED THIS PRAYER: ". . . so that they may be one as we are one" (John 17.11). This verse shows the Lord's impressive and important concern for the unity of the church represented by his disciples who served as the nucleus of the then emerging church. It is a unity, however, that is not to be made yet. The grammatical construction with the use of the Greek present subjunctive *hina ōsin* suggests that the prayer is for the disciples not to "become" one but to "continually be" one.[2] As such, this unity is a gift of the Father for the faith of the disciples. Leon Morris says, "It is a unity already given."[3] The church does not create its unity; it can only keep and strengthen it. Through Jesus's prayer we see that the keeping and strengthening of this unity demand the sustaining and strengthening grace of God. Hence, Jesus prayed for it. Of course, it did not take away the responsibility

---

1. This chapter was written and submitted by the author to the *EvQ* journal for publication, which at the time of the writing of this book the author was formally informed that the article would appear in January of 2016 issue. The author has written to the *EvQ* for permission to use, if needed, for this book. All credit to this chapter is, therefore, given to *EvQ*.

2. See Morris, *Gospel*, 727. He writes, "It is a unity 'in' the Father and the Son (v. 21). Christ is to be 'in' them (v. 23). We should be clear that the unity for which Christ prays is a unity which rests on a common basic attitude, that of abiding in Him and having Him abide in them."

3. Ibid. Macquarrie calls it the "unity of origin." Macquarrie, *Christian Unity*, 3.

of the disciples to work toward the keeping and strengthening of the unity they continued to enjoy in and through the effectual ministry of the Holy Spirit. The cooperation of the disciples with the Holy Spirit was indispensable. Therefore, the realization of Jesus's prayer depends both on the grace of God through the effectual ministry of the Holy Spirit and the responsibility of his disciples through cooperation with the Holy Spirit.

Scholars are divided on the interpretation of Jesus's prayer for the unity of his disciples. Ecumenical scholars argue that the appeal to unity is related to denominational unity in terms of denominational cooperation in and through world evangelization and mission. And so the ecumenical voices or "prophets" work hard to call churches and denominations to work together toward the realization of this prayer. They believe that the reunion and cooperation of the Christendom would mean the answer to Christ's prayer.[4] The problem of this interpretation is that it focuses on the outward unity of the church. On the other side of the spectrum are those who would like to think of the unity of the church in terms of a spiritual unity. They maintain the uniqueness of churches and denominations; but they still call everyone to have a unity in spirit—heart, mind, and will. And on that basis churches embrace an attitude of acceptance toward each other. The focus here is more inward than outward.

Both interpretations, however, are not mutually exclusive; it is not an "either/or" option but a "both/and" one. In other words, the unity of the church must be seen not only in terms of an inward unity (spirit—heart, mind, and will) but also outward (in terms of core biblical doctrines, Christian attitude of love and acceptance, ministry and mission participation and cooperation, and others that put flesh and blood to the unity of the church). The two are demonstrative of the objective and subjective aspects of the unity of the church. The objective aspect demonstrates the given unity derived from the work of God in Christ by the power of the Spirit and experienced by the church through faith. The subjective aspect demonstrates the active responsibility of the church in the context of grace to keep the given unity in and through its theology, history, life, ministry and mission. Sadly, the subjective aspect of the unity of the church is dwindling, if not dying. John Stott rightly observes,

> Today, however, many of us evangelical Christians acquiesce too readily in our pathological tendency to fragment. We take refuge in our conviction about the invisible unity of the church, as if its

4. Ibid., 727–28.

visible manifestation did not matter. In consequence, the devil has been hugely successful in his old strategy to "divide and conquer." Our disunity remains a major hindrance to our evangelism.[5]

This is where the catholic spirit of the church can contribute significantly toward the fulfillment of Jesus's prayer.

The catholic spirit is conduit to the unity of the church; it gives that unity its form both in faith and practice. Sadly the church since the Reformation has not strongly emphasized the necessity of unity among churches and denominations that have come or risen out of the Protestant Reformation. In fact, there has been a proliferation of the spirit of reformation among the Protestant churches. For example, reactionary to the Roman Catholic's abuses of ecclesiastical and political power, and to its distortions of biblical doctrines that led to Luther's 95 theses, the Protestants have believed that the church is always in need of a continual reformation, which sadly leads further to a number of eccentric denominations and independent churches within the Protestant circle both in the east and the west.

Have we in the Protestant churches lost our catholicity in the name of diversity? Or have we kept within our diversity the catholic spirit of the church?[6] If the latter is true, and I think it is, what then is the face of the catholic spirit within the Protestant churches? I firmly believe that it is in the spirit and work of "catholicization"[7] that we can keep and give face to our unity as disciples of Jesus Christ within our heritage of faith as Protestant churches and denominations.

What is Catholicization?

In the recent 2014 theological conference I attended and participated, sponsored by Asia Theological Association (ATA) in Seoul Korea, I presented a paper entitled, "Contextualization of the Life and Ministry of Jesus in the Four Gospels and, its Significance in Proclaiming the Gospel to Asian Cultures in the 21st Century." In that paper, I discussed the necessity of contextualization of the Gospel as exemplified by the evangelists themselves

---

5. Stott, *Evangelical Truth*, 141.
6. See Macquarrie, *Christian Unity*.
7. The word "catholicization" is defined in a dictionary as the process of making catholic. It is not used, however, here with reference to adhering to a Roman Catholic Church doctrine or becoming a member of the Roman Catholic Church.

through their gospel narrative accounts to various people groups.[8] I personally believe that contextualization is indeed a theological imperative for the church.[9] However, the work of contextualization is only one side of the spectrum of the work of the church. The other is the work of bringing churches from different cultures and contexts together in the spirit of unity as Jesus prayed in John 17.

In one of the informal discussions I had with people during the conference, a group of delegates talked and exchanged ideas on how we can work together to lessen, if not eradicate, the social divides within our various cultures, such as the caste system in India and other parts of Asia. That brought me to thinking of the need for us to work together in unity. Hence, my interest in the opposite direction came. If we are to address the disunity of various peoples within our cultures, we must first address the disunity we have within our circles or churches and denominations. Indeed, as John Stott said and let me repeat it here, ". . . our disunity remains a hindrance to our evangelism and mission."[10]

Catholicization takes the opposite (but not contra) direction of contextualization. The latter is focused on our attempt to dialogue with various cultures and contexts toward an effective communication of the gospel—outward focused; the former is geared toward the keeping and strengthening the unity of the church—inward focused. Both are integral parts of the work of the church. The church cannot afford to have one without the other. May our work on contextualization not blind us to the necessity of catholicization. I define catholicization as an attempt to provide a theological praxis of the unity of the church.[11] It puts emphasis not only on

---

8. Hallig, "Contextualization," 144–59.

9. Bevans writes, "There is no such thing as 'theology,' there is only contextual theology: feminine theology, black theology, liberation theology, Filipino theology, Asian-American theology, African theology, and so forth. Doing theology contextually is not an option, nor is it something that should only interest people from the Third World missionaries who work there, or ethnic communities within dominant cultures. The contextualization of theology—the attempt to understand Christian faith in terms of a particular culture—is really a theological imperative." Bevans, *Models*, 3.

10. Stott, *Evangelical*, 141.

11. For a thorough and good discussion on theological praxis, see Anderson's *Shape of Practical*. Theological praxis is usually taken into consideration in relation to contextualization, where people see the interrelation between theology and praxis in any doing of theology, i.e., text and context. Such understanding, however, is narrow. Theological praxis applies to the inherent relationship between theology (based on God's revelation in the Scripture) and life in its totality (lived experience) both in terms of life's essence

the theology of the unity of the church, but also on its practical relation (both implications and applications) to the life and ministry of the church. In the light of the liberal influence on contextualization and their various portraits of Christ, Yuan-Wei Liao writes:

> From the standpoint of Chalcedonian creed and the Reformation Confessions, many of them (*i.e., liberals*) seem to fall into the danger of denying the uniqueness of Christ and the supremacy of Christ-centered soteriology. While the Christian church should solemnly face the challenge of contextualization and indigenization, it is extremely important to bear in mind that standing firmly on "the faith that was once for all entrusted to the saints" is non-negotiable.[12]

This non-negotiable is a call for a work of catholicization that seeks to prevent us from detaching ourselves from the faith that was once entrusted to us. No work of contextualization should lead us to isolate ourselves from the body of Christ—the holy catholic church.[13] We must put the same effort on catholicization the way we do on contextualization. This is what young Filipino theologian Dick Eugenio echoed in his paper on postmodernism where he writes,

> We need to capitalize on *postmodernism's* emphasis on community, but establish the primacy of the church in the process. The church is the primary community to which Christ belongs. As Lovell Cocks writes, "The preacher is not the first place an artist, an individualist expressing truth through the medium of personality, but spokesman of the church's witness. He does not enter the pulpit to air his own views on religion, however original or striking, or to lay bare his soul in poetic abandon . . . His own faith gives him part in the company of witness . . . Here runs the true line of apostolic succession, in a witness that is at once the verdict of an individual man and the rolling 'Amen' of the Christian centuries." Theologians seem to have forgotten that cultural interpretations are not the last word. The community responsible for validating interpretations is the church, not cultures or nations. Theologians

---

and functions.

12. Liao, "Significance," 37. Liao's paper was later edited and published in the *JAET*. See, Liao, "Significance," 19. Italic is mine.

13. See Karkkainen, *Introduction*, 163–230, where the author discusses "contextual ecclesiologies." Karkkainen believes that it is here that the future of Christian theology lies.

need to identity [sic] the priority of their belongingness and allegiance: the church or their culture or nation?[14]

Catholicization offers a correction to all works of contextualization that set aside the theology of the unity of the church. There has to be a balance between contextualization and catholicization as Korean Reformed theologian Han Sang-Hwa puts it convincingly, and beautifully, in her concluding words on the *Currents In Christological Debates*: "Therefore, under the guidance of the Lordship of Christ, a future Evangelical Asian Christology of the 21st century should keep striving *to offer a* balance—to be biblically faithful, traditionally respectful, contextually relevant, and existentially nourishing."[15] I hope that this book will challenge us to work with equal intensity on the catholicization of the church in terms of both faith and practice as we do on contextualization.

The Gospel as Catholic

What is often neglected in the work of contextualization is the nature of the gospel as catholic. This I have emphasized in my own paper:

> Luke's Gospel exemplifies narrative contextualization that represents and challenges the context. Its concern for the marginalized and the outcasts of the society offers a paradigm for contextualization that is culturally and socially relevant. For Luke Christ is not confined to Israel and its people. He portrays the gospel as truly catholic. The life and ministry of Jesus, though particular, is relived in a wider and different context of its readers with their present faith community that addresses its unique challenges and needs.[16]

Similarly, Matthew testifies to the inclusivity of the Gospel. The life and ministry of Jesus is not exclusively Jewish: "Matthew's narrative therefore revolves around the theme of salvation not only for the Jews but also the inclusion of the Gentiles in the future kingdom. Such a two-fold theme is what is developed in the conflict of Matthew's narrative plot."[17] With

---

14. Eugenio, "Christ-centered," 273–74. Included is a quotation by Lovell Cocks, *By Faith Alone*, 111; quoted in McCracken, "Let the Preacher," 83. Italic is mine. The author used "postmodernity" instead of postmodernism.

15. Han, "Currents," 54. Italic is mine for clarity of expression.

16. Hallig, "Contextualization," 154.

17. Ibid., 149.

such inclusivity, no culture or nation has a monopoly of the good news of salvation. The Christian Gospel is a gospel for all nations.

One of the dangers of catholicization is the concept of mission imperialism or the internationalization of one's culture in the name of the gospel or the church. Sadly contextualization is in part a reaction to such imperialistic concept. Some missionaries are tempted to carry with them not only the catholic gospel but also their culture. They find it hard to unwrap the gospel for a new audience and allow the contextualization process to take place in partnership with, if not in the hands of, the local people. This attitude is due to a limiting definition of the catholicity of the church in terms of an evangelistic inclusion of all persons without regard to the unity of the church. The gospel, however, is not only a message for all nations but it is a message that defines a new community out of nations. Peter understands this truth clearly when he writes, "But you are a chosen people, a royal priesthood, a holy nation, a people belonging to God, that you may declare the praises of him who called you out of darkness into his wonderful light" (1 Pet 2.9). The church inclusive of Jews and Gentiles is more than geographical expansion or historical organization; the church is a spiritual people—chosen, royal, and holy—called to declare the glory of God in and through its unity.

The catholicity (and unity) of the church is a clear implication of the catholic gospel as Paul puts it succinctly: "There is neither Jew nor Greek, there is neither slave nor free, there is neither male nor female; for you are all one in Christ Jesus" (Gal 3.28).

The Unity of the Church

Paul's letters to the Corinthians tell us that the church is not exempt from problems and controversies. Early on the church has been dealing with all kinds of challenges both inside and outside. Many of the challenges, for example, in the early church were threats to the life and unity of the church. The church through the Apostles responded carefully in and through the leadership of the Holy Spirit. The responses put emphasis on the catholicity of the church that helped keep and strengthen the unity of the church.[18]

---

18. The Church developed what later came to be known as the marks or notes (as used by the Roman Catholic Church) of the Church: Unity, Holiness, Catholicity (universality), and Apostolicity. The development of these marks was gradual until the marks were formally stated for the first time in the Creed of Constantinople in 381, which listed

In today's context, the church needs to work on this same important mark (i.e. catholic) of the church that had helped keep and strengthen the unity of the then catholic church (this should be differentiated from the Roman Catholic Church). From the beginning the church has been catholic (universal and united). The Reformation was not intended to destroy the catholic church; the opposite was true. Martin Luther was neither hoping nor attempting to divide the church, but only to purify it from false doctrines and wrong practices. After the Reformation, the Reformers, who were later labeled as Protestants, accepted the original marks of the church including "catholic," but of course added two others—the Scriptures (sola) and the (two) Sacraments. As such the Protestants remained catholic.

Later, however, catholicity has been a challenge to Protestant churches. With the growing churches and denominations, divisions in the church multiplied—some are minors that can easily be addressed; others are majors that need to be taken seriously. If we are to be catholic as our forefathers were, catholicization must not be an option. Catholicization is a must. We in the Protestant churches have been long divided by our differences and "distinctives" in terms of both theology and practice. There is very little effort, if not none at all, on catholicization. And sadly it is rarely part of the academic debates and discussions or even one of the ecclesiastical or missiological challenges. If we want to make Jesus's prayer for unity not only a spiritual reality but an empirical one, a new reformation is needed but this time towards a catholic movement. Catholicity is a way to the unity of the church. Nazarene theologian H. Ray Dunning believes that "catholicity is another aspect of unity."[19] Catholicization is anchored in four "distinctives" of the unity of the church.[20] Together they serve as the foundation of catholicization.

The Trinity

The unity of the Christian church is rooted in our confession of the triune God. T. A. Noble writes,

---

the predicates as "one," "holy," "catholic," and "apostolic." For more discussion, see Dunning, *Grace*, 529.

19. Ibid., 532.

20. The first two "distinctives" are ontological in nature; the other two are more functional.

> The great revival of the Trinitarian theology in the late twentieth century helped us understand that the doctrine of the Trinity is not just one Christian doctrine among others. It is the comprehensive doctrine that gives unity to the whole Christian faith. Without it, the gospel itself collapses into incoherence.[21]

The historical and theological development of the Trinity has brought the church to the source of the Catholic spirit and faith.[22] As Paul says, "There is one Lord, one faith, one baptism" (Eph 4.5). A fuller understanding of this verse revolves on the Christian understanding of God. Behind "one Lord, one faith, and one baptism" is the triune God. The unity of the church is inconceivable outside the primary Christian doctrine of the Trinity.[23] The controversies and commitments[24] that surrounded the doctrine of the Trinity have helped shaped the Christian understanding of God in terms of not only the "oneness" of God but also his "threeness": one God; three Persons. The Trinity is the catholic faith. The Athanasian Creed or the "*Quincunque Vult*" states, "And the Catholic Faith is this, that we worship one God in Trinity, and Trinity in Unity."

Through the Trinity the church fathers were able to preserve the unity of God, and in doing so they likewise preserved the unity of the church, or rather the unity of God in Trinity preserved the fathers and the church. Kenneth J. Howell rightly observes,

---

21. Noble, *Holy Trinity*, 128.

22. For more discussion on the trinity and its historical development and today's application, see Leupp, *Renewal*.

23. Ibid., 127–43. Leupp writes, "Few of theology's main constituent parts other than ecclesiology lend themselves so readily to a Trinitarian makeover, or at least scrutiny. There is a desire to fashion the many of the church, the cloud of witnesses (Heb 12:1) who are easily observed on Sunday morning, into a congregation recreated in the triune image." Ibid., 128.

24. Dunning notes, "There were three basic commitments of the Early Church that entered into the discussion. They existed in tension with each other, and in fact, they appeared to be mutually exclusive. First there was monotheism, which derived both from the Hebrew faith and the dominant Hellenistic philosophy. 'The doctrine of one God, the Father and Creator, formed the background and indisputable premise of the Church's faith.' The second component was its faith in the deity of Christ as witnessed to in the New Testament. Third was their experience that God is Spirit, 'immanent in the whole creation as the Hebrews had known him to be, but now newly experienced and understood as the Holy Spirit of the God and Father of the Lord Jesus Christ.'" Dunning, *Grace*, 212.

> The implications of God's trinitarian Being are profound. The unity of Christians then is not a human creation, much less a negotiated peace. The unity God desires for the church is a gift of God Himself. The search for unity is not really a process of compromises but a voluntary relinquishing of mistaken ideas about unity to embrace a greater truth that can liberate Christians from our time-bound ideas. The unity we should be seeking is the presence of God Himself in the hearts of the faithful to bind them together more fully and to enfold them more completely into the body of Christ.[25]

Moreover, the affirmation of the catholic faith, vis-à-vis the Trinity, protects the church from any syncretistic understanding of God, for example paganism or animism—still prevalent in many cultures now, and if uncritically used and adapted today could still serve as a threat to the life and unity of the church. The different Jesuses of unguarded contextualization coming from the fences of both liberals and conservatives with their uncritical use of cultures pose a challenge to the life and unity of the church today. Christological heresies arise from lack of respect, or at least theological reference, to the catholic faith.

Important in the discussion on the doctrine of the Trinity is the uniqueness of Jesus Christ and the person of the Holy Spirit. The unity of the church is grounded objectively in Christ.[26] Christ is rightly the Lord of the church because he gave his life to it and in doing so gave life to it. Dunning rightly says, "It is inappropriate to say that Christ founded the church or that He was part of the church; He *was* the church."[27] The relationship between the church and Christ is indissoluble. The very existence of the church is because of Christ. Without Christ, there is no church. In this sense the unity of the church is Christocentric. This Christocentricity must be understood in the wider context of the Trinity. Therefore, an understanding of Christ outside his relation to the other members of the Trinity would likewise alter the unity of the church. Dunning also points out that the subjective ground of the unity of the church is the work of the Spirit.[28] The Holy Spirit is the Effector of the grace of God in Christ Jesus, and so of the unity of the church. This is why Paul describes the unity of the church as the unity of the Spirit.

25 Howell, "Culture Divided," lines 90–97.
26. Dunning, *Grace*, 531.
27. Ibid.
28. Ibid., 532.

Catholicization puts emphasis on the triune God. It points every believer to the eternal relation in God. In the Catholic Faith, there is no African God, Asian God, American God, Australian God, or Anglo-Saxon God. There is only the God of Abraham, Isaac, and Jacob; the incarnate Word, who lived, died, and resurrected for all of us; and the abiding and ever present Holy Spirit in us. There can be no variance of God in the nations. The gods, or rather idols, of the nations are excluded for there is only the triune God. However, the Trinity invites everyone. It gives room to all who would believe in Christ. The phrase "in Christ" also means "in God" and "in the Spirit." The Trinity does not discriminate anyone. Peter testifies to this truth when he said, "Can anyone keep these people from being baptized with water? They have received the Holy Spirit just as we have" (Acts 10.47). Thus, the Trinity is both exclusive and inclusive.

The Scripture

The unity of the church is created by the Word. The Scripture does not only serve as the source of theology, but it also serves as the substance of theology. Catholicization embraces the Protestant Hermeneutical Principle—*Sola Scriptura*—both in terms of source and substance. Heretics are born out of their deviation from the Word of God. The Holy Scripture stands as the foundation of the Christian faith and practice. Martin Luther's 95 theses were all grounded upon the Scripture. I pointed this out in a paper I wrote,

> With his 95 theses, Luther signaled the beginning of a long struggle for theological truths. But Luther's theological cry was rooted upon the principle of "sola scriptura." He had made the Scripture the sole authority both in the dogma and praxis of the church. He denied any authority, including that of the Pope, the council, and the church. The church's understanding of the Scripture in the light of its tradition, for Luther, had greatly marred the biblical teachings, especially its conception of the righteousness of God in Christ. He used the Bible as a means to judge both the theological dogma and praxis of the church. When called upon to recant his teachings against the church's doctrine and authorities, including that of the Pope, Luther declared, "Unless I can be instructed and convinced with evidence from the Holy Scriptures or with open, clear, and distinct grounds and reasoning—and my conscience is captive to the Word of God—then I cannot and will not recant,

because it is neither safe nor wise to act against conscience." He added, "Here I stand. I can do no other. God help me! Amen."[29]

The Holy Scripture defines and engenders the catholic faith. Other sources of theology must yield to the authority of the Scripture.[30] The church should not do catholicization on the basis of international political ideologies, economic superiorities, universal philosophies, or institutional offices. Works of catholicization must be Scripture-based. The Holy Scripture as the Word of God is the only valid source for catholicization or any work of theology. This, of course, does not mean that we can no longer use supplementary sources.

While the Bible was given in and through Jewish' cultures and contexts, its message is not exclusively for the Jews. Both hermeneutics in general and any hermeneutic in particular must take into consideration the catholicity of the Holy Scriptures. Evangelical narrative critics, for example, refuse to read the Bible from a purely narrative criticism or literary approach. They recognize the fact that the Bible is Scripture and must be read as such.[31] To read otherwise leads to incomplete, if not wrong, interpretation.

Both the church and its unity are engendered by the Word. Subjectively the church must keep and strengthen its unity in and through the Holy Scripture.

The Creeds

The unity of the church is confessed and preserved in and through the creeds. The challenges brought by the theological controversies and heresies in the fourth-century and onwards were behind the formulations of the Christian creeds. Four important creeds come to front in terms of their influence in the shaping of the catholic faith: the Apostles' Creed, the Nicene Creed, the Athanasian Creed (*Quicunque Vult*), and the Chalcedonian Definition

---

29. Hallig, "Luther's," 7. The quotation includes the following references, Kaulfuss-Diesch, ed., *Das Buch der Reformation*, 243–46.i

30. A number of supplementary sources are available to theology, such as reason (Science and Philosophy), tradition (History and Culture), and experience (Politics and Commerce).

31. See Kurz, *Reading Luke-Acts*, 159–66. Kurz considers the Bible in general and the Gospels in particular as biblical narratives that must be studied not only as literature but also as Scripture. See also Kingsbury, *Conflict in Luke*; Darr, *On Character Building*; Tannehill, *Luke*.

(also Confession or Creed of Chalcedon). At the heart of the controversies were the doctrines of the Trinity in general and Christology in particular. Yuan-Wei Liao notes this,

> It is therefore completely understandable that the theological controversies on the doctrines of the Trinity and Christology were closely connected in the fourth and fifth centuries. For one of the key issues in holding trinitarian faith is the doctrine of Christ as fully God and fully human. Also, the solution of the trinitarian problem seemed to elevate the Christological problem. To be specific, if Jesus is "same substance" with God, what would be the relation of his deity to his humanity? Facing so many deviations and even heresies along the way, such as Docetism, Gnosticism, Arianism, Apollinarianism, Nestorianism, Eutychianism, and son on, with issues further, for the purpose of safeguarding *analogia fidei*.[32]

The strength of the creeds is primarily in protecting the church from any theological rift that threatens the life and unity of the church. The creeds were able to differentiate, serving as the yardstick of faith, biblical Christian doctrines from pseudo-Christian doctrines developed in and through personal or private reading of the Scripture. As a result the catholic faith was formulated and has ever since served as the *regula fidei* of the church.[33]

---

32. Liao, "Significance," 29.

33. Zahn defines, *Regula Fidei* (literally means rule of faith) as "a term used so frequently in early Christian literature from the last quarter of the second century that an understanding of it is necessary to a correct idea of the religious conceptions of that period. Different forms with more or less the same meaning occur. *Ho kanon tēs alētheias* ("the canon of truth "), *regula veratatis* (rule of truth), probably the oldest form, was used apparently by Dionysius of Corinth (c. 160), then by Irenseus, Clement of Alexandria, Hippolytus, Tertullian, and Novatian; *ho kanon tēs pisteōs, regula fidei*, by Polyerates of Ephesus, Clement of Alexandria, Tertullian, and by the later Latin writers. The equivalent use of these two expressions is important for the determination of the original significance attached to them. The truth itself is the standard by which teaching and practice are to be judged (cf. Ireneeus, *Hr*, II., xxviii. 1; *ANP*, i. 399). It is presupposed that this truth takes for the Christian community a definite, tangible form, such as the law was for the Jews (Rom 2:20), in a body of doctrine not merely held and taught by the Church, but clearly formulated. Besides the expressions already discussed, another is worth mentioning, found only in Greek writers and the versions from them *ho ekklēsiastikos kanon* or *ho kanon tēs ekklēsias* (Clement of Alexandria and Origen). The ante-Nicene church never considered as the Rule of Faith the Bible or any part of it. Certain expressions of recent writers show that it is not unnecessary to point out that the word *kanon*, with or without qualifying additions, is never used until after Eusebius to designate the Bible, and that even after the word had begun to be applied to the collection of Scriptural

Through the creeds the church was able to protect herself and preserved its unity. The series of creeds gradually crystallized church doctrines based on the raw materials the Scripture provided and the theological reflections of the church in the context of its catholicity. The Protestant Reformers, however, rejected creeds that do not adhere to Martin Luther's emphasis on the principle of *sola scriptura*. The catholic faith in terms of the creeds is subservient to the Scripture. The catholic function of the creeds is acceptable and valid only in relation to the fixated tradition (the Scripture in terms of tradition). As such the church is one and catholic in and through its faithful confession of the historically and theologically formulated creeds. In this sense the unity of the church is beyond its present membership; it embodies the "triumphant church"—past, present, and future.

Worship

The unity of the church is celebrated in our corporate worship. Roman Catholic theologian Yves Congar puts the relationship between faith and worship beautifully in the following words,

> The confessing community lives out its faith by celebrating it. It is not coincidence that in Scripture the doxologies are the best expression of the dogmatic content of faith. The church prays, sings, and celebrates its faith. Dogma is only a landmark, holy though it may be, in the church's experience of the fullness of its faith which it attains by celebrating it. There is nothing more profound and decisive than faith lived out, expressed in spiritual life and prayer. Now despite the difference in dogmatic formulae, that faith is the same, and it is lived and prayed out similarly in both West and East.[34]

---

books, the sense mentioned. Above is never given to it by the Greeks. This is explained by the fact that the early Church used this word for something else-the baptismal formula. It is quite evident that in the oldest and most explicit witnesses for the use of the word, Irenaeus and Tertullian, this was known primarily as the rule of faith. When the former (I., ix. 4) says "he who retains unchangeable in his heart the rule of the truth which he received by means of baptism," the expression "rule of truth" cannot mean any sum total of truths as to which instruction has been conveyed before or after baptism, but only a formula which the neophyte has made his own by a profession of faith made at the time of baptism. This was "the faith," which the convert received from the teaching Church and was to keep as the standard for his subsequent life and for the testing of all doctrines presented to him. . . ." Zahn, "Regula Fidei."

34. Congar, *Diversity*, 100.

The catholic faith formulated in the creeds is celebrated in the liturgical life of the church. In and through the corporate worship, the unity of the church is expressed and lived out as a community by the one confessing church.[35]

Worship is an example of the theological praxis of the unity of the church—a unity that comes from or rooted in the catholic faith. Local worship services are celebrated in the spirit and faith of the catholic church. No local church worships God in isolation; worship is done both in relation to the triune God and the church. Wesleyan theologian Thomas Oden emphasizes that worship is a community affair not only of the present but also of the past: "The experienced liturgist comes especially to appreciate those recurrent signposts and familiar pathways that remind the community of its historical experience and continuity through time."[36] No believer, regardless of his/her national identity, should be alienated in any liturgical services of the catholic church. If Paul were to worship with us today, would he feel at home as a member of the community of faith?

The church is a worshipping community of faith.[37] In and through worship, the church lives out its unity. In fact, worship brings the other three together in action—it celebrates the relationship of the church with the triune God, the transforming and creative power of the Word, and the historical and theological catholic confessions. Worship is a life arena of the unity of the church.

Why Catholicization?

We still all live today amid a highly secularized society where individualism is at its utmost. Although some postmodernists react to hyper-individualistic axioms of modernity, the same spirit appears to remain. Religion is no longer defined as a spiritual social organization, but a personal, even

---

35. Pius XII warns the Roman Catholic Church on the relationship between faith and worship: "However, since the liturgy of the Church does not engender the Catholic faith, but rather springs from it, in such a way that the practices of the sacred worship proceed from the faith as the fruit comes from the tree, it follows that the holy fathers and the great doctors, in the homilies and sermons they gave the people on this feast day, did not draw their teaching from the feast itself as from a primary source, but rather they spoke of this doctrine as something already known and accepted by Christ's faithful." Quoted in Dulles, *Craft*, 207.

36. Oden, *Pastoral Theology*, 94.

37. See Dulles, *Models*.

a very private, experience. My American theology professor Roderick T. Leupp says, "It is so private that where different views of God or the Absolute are concerned, none is any better than any other."[38] Views on absolutes and concepts on standards are seen as suspects, and they are considered as primitive and an infringement on personal freedom. Leupp trumpets such an alarming secularism as oppose to Christian orthodoxy,

> Orthodoxy of any sort, especially Christian orthodoxy, is becoming increasingly out of fashion for shapers of public opinion. Those who cling to any orthodoxy are accused on blocking intellectual and social progress, and of trying to breathe light into a dying day. The very most scoffers will admit is that a deep-rooted religious identity can sustain one in a psychological crisis. But those days are gone forever, skeptics say, when orthodox Christianity literally provided the value structure and intellectual cement of the Western world. All observant Christians, and many secular sympathizers, will be disturbed by the radical relativism of our day. Inevitably, it will lead to nihilism, the abolition of all values whatsoever. Christian influence in such vital areas as medicine, education, and culture has perhaps never been lower. Visible and empirical measures of Christian expressions may be inching ever upward, but to what end? The Christian influence in the public forum, the Christian weight in the marketplace of ideas, seems battered, compromised, and ineffectual.[39]

The call for the church to navigate men and women to the right direction has never been this loud and clear. With numberless victims of secularization that we have seen, the church cannot just watch and pray. We must be what Jesus prayed for us to be: "May they be brought to complete unity to let the world know that you have sent me and have loved them even as you have loved me" (John 17.23b). This prayer is directly for us. Jesus knew what the power of the unity of the church can do in terms of leading men and women to the right understanding and *pathos* of life.

Our disunity will only, and indeed continually, be a hindrance to our evangelistic calling. As Jesus's disciples and witnesses to the transforming power of the gospel, we are indebted to the world; we owe men and women living in a world of disconnections and divisions our unity. The apostle Paul said, "Though I am free and belong to no one, I have made myself a slave to everyone, to win as many as possible" (1 Cor 9.19). The Reformers

38. Leupp, *Knowing the Name*, 23.
39. Ibid., 23–24.

in the sixteenth century and their heirs onward were all catholics both by faith and practice.[40] The Protestant heritage is a catholic heritage. The challenge is for Evangelicals, as we are all known today, to remain catholic and so work on catholicization—keeping and strengthening our unity through faith and practice.

Let me go back to the informal conversation I had with a small group of co-workers in the Lord at the ATA conference in Seoul, Korea. I owe them my gratitude for "conscientisizing"[41] my spirit in relation to the issues within our cultures, that is, the social divides our people experience in various forms. I agree to what one of us in the group said that we all experience discrimination either subjectively or objectively. I know that the journey to the solutions we want to offer to our people is not easy and short, but a hard and long one, or may even be impossible or too idealistic in this world; but we have to begin somewhere and embrace the optimism of God's grace in and through the unity of the church. What a better way to begin it among ourselves—the catholic church. Let's celebrate the gift of unity the triune God has given us, and then, in and through that unity work towards the world by giving them a better alternative to either our traditional cultures that embrace and promote social divides or the present secularization or post-modernization of the world that keeps us apart.

Conclusion

Jesus prayed for it, the church's fathers protected it (by formulating the creeds), the Scripture demands it, and the world cries for it. Kenneth J. Howell believes that there is a clear biblical-theological mandate for the unity of the church—the triune God and the Incarnation:

> There is a mandate for unity, not only because it is taught in the New Testament, but because God Himself is a unity of three Persons in one nature. Yet, the necessity for Christian unity also lies in the Incarnation, in the act of God becoming man. When John proclaims that the Word (*Logos*) became flesh, it was a declaration that God intended to unite all humanity in the person of His Son, the Word of God. Over time the church realized the full significance of this truth by proclaiming Jesus Christ as fully God and fully man. Had the apostles proclaimed Jesus as half God and half man, the gospel

---

40. See Wesley's, "Catholic," 299–309.
41. A borrowed term from Laroya, "Liberatory," 29–30.

would not have changed the world. It would have been just another variation on the theme in Greek mythology in which the gods became human by becoming less divine and humans became like the gods by shedding their mortal humanity. But when Christians proclaimed Jesus as one-hundred percent God and one-hundred percent man, they offered the first real hope of uniting all humanity into one. That was the very message that the sagacious St. Athanasius saw in the *On the Incarnation of the Word* as the lynchpin of our faith. By the Logos becoming man and dying for all, the God-Man Jesus Christ absorbed all humanity into Himself and provided the foundation for unity in the church.[42]

Catholicization is a challenge for the church to live out its unity. Both the life and ministry of the church depend on the unity of the church. Disunity destroys, if not kills, the church. A way to keep and strengthen the unity of the church is to provide it a theological praxis—catholicization. Catholicization is not just a call for outward manifestations of the unity of the church, but also for a strong theological foundation that is not only cognitive but also practical. I agree with Filipino contextual theologian Timoteo D. Gener in saying, "Conversely, theology pursued out of sheer passion for systematic thought and divorced from lived experience is, at the very least, a deficient theology."[43]

Theology is undoubtedly necessary; but what kind of theology is the more adequate question we should all ask. Contextualization is not enough—it is only helpful in relation to communicating the gospel to our various cultures. Catholicization brings our unique differences and the inherent beauties in our cultures into "one, holy, catholic, and apostolic" church, where no one is inferior or superior. Indeed the grander unity of the church is beyond the bringing of the sundered denominations together.[44] The catholic church is many but one, different but the same, and varied but united. Catholicization holds this complex paradoxical ontology and function of the unity of the church.

---

42. Howell, "Culture," 3.
43. Gener, "Revisioning," 140.
44. Morris, *Gospel*, 728.

7

The Catholic Life and Witness
Ten Practical Life and Witness Applications

Jesus said, "You are the salt of the earth. But if the salt loses its saltiness, how can it be made salty again? It is no longer good for anything, except to be thrown out and trampled underfoot. You are the light of the world. A town built on a hill cannot be hidden. Neither do people light a lamp and put it under a bowl. Instead they put it on its stand, and it gives light to everyone in the house. In the same way, let your light shine before others, that they may see your good deeds and glorify your Father in heaven" (Matt 5:13–16). Catholicity is more of a life than a statement of faith to be confessed to the world. The catholic faith does not end in doctrines or dogmas, which are theological expressions of the life and witness of the church. To limit the catholic faith more to words of confessions than to life leading to worship (*liturgia*) and witness (*marturia*) makes catholicity an abstraction without any practical-life relation whatever. It turns the catholic church into a social or religious club governed by laws and regulations in the context of its group-identity. Reflecting on Matt 5:11–16, R. T. France writes, "From a general description of the disciple character, the Sermon now turns to a direct address to Jesus's disciples, and indicates the effect that character is to have in the life and witness."[1] This same relation gives life to the catholic church. Having defined the catholic mark of the church historically and theologically, we are now ready to address its practical relationship to life and witness.

---

1. France, *Gospel*, 111.

The Catholic Life and Witness

Catholic theology is not an end in itself; it is only a means to the life and witness of the church. Jesus said, "The thief comes only to steal and kill and destroy; I have come that you may have life, and have it to the full" (Matt 10:10). This means that Jesus did not come to deliver to us theology or theological confessions; he came to give the world life. Wayne Grudem emphasizes this truth in his systematic theology book where he says,

> Defining systematic theology to include "what the whole Bible *teaches us* today" implies that application to life is a necessary part of the proper pursuit of systematic theology. Thus a doctrine under consideration is seen in terms of its practical value for living the Christian life. Nowhere in Scripture do we find doctrine studied for its own sake or in isolation from life. The biblical writers consistently apply their teaching to life. Therefore, any Christian reading this book should find his or her Christian life enriched and deepened during this study; indeed, if personal spiritual growth does not occur, then the book has not been written properly by the author or the material has not been rightly studied by the reader.[2]

Catholic, catholicity, and catholicization are ecclesiological principles that define not only the wholistic and catholic theology of the church, but more so the church's organic and catholic life and witness under the catholic covenant of God with Abraham that was fulfilled in his offspring Jesus Christ. They define the covenant of God as a covenant of life for all nations. Such covenant was demonstrated and delivered by God in and through his servants and messengers in the Old Testament and by his son and his disciples in the New Testament to which the church now stands not only as its people but also as its witness.

The relationship between theology and life is one that is indissoluble. The Christian life and its witness are lived in the light of the historical and theological confessions of the church that are based on the faithful interpretations of the Holy Scriptures. Both theology and life are necessities of the Holy Scriptures vis-à-vis the church: the former is confessional or doctrinal (dogma); the latter is practical or existential (praxis). Dogma without relation to life and practice is dead orthodoxy; life and practice without theology is pure speculation. Without the Holy Scriptures, dogmas are expressions of human religion, and life and practice are predictions of science. Hence, God's redemptive purpose is achieved in and through the inherent

---

2. Grudem, *Systematic Theology*, 23.

triangulate relation of the Holy Scriptures, Christian theology, and the life of the community of disciples. While this chapter focuses on the practical or existential aspect of the catholic mark of the church, interactions with the Scripture and theology are implicitly assumed if not explicitly shown.

Life and the Body of Christ

The catholic life is perfectly demonstrated in the image of the church as the body of Christ in terms of both relation and function. The image of the body of Christ communicates the union of believers with Christ as the head of the church. The church neither exists nor lives on its own. Its life is connected to and flows from Christ. Apart from Christ, the church does not exist. As such the church is ontologically united with Christ. This unity is not a simple unity; it involves layers of interdependent truths that define the union.

Union with Christ is made possible first and foremost by one's personal faith in Christ regenerated by grace. This is rightly called the subjective faith—a willful act of man's response to the grace of God in Christ Jesus. It is this faith that engenders the unity of the Spirit, who seals the union of the believer with Christ. The believer enters into a covenant relationship with God in and through Jesus Christ, the offspring of Abraham, and it happens by the same faith that Abraham had. This faith that unites believers with Christ is not a one-time act of believing in Christ. Faith engenders the dynamic relationship with Christ, so that we *love him*, we *know him*, we *worship him*, we *obey him*, we *give/offer to him*, we *serve him*, we *listen to him*, we *fellowship with him*, we *pray to him*, we *learn from him*, etc. Apparently, faith in Christ is more than a confession of his Lordship and/or his being the Savior; it submits in and through obedience to the Lordship of Christ; and that continually in and through his sanctifying work in us and his saving work through us; hence, faith is ever active and dynamic.

Union with Christ brings every believer into a communion of believers. This is the second layer of the unity of the church. It is a unity that is created by the Holy Spirit. The same Spirit who bore witness with the spirit of believer in faith unites all believers into a spiritual communion—the body of Christ. This body of Christ refers to a group of believers called and gathered for fellowship, worship, and witness. It particularly points to a local church, for example, the *church* in Antioch, the *church* in Jerusalem, and others. The local church is also a communion of relation. Such relation is expressed in the various commands for the church vis-à-vis one another—love one *another*, pray for one *another*, build up one *another*, and other commands for the church. The New Testament uses the word "church" to refer to people. The fellowship of believers centers on people—the building up of one another. It is people together, united in Christ, that make a church.[3] Everything that the church does is for the strengthening of faith and fellowship. Believers keep the unity of the church when everybody is committed to all the members of the body.

The third layer is the catholic church. The catholic church is a communion of churches or congregations. The local church is a unit of the catholic church. Local churches are also united in Christ. This is the intra-communal aspect of the body of Christ. The catholic church brings people separated by place, history, language, and culture together in the great fellowship of churches in Christ. Every church is in Christ. This is captured by John Oxenham in the hymn he wrote in 1908,

> In Christ there is not East or West, In him no South or North;
> But one great fellowship of love throughout the world wide earth.
> In Him shall true hearts everywhere, Their high communion find;
> His service is the golden cord, Close binding all mankind.
> Join hands then, brothers (and sisters) of the faith, What-e'er your face may be;
> Who serves my Father as a son Is surely kin to me.
> In Christ now meet both East and West; In him meet South and North,
> All Christly souls are one in Him Thro'-out the whole wide earth.[4]

---

3. Powell, *Church*, 45.
4. Oxenham, "In Christ," 678.

Jack M. Tuell likewise describes the unity of the church beautifully in his description of the church in the context of the local United Methodist church,

> To be a member of a local United Methodist church is to be a member of the total United Methodist connection (Par. 210) and a member of the Church Universal (Par. 208). This means that becoming a member of the church means becoming a member of a fellowship without boundaries of time or geography, a fellowship extending around the world and through the centuries of history, a fellowship made up of those who call Jesus Christ "Lord" and who come together to carry out his purpose in the world. Every local church, then, everywhere, is open to all persons, regardless of race, color, national origin, or economic condition, when they take appropriate vows of membership.[5]

The believers in a narrow sense make a local church; the congregations in a broader sense make up the catholic church. So that commands to believers and local churches are likewise applicable to the catholic church unless they are particular or personal in their given contexts.

Moreover, believers and churches all belong to the greater community of faith—the community of the kingdom. The kingdom of God transcends the boundary of the catholic church to include the world. While the church is in the world, it also exists for the world.[6] It is in the light of the kingdom that the church is called to minister to the world to bring the kingdom of God here on earth as in heaven.[7] In the missional aspect of the catholic church, believers must embrace the kingdom-mindset. Believers are members of the kingdom; we are kingdom-people. We live in the world not only as representatives of our churches or denominations but also as ambassadors of the kingdom. Regardless of our church identity, we work for the kingdom and are under the authority of the King—our sovereign Lord. Our kingdom identity is inherent not implied in our union with Christ. One who belongs to Christ belongs to the kingdom; to be in Christ is to be in the kingdom.

---

5. Tuell, *Organization*, 46.
6. Ibid., 19.
7. For an insightful integration of the gospel (and so the church) and the kingdom, see the recent work of N. T. Wright, *How God Became King*.

The following diagram demonstrates the layers of interdependent truths of the body of Christ in terms of its complex dynamic and organic relationships of being in Christ,

Such is the Christian life—a life of relation; not of isolation. The relations (church, catholic, and the kingdom) within the relation (in Christ) function as an organic entity but never independently. The emerging organic churches, for example, today must not function as independent churches or isolate themselves from the whole body of Christ past, present, and future.[8] The outward form and structure may vary, but the inner spirit of the church must remain in the relation of relations. Otherwise, they become emerging organic churches in disguise, who in reality are perhaps "new age" groups.

Life and the Catholic Responsibility

Catholicity is more than our identity; it involves our responsibility to the church of Jesus Christ. The Christian life is properly understood not only in terms of divine grace but also in terms of human responsibility. The existential aspect of the catholic life put emphasis on the subjective experience. Differentiating objective experience from subjective experience, T. A. Noble warns us of the danger of isolating subjective experience from the objective experience,

> Christian doctrine then is the expression of that knowledge of God we all share in the body, the church. "Experience" is not therefore a distinct source of doctrine any more than "Reason" is. The One we experience is the God who makes himself known to his people by his Spirit, but never apart from his Word. Therefore, it is best to say that there is only one source of Christian doctrine, the Word of God. God's revelation in the Word made flesh—known to us

---

8. For a discussion on the emerging church, see Brewin, *Signs of Emergence*.

through the authoritative witness of the apostles and prophets in Holy Scripture, and experience by us within the space-time creation by the Spirit—is the only reliable source of truth about God. Any other knowledge we think we have is shadowy and liable to be distorted and misleading. But our expression of the Word of truth, that is, church doctrine, is shaped by our rational, spiritual experience of God in and through his Word, by our rational reflection upon that.[9]

In other words, our subjective experience is subject to the influence and control of the objective experience or knowledge that we have from God in Christ by the Spirit. The subjective experience is only an overflow of the objective experience.

But what is the subjective experience that we are referring to in the context of the catholic life? It refers to the Spirit inspired and empowered active-responsibility of keeping the unity of the church for life and witness. Such responsibility is in obedience (hence an expression of faith) to the command for every believer to "keep the unity of the Spirit" (Eph 4:3). What are the practical actions that must be taken to make the command a reality? Of course, we all can think of a thousand ways to do it, but allow me to suggest at least three, namely, prayer, participation, and promotion.

Prayer is the most practical action but often done pretentiously. Prayer is a spiritual activity that people without the Spirit or uninspired by the Spirit will always find challenging if not frustrating. Spiritual people, however, cannot help but engage themselves in the discipline of prayer believing that it changes things and circumstances in and through divine intervention and interaction with men and women both inside and outside the church.[10] The history of the church is replete with men and women who prayed; they all kept the life and unity of the church in and through their prayers. The historical vicissitudes of the life and history of the church were influenced in one way or another, or were caused (in a subjective sense) by the persistent prayers of the believers. If we are to keep the unity of the Spirit, we all must engage in *personal and private* prayer, *corporate or community* prayer, and also *ecumenical* prayer for the unity of the church. To some prayer is very simplistic; but in the true sense and spirit of prayer, it is the most self-sacrificing act a believer can engage himself/herself in behalf of the church, and the most productive and blessed one. It is in the neglect

---

9. Noble, *Holy Trinity*, 15.
10. See Foster, *Celebration*, 33–46.

of prayer that churches suffer from the acts of the flesh: divisions, factions, quarrellings, envy, hatred, jealousy, fits of rage, discord, selfish ambitions, and dissensions (cf. Gal 5:19–21).

Participation in the catholic life of the church is another action that demonstrates responsibility. Participation refers to the total engagement of the believer in the life and mission of the catholic church in the context of its relation in Christ. The Protestant principle of the priesthood of all believers calls for the participation of all believers in the life and mission of the church. There is a strong sense of corporate calling among protestant churches giving the responsibility not only to the elite clergy of the church but also to the common Christians in the pew. Christ commissioned the whole church to "go and make disciples of all nations" (Matt 28:19–20) in addition to his command for the church to "love one another." Moreover the Holy Spirit has been given to all members of the church, Jews and Gentiles alike, and the gifts of the Spirit made available to the body of Christ in variety for various functions and purposes. Donald G. Bloesch rightly reminds us,

> The church fundamentally is a community of charisms. This is not to deny that every church needs form and structure as well, but the church is essentially a fellowship, not an institution. Truth is imparted neither from the top down nor from the bottom up but from the risen Christ in whom we live and move and have our being. Christ speaks to us in his Word and also in our conscience. He is above us, within us and in the midst of us ... The true church of God needs to be brought into obedience to the Word and at the same time animated by the Spirit.[11]

As a community of charisms, every member of the church has his/her call and personal ministry or ministries. As Hans Küng says,

> The fellowship of believers, the collegiality of all believers, of all those who had charisms and fulfilled their own ministries, the collegiality of the whole Church, in short, gave place to the collegiality of a special ministry within the community: the collegiality of the leaders of the community, the *episkopoi* or elders, who increasingly began to see themselves as distinct from the community, from the "people"; this is where the division between "clergy" and "laity" begins.[12]

---

11. Bloesch, *Church*, 209–10.
12. Küng, *Church*, 410.

Participation in the life and mission of the church is neither an option for the "laity" nor a career for the "clergy." Participation is a divine call for all.

Promotion is in reality an overflow of both prayer and participation. Prayer and participation should lead the church, the people of God, to the fulfillment of the Great Commission—the Great mission of the church of Jesus Christ. Every believer must be a missional believer; every Christian is a missionary indeed. I will give attention to this in detailed in the following section.

Life and Evangelism/Mission

The numerical growth of both the local churches and the catholic church is dependent on the works of evangelism and mission. Without evangelism and mission the church would soon become extinct.[13] Christ had entrusted the multiplication of the community of disciples to his followers by giving them the Great Commission which would be fulfilled in and through their participation in evangelism and mission. To be catholic means to go into the world and to preach the catholic gospel of Christ to all nations. Evangelism and mission are catholicity in action in the world effected in and through the spirit of unity. "The reality of Christian unity is a fundamental spiritual truth, tied together with the foundational purpose of the church's mission in the world."[14] The promotion of the catholic faith empowered by the unity of the church takes place in the active witness of the church in the world. This is where the ecumenical movement made its early historical contribution—a mission built in unity. Pierson writes,

> While it is clear in the New Testament that there is only one church and that the unity of all believers is an objective fact based on the work of Christ, the modern ecumenical movement finds its major biblical basis in John 17, where Jesus prayed that all who believed in him would be one so that the world might believe. Thus unity would be linked to mission. And in fact the historical roots of ecumenism are found in movements of renewal and mission beginning with Pietism and Moravianism in the eighteenth

---

13. Coleman, "Evangelism," 343. Dyrness notes that, "Mission lies at the core of theology—within the character and action of God himself. There is an impulse to give and share that springs from the very nature of God and that therefore characterized all his works. So all that theologians call fundamental theology is mission theology." Dyrness, *Let the Earth*, 11. See also Moreau, "Mission," 636–38.

14. Platt, "Unity," 988.

century. An example was the correspondence among Francke, the Lutheran Pietist in Germany; Mather, the Congregationalist in New England; Chamberlyne and Newman, the secretaries of the Society for the Propagation of Christian Knowledge; Boehm, the court chaplain at St. James Chapel; and Ziegenbalg, the Lutheran missionary in India in which they sought greater unity in order to carry out the mission task. Later, Anglicans cooperated with Lutherans in the mission in India. And because of his desire to work for renewal, unity and mission together, Zinzendorf would be called an "ecumenical pioneer."[15]

However, evangelism and mission are greatly hampered when the world does not see the unity and catholicity of the church. When churches fail in the call to unity so that there is lack of the catholic spirit among believers, our Christian witness is put on question. Platt asks, "What does the absence of reference to organization or ecclesiastical forms in the New Testament texts indicate about unity?,"[16] and to which he cogently answers, "Surely, it eliminates any basis for dogmatic imposition of structures. At the same time, all Christians are called to make the practical expression of Christian unity a high priority, or suffer the consequences of ineffective witness and outreach."[17] Indeed, a church divided will never have attraction in the world today. Part of the reasons why there is a growing number of people being attracted to other religions especially in the West today is the ability of these religions to project a united front with a strong united spirit for what they believe and advocate; while Christianity is so divided in so many issues notwithstanding "faith nominalism." The human spirit is naturally drawn to unity; everybody is a person who values relationships and belongingness to a group. Maslow's theory of the hierarchy of human needs shows how men and women need fellowships and belongingness, which some of the world religions based their "missionary" efforts and take advantage of humanity's basic needs by offering a unity anchored in their own philosophical theories or political ideologies. Below is Maslow's diagram of the hierarchy of human needs:[18]

---

15. Pierson, "Ecumenical," 300.
16. Platt, "Unity," 988.
17. Ibid.
18. See Maslow, *Motivation*. Also Maslow, *Farther*.

Next to the fundamental and basic needs of men and women—the physiological or physical needs—is the need for relationships—belongingness and love. The church of Jesus Christ offers genuine fellowship built in the spirit of divine love and human compassion. Indeed, the church is essentially a fellowship; not an institution nor a religion. We offer the world an inclusive fellowship that is beyond family ties and racial heritage; we offer them the catholic church.[19] The catholic life is communicated in and through the catholic spirit. When such spirit is not cultivated and nourished, the church witness is weak, if not totally useless.

The catholic spirit is the very essence of evangelism and mission; without the catholic spirit our evangelistic and mission endeavors would mean nothing. The catholic spirit is what defines the catholic witness that Jesus prayed for,

> My prayer is not for them alone, I pray also for those who will believe in me through their message, that all of them may be one, Father, just as you are in me and I am in you. May they also be in us so that the world may believe that you have sent me. I have given them the glory that you gave me, that they may be one as we are one; I in them and you in me. May they be brought to complete unity to let the whole world know that you sent me and have loved them even as you have loved me (John 17:20–23).

Indeed, our unity or disunity affects our witness—evangelism and mission. It promotes or hinders the life and growth of the church. The witness of the church is essential to the life cycle of the church. Phillips writes,

---

19. For a case of inclusive evangelism in the OT, see Brueggemann, *Biblical Perspectives*, where he talks about outsiders of the faith, forgetful insiders to the faith, and children of the faith.

Barth elaborates the church's ministry of "witnessing" broadly under the twelve basic forms: praise, preaching, teaching, evangelization, foreign missions, theology, prayer, the cure of souls, personal examples of a Christian life, service to the needy, prophetic action in the world, and fellowship among races and classes. Through these forms of witnessing the church is not simply proclaiming but also making disciples. Consequently, the Christian community is constantly renewed as converts themselves become new disciples and begin witnessing to the gospel.[20]

Life and Catholic Confessions

The exposure I had with the catholic confessions or the Christian creeds was very minimal. My Roman Catholic experience was short lived. I came to know Christ at a very young age (14) which cut short my Roman Catholic life including its faith and its own traditions. The church that I attended and grew up with was also not into the catholic creeds and their public confessions. As a result, I knew very little about the Christian creeds. Sadly, I could not even recall a time in my college days at the Bible school I attended or even during my seminary life when I studied seriously about the creeds—its history, development, and impact on the life and mission of the catholic church. It was during my graduate study at an independent Reformed seminary in South Korea where I had my first formal exposure to the historical creeds of the church. At Reformed churches, I had recited the Apostles' Creed almost every Sunday. As a result I slowly began to appreciate the rich heritage of my faith as a protestant, evangelical, and catholic Christian. And here I am engaged in writing about it and to which I am grateful.

Our studies above should convince us all that the catholic creeds have to have their place in the life and mission of the church. The recital of the creeds in churches every Sunday is not enough. They need more expressions in the life of the church. For examples, catechisms and doctrinal studies have to be a part of the theological programs of the church and should embody the catholic faith and how they affect the life and witness of local churches in particular and the catholic life and witness in general. Catholic churches have to embrace the catholic faith and promote the catholic spirit among their congregations. The sectarian spirit has to be discouraged if not

---

20. Phillips, "Neo-orthodox," 674.

dissolved or dispensed. The world needs the whole church of Jesus Christ. If there is no salvation outside the church, then the world has to have the whole church and what it represents including its theological traditions based on the Scriptures. The failure of the church would mean a tragedy for the world. The gospel is more about the catholic faith than about denominational 'distinctives.' There is no variance of the gospel of salvation in the churches of Jesus Christ world-wide. Men and women in all nations will only find one and the same gospel the church proclaims: "There is only one Lord, one faith, and one baptism" (Eph 4:5).

Each statement of faith of all catholic churches must affirm and embody the historical and theological catholic creeds shared by the catholic church based on the Holy Scriptures. No church of Jesus Christ must have its unique and independent doctrine or doctrines that do not adhere or relate to the catholic faith. Sectarian doctrines and the catholic church do not go together. Distinct expressions or doctrinal emphases of the catholic faith may vary but the spirit of the doctrines must affirm the established doctrines of the catholic church; by such spirit they found a home in the catholic church. Every church is under the authority not only of the Holy Scriptures but also of the other churches within the body of Christ: "Dear friends, do not believe every spirit, but *test the spirits* to see whether they are from God, because many false prophets have gone out into the word" (1 John 4:1). It is the responsibility of the catholic church to test in and through the Word and the Spirit the doctrines of all churches under its folds.

The Word serves as the primary source of various theologies of Christian churches but it is the catholic tradition that affirms the traditions of all Christian churches in the light of the catholic and faithful interpretations of the Word. Hence, both the Word and the catholic church together serve as the canon of Christian statements of faith in matters of both faith and practice. The former is the primary canon of faith; the latter is the secondary canon of faith. Both, however, are necessary in affirming a Christian statement of faith. Therefore, churches do not only stand on the Scriptures but also on the collegial testimony or witness of the rest of the body of Christ—the catholic church. By example, the Articles of Religion (Thirty-Nine Articles) of the Church of England demonstrate it,[21]

1. OF FAITH IN THE HOLY TRINITY

---

21. Anglican, "Articles."

2. OF THE WORD OR SON OF GOD, WHICH WAS MADE VERY MAN
3. OF THE GOING DOWN OF CHRIST INTO HELL
4. OF THE RESURRECTION OF CHRIST
5. OF THE HOLY SPIRIT
6. OF THE SUFFICIENCY OF THE HOLY SCRIPTURES FOR SALVATION
7. OF THE OLD TESTAMENT
8. OF THE CREEDS
9. OF THE ORIGINAL SIN; BIRTH-SIN
10. OF FREE WILL
11. OF THE JUSTIFICATION OF MAN
12. OF GOOD WORKS
13. OF WORKS BEFORE JUSTIFICATION
14. OF WORKS OF SUPERREGATION
15. OF CHRIST ALONE WITHOUT SIN
16. OF SIN AFTER BAPTISM
17. OF PREDISTINATION AND ELECTION
18. OF OBTAINING ETERNAL SALVATION ONCE BY THE NAME OF CHRIST
19. OF THE CHURCH
20. OF THE AUTHORITY OF THE CHURCH
21. OF THE AUTHORITY OF GENERAL COUNCILS
22. OF PURGATORY
23. OF MINISTERING IN THE CONGREGATION
24. OF SPEAKING IN THE CONGREGATION IN SUCH A TONGUE AS THE PEOPLE UNDERSTAND
25. OF THE SACRAMENTS
26. OF THE UNWORTHINESS OF THE MINISTERS, WHICH HINDERS NOT THE EFFECT OF THE SACRAMENT

27. OF BAPTISM

28. OF THE LORD'S SUPPER

29. OF THE WICKED, WHICH EAT NOT THE BODY OF CHRIST IN THE USE OF THE LORD'S SUPPER

30. OF BOTH KINDS

31. OF THE ONE OBLATION OF CHRIST FINISHED UPON THE CROSS

32. OF THE MARRIAGE OF THE PRIESTS

33. OF EXCOMMUNICANICATE PERSONS, HOW THEY ARE TO BE RESTORED

34. OF THE TRADITIONS OF THE CHURCH

35. OF THE HOMILIES

36. OF CONSECRATION OF BISHOPS AND MINISTERS

37. OF THE CIVIL MAGISTRATES

38. OF CHRISTIAN MEN'S GOODS, WHICH ARE NOT COMMON

39. OF A CHRISTIAN MAN'S OATH

All together they affirm the authority of the Holy Scriptures and the role of the traditions of the church, which *are* not repugnant to the Holy Scriptures. However, it should be noted that articles are subject to change on three united grounds: (1) on the truth that men and women (councils) might have erred, (2) on the basis of clearer and stronger interpretations of the Holy Scriptures; and (3) on the united consent of the church's councils.

Therefore, the Christian life is lived not only in the light of Scriptures but also in the light of the faithful traditions of the church. Every believer comes to the truths of the Scriptures in and through the traditions. Thus it is the responsibility of every church to strengthen its tradition towards the catholic tradition. Older traditions have to give room to fresh interpretations of the Scriptures and see how they can be integrated into the already established traditions. Likewise, new and fresh development of traditions must be built or constructed on the wisdom of older traditions. Only by doing so that that the catholic church can offer a better alternative to a divided church toward a more united church of Jesus Christ. One, for example, does not have to be a Wesleyan or Pentecostal to embrace the biblical doctrine of holiness or put more emphasis on the active ministry of the Holy Spirit.

In the same way, churches of Wesleyan and Pentecostal traditions do not have to become Reformed or Lutheran to appreciate the doctrines of divine sovereignty and election. We all can enrich our Christian confessions in the context of the catholic tradition.

Life and Catholic Witness

Unity is not an option for the church. While unity is a gift of the Spirit—for it is he indeed who is responsible for the unity of the church, the people of God are commanded to keep the unity of the Spirit. Unity is essential not only to the life of the church but also to its witness to the world. It gives substance to both our witness and our message. The church is a community of reconciliation: On the one hand, the church has been reconciled to God and to one another; on the other hand, we preach reconciliation to the world. It is only the reconciled church that can tell the world about reconciliation. As such, the church does not only talk about unity—calling the world to a union with God—Father, Son, and the Spirit; it also lives out its unity—showing the world the unity of the Spirit.

Evangelism and mission outside the catholicity of the church are shallow and hypocritical works of the church in the world. Michael Green writes,

> Evangelism is neither Christian proclamation done nor Christian presence alone. It is both. There has been a disastrous tendency for some Christians to concentrate on proclaiming the gospel without showing it; so to emphasize the preaching that the feeding, the healing, the educating, and the liberating fall into the background. In reaction, those who have concentrated on a 'social gospel' have been content to get among people and embrace them with the arms of Christ's love without bearing any overt witness to the one in whose name they do it. The very idea of separating the spiritual from the social gospel does despite to the New Testament. Jesus went about doing good and preaching the good news of the kingdom. His followers must aim for the same balance. There is only one gospel—of a God who preaches people in their need, with every aspect of their lives in this world and the next. This message must be both proclaimed and lived out. Presence done and proclamation alone are equally useless. The early Christians employed both. So must we.[22]

---

22. Green, *New Testament*, 11–12.

The church and the gospel are not to be separated. The two go together. The vessel that holds the gospel is the church. As Christ and the kingdom are inseparable, so are the church and Christ. Men and women hear and believe the gospel of Christ in and through the church.

Evangelism and mission are the outward expressions of the witness of the church; character in general and integrity in particular are inward expressions of the witness of the church. Both character and integrity demonstrate the unity of the church—a unity that is based on communal relationship among churches as the body of Christ. It is a relationship that Augustine called as *"caritas"*—that love of God that is "poured out into our hearts through the Holy Spirit who has been given to us" (Rom 5:5)—in contrast to the worldly concept of *concupiscentia* or *cupiditas* —a self-centered love including not only sexual desires, but the greed for possessions, for fame, and for self-glory.[23] *Caritas* is the inner power or essence of both character and integrity of the church in the context of both local and catholic. Thus the unity of the church is a unity of love; and when related to mission, it refers to a witness of love that should captivate the heart of those that are outside the faith who are looking for something greater than self and society that are void of *caritas*. The catholic church is a community of love that transcends not only the uniqueness of each church but also the differences within the body of Christ. And when the world sees such a fellowship of love in the body of Christ, it cannot deny that the church is indeed Christ's community of disciples, and that the gospel is a gospel of love and life.

Life and Christian Fellowships

The catholic life is a life of fellowship—a fellowship that is open and one. Christians are all one in Christ and in the church. As it is commonly said, "united we stand, divided we fall." A church divided will not stand for long and will definitely not be able to impact the world in and through its witness (cf. Luke 11:17). The survival of the church depends subjectively on the fellowship of the church. The prayer of Jesus for the church to be one in fellowship based on a relationship of love is indeed a catholic prayer that has its existential and missional impact. The unity of the church cannot just be locally lived out without reference to the catholic church. While pursuing the unity of the local church, Christians must be aware of the catholic

---

23. See Noble, *Holy Trinity*, 108–27.

life and fellowship and pursue the same spirit of unity to strengthen the body of Christ universal. As such, we are not only a church; we are catholic—the *ecclesia catholica*.

Local churches exist and live in a broader base and wider scope of fellowship—the catholic fellowship—embodying the catholic life in and through unity toward mission. Western churches, for example, cannot for long take single responsibility for the life and witness of the church. It would be a grave error to always see other nations as mission fields. Such attitude is only a disservice to the church of Jesus Christ. An unhealthy mission can only lead to an unhealthy church. The church is not defined by its affluence and political power, but by its ability to enrich and empower others to create a fellowship that is truly Christian and catholic. It is only in such fellowship that all local churches live out the catholic church, and together contribute to the work of God toward the catholic mission. For example, the Conservative Baptist Church in the Philippines started with the commitment of a Filipino believer who took the call to plant churches and was supported by the church in the US through its mission department. From one man to a church, to churches, to group of churches, to denominations, and now the church has been sending missionaries outside the Philippines. A church was born and a mission began in and through the sacrifices of local men and women. Genuine fellowship embraces shared leadership or broader partnership in the body of Christ. Missionaries who are not willing to hand over positions of leadership in local churches and trust their fellow local Christians only do disservice to the life and mission of the catholic church. Fellowship is deepened by cooperation and partnership in the life and witness of the church. Strong local fellowships lead to a strong catholic fellowship. This means that the catholic fellowship is inclusive. This inclusivity is not only in terms of membership but also in terms of leadership. Superiority and inferiority do not have room in the fellowship of the church. They destroy the very essence of catholic fellowship—inclusivity.

Life and Christian Liturgy

The Westminster catechism states that the chief end of men and women is to glorify God.[24] This is made possible in and through faith. By faith, men and women are awakened spiritually in and through the Word and the Spirit so that they can live ultimately to glorify God. This is true of

---

24. See "Westminster."

the church. The church exists primarily for the glory of God. It does not exist only to live and to do the mission of God, both of which are essential, but the church lives and does missionary work for the glory of God. Both creation and redemption will end in the glory of God. The glory of God in relation to himself is centered on his holiness, which is revelatory of who God is—his very nature. This is to say that the works (creation and redemption) of God will ultimately serve the person of God, that is, what God does serves who God is.

The church is not only a witnessing community but also a worshipping community. The catholic faith makes this very explicit: "And the Catholic Faith is this: That we *worship* one God in Trinity, and Trinity in Unity." Indeed, the end of theology is liturgy. The church's relationship with God is one of worship. Faith and obedience lead to worship. Rightly so, because worship is the very conduit of life. If theology is to give life then it should lead men and women to worship God in and through whom we all receive life. The catholic life flows out of the catholic worship.

Hence, Christian worship is beyond individual act of worship; it finds its ultimate expression in the catholic worship. Worship is more communal than individual. To be a Christian is to be in a community—a community that is not only local but also catholic; to worship God, then, is a community affair. Local worship services are always done in the context of the catholic church. Whenever churches worship God, they do so in the spirit of the catholic church. Our prayers, offerings, and other activities in the church are never done in a selfish manner, but always in the context of the community. Jesus emphasized this in his instruction on prayer,

> *Our* Father in heaven, hallowed be your name; your Kingdom come, your will be done, on earth as it is in heaven. Give *us* today *our* daily bread. Forgive us *our* debts, as *we* also have forgiven *our* debtors. And lead *us* not into temptation, but deliver *us* from the evil one. (Matt 6:9–13)

The Christian life is a community life—a catholic life indeed. The catholic spirit takes self-centeredness away from the life of the church. Local churches can also be guilty of self-centeredness. The absence of the catholic spirit in the church gives room to self-centered worship and witness, which are contradictory to the Christian faith. We must always remind ourselves that whenever we worship we worship as catholic. We do not approach the throne of God as individuals but as members of the community—Christ's body. This is to say that we are not just Christian; we are catholic. Thus, Christian worship is catholic worship.

The individualism of the West was too costly for the church. There arose a theological need for the church to recapture its catholic spirit. Pietism, for example, should not be an individual or personal pursuit for holiness or spirituality. Pietism is only Christian and holy when done in the catholic spirit of the church. In that sense, catholicity defines Christian spirituality or church spirituality. The missing link among the pietists has always been the catholic spirit. No wonder why many of the pietists became separatists. Their pursuit of spirituality had led to another form of religion—a religion of isolation and seclusion. Such spirit is not Christian; it is contra catholicity. Christianity and its virtues are hardly about individuals. Love, for example, is impossible to exercise or live out outside a community. Love is given life only in a community and never without it; otherwise it is no longer love. Worship is community.

Life and Christian Apologetics

As early as the early church, Christians have been engaged in apologetics. The apostle Paul himself exhorted young Timothy with the following words, "Timothy, my son, I am giving you this command in keeping with the prophecies once made about you, so that by recalling them you may fight the battle well, holding on to faith and a good conscience, which some have rejected and so have suffered shipwreck with regard to the faith" (1 Tim 1:18–19). In the same way Paul exhorted Titus, "He must hold firmly to the trustworthy message as it has been taught, so that he can encourage others by sound doctrine and refute those who oppose it" (Tit 1:9). There have been inquirers and challengers of the Christian faith since the early beginnings of the church. The church must stand firm in the faith and fight for it. Heresies are born out of doctrinal or theological deviations from the explicit biblical doctrines of the church in and through private and eccentric interpretations of the Holy Scriptures if not by intentional distortions or deconstructions of the Christian faith. Again, Jesus warns us that heretics come in sheep's clothing but inwardly they are ferocious animals (cf. Matt 7:15). Apologetic then is a biblical mandate. The catholic church needs apologetics not only for meeting the faith inquirers but also for confronting the heretics or the enemies of the faith. In addition, apologetic is necessary not only for the above two reasons, but also for a more contemporary reason—dialogue. Jerry H. Gill proposes this type of apologetic in his book, *Faith in Dialogue: A Christian Apologetic*, where he writes,

> Against the backdrop of these standard postures toward apologetics, I should like to invite the reader to take up a more dialogical posture when reasoning about Christian faith, whether approaching it as a believer or as an unbeliever. It is my conviction that the only apologetic appropriate both to the nature of Christian belief and to the pluralistic character of our times is one which is open enough to acknowledge the limitations of religious knowledge and faith as well as to affirm their reasonableness. We must remember that even believers "see through a glass, darkly," and that there is no inherent contradiction between confidence and humility.[25]

Whether it is to respond to faith inquirers, or to defend the faith from heretics, or to dialogue with non-believers in the context of their own world and the Christian faith, the catholic church must take a strong apologetic stance to be able to survive and pass on or hand over what we believe to the next generation/s. John Stott rightly says,

> Evidently we are not only to stand firm in the gospel ourselves, but fight for it in the public arena as well. "Contending for the Gospel" might be described as a combination of evangelism and apologetics. It is not enough to proclaim the good news; we have also to defend it and confirm it (verse 7 and 16). The apostles did not separate these tasks. Neither must we. There was a strong element of apologetics in all their evangelism. The apostle Paul could even sum up his ministry by two Greek words which can be translated "we persuade people" (cf. 2 Cor 5:11). And Luke describes him doing so—arguing the gospel, reasoning with people out of the Scriptures, and convincing them of its truth.[26]

The catholic spirit is apologetic. While there are among us formal apologists, the rest are informal apologists.[27] Apologetic must come alongside evangelism, discipleship, and mission. Perhaps the defending of the catholic faith comes as an instinct when we are under open attack, but often the enemies come in more cunning ways. The church must be vigilant and ever ready to defend (cf. 2 Tim. 4:2); or, perhaps we need to be more intentional

---

25. Gill, *Faith in Dialogue*, 12.

26. Stott, *Evangelical Truth*, 138.

27. Green uses the word "informal" in reference to the work of evangelism we all do in the church. Green, *Evangelism*, 211.

in our apologetic for the catholic church. Gill offers the church two compelling reasons for apologetics:

> (1) it is necessary and valuable for Christian faith to provide a rationale for itself in relation to the general human search for truth—that is, for the individual believer to "give a reason for the hope that is within" (1 Pet. 3:15)—and that (2) it is *not* necessary or possible for a person, whether a Christian or not, to provide *proof* for his or her belief in order for it to be responsible belief. Justified belief must be sincere and open on the one hand, reasonable and responsible on the other hand. Honest Christian faith need not be more and can surely be no less.[28]

Life and Christian Holiness

The command of God for Israel to be holy just as he is holy (Lev 11:44–45; 19:2; 20:7), and its repeat in the New Testament for the church of Jesus Christ: "But just as he who called you is holy, so be holy in all you do; for it is written: 'Be holy, because I am holy'" (1 Pet 1:15–16) establishes the necessity of holiness. While it is associated with things and rituals (particularly in the Old Testament), holiness is primarily a character—it is a divine character out of God's holy nature that he requires for his people both in the Old Testament and the New Testament. (cf. Eph 1:4; 1 Pet 2:9).[29] The church today is not exempt; the command to be holy remains the same. The catholic church must be a holy catholic church. Indeed it is proper to describe the church as "one, holy, catholic, and apostolic church." Each adjective aptly qualifies the nature of the church.

And so it is fitting for the church in and through the Apostles' Creed to confess: "I believe in . . . the *holy* catholic church." Such is not only a confession but an affirmation of the holy calling of the church to live its relations and roles as the church of Jesus Christ in and through holiness. Holiness is not reserved only for the Puritans, Pietists, Moravians, Wesleyans, and many others; but it is a call, or better, a life for every member of the catholic church indeed. The biblical doctrine of holiness differentiates the catholic church from other religions or organizations in the world for it is a holiness that is not defined by ecclesiastical offices, religious isolations, spiritual trans-meditations, rituals and relics, but by its relationship with

---

28. Gill, *Faith in Dialogue*, 156.
29. See also Rees, "Holiness," 269–70.

the Holy God in and through obedience to the Holy Scriptures leading to holy lives by the power of the Holy Spirit. And it is only possible in and through faith in Jesus Christ; hence, Christian holiness is always and only understood and applied in Christ.

Theologians are right to affirm that the biblical doctrine of holiness is not a distinctive doctrine of a church, but one that belongs properly to the catholic church. T. A. Noble writes,

> In keeping with Wesley's "catholic spirit," we will not present his doctrine of Christian sanctification as merely a series of sectarian "distinctives" of interest only to Wesleyans, but as a view that stands within the mainstream tradition of the Christian church. Sadly, the Wesleyan view too often been presented in a sectarian way. In the disputes among evangelical Christians in the nineteenth and twentieth centuries, it was often attacked as "sinless perfection," and some of Wesley's heirs deserved to be rebuked for that distortion of his teaching. But unlike his more unbalanced followers, John Wesley was widely read and deeply immersed in the church Fathers and was an Oxford scholar who read the Fathers and the Scriptures in the original languages. He insisted on using the easily misunderstood word "perfection" because his commitment to Scripture as "a man of one book" (*homo unius libri*). The Bible was Wesley's source of authority for his doctrine of Christian "perfection" was not, therefore, a new doctrine; it was simply his formulation of the doctrine within the mainstream tradition of the church catholic. The aim here therefore is not just to carry on a conversation within the Wesleyan tradition, but across the church.[30]

No church of Jesus Christ should claim that they are not called to holiness. Holiness is a requirement, if not a demand, for all the members of the body of Christ whether Wesleyan or not, Reformed or not, Franciscans (an order in the Roman Catholic) or not. Holiness is neither a special task assigned to a church nor a denominational emphasis vis-à-vis the gospel of Jesus Christ. It is a misreading of the Reformation to think that Luther's gospel was merely centered on justification by faith without implications or relation to God's demand for holiness among Christians. Understandably the Reformation was primarily doctrinal and eventually also political; but it is wrong to think of it as non-practical or non-existential. Both Luther and Calvin called their followers to the necessity of holiness in living the

---

30. Noble, *Holy Trinity*, 3.

Christian life. For the Protestants, justification by faith leads to sanctification as well. Luther's famous dictum that Christians are *"simul justus et peccator"* testifies to the spirit of the doctrine. The dictum is in recognition of the tension that Christians find themselves in in this sinful world with sinful people.

The church is a holy church; it must live holy indeed. That holiness may not have its absolute perfection here on earth is something that we all agree. But there has to be at least a degree of holiness as we all grow in the Word and by the Spirit. T. A. Noble is right to suggest that we call it as "Christian Perfecting" rather than the traditional "Christian Perfection,"[31] although a faithful reading of the Wesleyan doctrine of holiness already communicates that without calling it as such.

In sum, the church of Jesus Christ is called to be holy as God is holy. And so, to say that 'we are catholic' is to embrace our holy calling—the call to holiness. We all can confess with confidence and humility that we are the holy catholic church—the body of Christ.

Life and the Kingdom of God

As earlier discussed, the kingdom of God is a reference to God's dynamic reign in the lives of men and women who come under the authority of God as King by faith in and through the Lordship of Jesus Christ. But the kingdom does not only refer to God's saving presence and that assurance or promise of eternal life, which is traditionally understood in terms of an apocalyptic or eschatological reality of the redemptive work of God, i.e., heaven, contra the narrow-minded nationalistic and political establishment of the kingdom to Israel. A more fitting interpretation or understanding of the kingdom, however, points further to the universal redemptive activity of God in and through the church here on earth as it is in heaven.

The catholic life then is related not only to the proclamation of the Kingdom, but also to its earthly fulfillment expressed in and through the various ministries and missions of the church that bring the Kingdom of God within the reach of men and women seeking righteousness on earth as it is in heaven. The kingdom-mindset answers indeed the theological challenge of Bultmann's demythologizing of the Kingdom. It portrays the existential relevance of the Kingdom for the present. C. C. Caragounis writes,

---

31. See Noble, *Holy Trinity*.

> The Kingdom of God need not be demythologized. But it is instructive to note that the early church, addressing primarily Gentile converts, avoided using a term loaded with Jewish national or apocalyptic connotations which might introduce confusion, seeking instead other dynamic equivalents such as "eternal life" or "salvation" as more appropriate, though "Kingdom of God" did not disappear entirely from its lips. The church continued to proclaim the legacy of its Master, but in dynamic forms. Every age has to find its own appropriate forms for expressing the ever-relevant message of Jesus on the Kingdom of God. The forms may change but the essence remains.[32]

The kingdom of God is not an abstraction of the theology of the early church, but a concrete expression of the universal incarnation of the dynamic reign of God in and through the church, where the world "could find the fulfillment of its ultimate desires for righteousness, justice, peace, happiness, freedom from sin and guilt, and a restored relationship to God—an order which God was King."[33]

Interestingly, N. T. Wright's redefinition of the gospel in terms of the kingship of God, here on earth as in heaven, highlights the catholic life of the church vis-à-vis the Kingdom of God. The kingdom aspect of the catholic gospel leads the church to its socio-political and socio-economic relevance in the world. The Kingdom of God though an inner spiritual reality that is experienced by the church, its outward life expression shows its dynamic, growing, and transforming influence or impact in the world. The church in and through its kingdom life serves as the community of justice and righteousness for the world where men and women can truly experience them here and now on earth as it is in heaven indeed.

Part of the Kingdom of God is its accommodation of the cultures of the world. It is only in the kingdom where cultures will find their ultimate expressions unadulterated by their ungodly forms, such as the pride of cultures, idolatry in cultures, and other pagan spirits in them. Contextualization finds its home in the church in and through its kingdom life. Contextualization outside the kingdom is similar to the narrow-minded nationalistic hope of the Jews.

The catholic church does not serve itself, but the world. It exists for the world not only as the preacher of the redemptive aspect of the Kingdom through faith in Christ but also as the catalyst of righteousness and justice

---

32. Caragounis, "Kingdom," 430.
33. Ibid.

in the world in the name of the kingdom. By doing so, the church proclaims the two-fold meaning of the gospel of Jesus Christ—justification by faith and the Kingdom of God.

Conclusion

Catholicity is a life—a life that the church must live. It was not an invention of Ignatius, but a holy recognition of the life of the church along with its unity, holiness, and apostolicity. Hence, the church is "one, holy, catholic, and apostolic." Indeed, "wherever Christ is, there is the catholic church." We can add further and say that wherever the (local) church is, there is the catholic church as well. The above practical life applications show the dynamic and rich catholic life of the church.

Sadly, catholicity has not been given serious attention among protestant churches. For centuries, we have preoccupied ourselves with our own denominational unique identities and theological differences at the expense of our unity and catholicity. Admittedly, the catholic spirit needs to be rekindled and renewed among the churches within the catholic church. We cannot keep on putting the life and witness of the church at risk for weak catholicity or lack of the catholic spirit. The Reformation was never intended to destroy the catholic church; on the contrary. The Reformation, in fact, was the vanguard of the catholic life of the church. It was corrective of the false catholicity looming within the undivided church's hierarchy and the then theology of the church.

We do need to celebrate the gains of the Reformation—biblical, theological, intellectual, philosophical, social, political, educational, scientific, and technological, and many others. We have gone a long way indeed, but we must humbly admit that we have weakened the catholic life of the church. Indeed, we need a new Reformation but this time back to the catholic church. May the 500th year celebration of the Reformation in October of 2017 be in the spirit of the catholic church. May all Christian churches around the world declare with confidence and humility that "we are catholic"; and, onwards we will sing it, shout it, preach it, and live it.

8

Conclusion

The Catholic Spirit

WHEN ASKED BY AN expert of the law, "Teacher, which is the greatest commandment in the law?" Jesus replied, "Love the Lord your God with all your heart and with all your soul and with all your mind. This is the first and greatest commandment. And the second is like it: 'Love your neighbor as yourself.' All the Law and the Prophets hang on these two commandments" (Matt 22:37–39). The conclusion of all the matter is love; yes, it is all about love. Catholicity must end in love as well, if not, then it is unscriptural. And as such, catholicity is indeed Christlikeness. To say that, "We are catholic" is to say, "We are Christlike" for where Christ is, there is Christlikeness, and to be Christlike is to love—love God and love your neighbor as yourself. The Apostle Paul proclaimed likewise that the Christian faith is that which works itself in love: "For in Christ Jesus neither circumcision nor uncircumcision has any value. The only thing that counts is faith expressing itself through love" (Gal 5:6). If the Christian faith means being "in Christ," then faith only means one thing—love; indeed, faith must express itself in love. John Wesley rightly calls this as the catholic spirit: "For love alone gives the title to this character—catholic love is a catholic spirit."[1] Indeed, this is the catholic spirit—faith working through love. For our purposes, a better summary of the catholicity of the church is the concept of the catholic spirit in terms of faith expressed in love. What Paul said in 1 Corinthians 13:13, which summed up his whole discussion on the church and the Spirit that

---

1. Wesley, "Catholic," 309.

Conclusion

puts emphasis on the greatness of love captures it: "And now these three remain: faith, hope, and love. But the greatest of these is love." Gordon Fee beautifully sums this verse up in the following words,

> Together these words embrace the whole Christian existence, as believers live out the life of the Spirit in the present age, awaiting the consummation. They have "faith" toward God, that is, they trust him to forgive and accept them through Christ. Even though now they do not see him (or see, as it were, "a reflection in a mirror"), they trust in his goodness and mercies. They also have "hope" for the future, which has been guaranteed for them through Christ. Through his resurrection and the gift of the Spirit, they have become a thoroughly future-oriented people; "as if not" (cf. 7:29–31), not conditions by the present with its hardships or suffering. They are on their way "home," destined for an existence in the presence of God that is "face to face." And they have "love" for one another as they live this life of faith and hope. In the present life of the church "these three remain (or continue): faith, hope, and love.[2]

Let me offer my summary and conclusion of the catholicity of the church in the same fashion. There is nothing that better encapsulates the catholic spirit than Paul's triadic formula of the Christian faith and life in the context of the church and the Spirit. Catholicity is perfectly defined by the triad of faith, hope and love. By faith the catholic church is reconciled to God and to one another to share to the world the very same faith that offers men and women the same reconciliation, in hope the catholic church stands that in God's time those who believe regardless of race and religion will be one in Christ, in fellowship, and in worship of the triune God both here on earth and in the life to come in heaven, and through love the catholic church embraces and accepts one another and by the same spirit of love serves the world altogether.

The Catholic Spirit and Faith

Catholicity is one of faith; it is neither an institution nor a movement. Platt rightly asks the question and it is worth repeating it here, "What does the absence of reference to organization or ecclesiastical forms in the New

---

2. Fee, *First Epistle*, 650.

Testament texts indicate about unity?"[3] Platt answers, "Surely, it eliminates any basis for dogmatic imposition of structures. At the same time, all Christians are called to make the practical expression of Christian unity a high priority, or suffer the consequence of ineffective witness or outreach."[4] We also cannot turn catholicity into an ecclesiastical law or a canon of the church. Catholicity in terms of faith defines the church. We are catholic because we believe.

Objective and Subjective

The catholic spirit embraces both the objective and subjective aspects of faith. The objective aspect focuses on the centrality and sufficiency of the Holy Scriptures. There is no faith where there is no Scripture: "Consequently faith comes from hearing the message, and the message is heard through the word of Christ" (Rom 10:17). The catholic tradition is grounded primarily on the sole authority and message of the Holy Scriptures. The Reformation's cry and call for the church to be *sola scriptura* must remain as the center of the life and mission of the church. Catholicity is not so much about the church than it is about Christ. The Holy Scriptures bears witness to the catholicity of the church (see chapter 3) and how it is rooted in God's revelation of himself to the Patriarchs and the Prophets, and to Christ and the church. Catholicity is the very essence or spirit of revelation or God's redemptive work. Moreover, our study of the traditions of the church in chapter 4 reveals that when the church deviates from the clear teachings of the Holy Scriptures, doctrinal and theological distortions happen. While the theological constructions and expressions of the doctrine of the church are gradual and progressive, the Holy Scripture is final and fixed. The catholic church must be faithful to the Holy Scripture—it being the sole repository of God's redemptive revelation. This means that the Holy Scripture is the only valid source of Christian theology; other sources, whether experience, tradition, reason, etc., are only supplementary in function. When the Scripture is properly interpreted and correctly established in doctrines, true catholicity must uphold the sufficiency of the Holy Scripture in matters of both faith and practice. The catholic church does well to submit to its authority, to be faithful to its doctrines and teachings, to obey its commands and exhortations, and to submit to its ethical and moral standards.

3. Platt, "Unity," 988.
4. Ibid.

Conclusion

The subjective aspect involves hermeneutics and theology. One caution is proper: while interpretation and theology are needed for a sufficient grasp of the Scripture toward proper and profound understanding of the Word of God, the Holy Scripture remains to be the perimeter of any hermeneutical and theological undertakings. The tasks of hermeneutics and theology belong to the church in cooperation with the Holy Spirit and in consonant with the Word. Cooperation with the Spirit happens as the church engages itself by faith in the tasks of interpretation and theology anchored in the Word; for where the Word is, there is the activity of Holy Spirit. The work of the Holy Spirit is indispensable to both. But the activity of the Holy Spirit in the hermeneutical and theological tasks of the church necessitates faith. Faith is an invariable requirement for faithful interpretations of the Scripture and constructions of Christian theology.[5] Faith, however, does not guarantee correct interpretation and sound theology. Hermeneutics and theology are likewise subjective disciplines that require biblical and theological knowledge (not excluding philosophy and other fields of academic disciplines, such as sociology, psychology, and others), exegetical and hermeneutical skills (both in terms of science and art), diligence, prayer, and patience (and other attitudinal requirements), notwithstanding experience and maturity (personal and corporate, ministry and society), and the list goes on.[6] Indeed, both hermeneutics and theology are complex disciplines, and they are ever under construction and reconstruction.

Dogma and Practice

The catholic spirit of the church also embraces both dogma and practice as expressions of the Christian faith. The former relates faith with the confessions (local or denominational) of the church, the traditions (historically and theologically universal) of the church, and the theology (pilgrim or ongoing theology) of the church. Historically, the dogmas of the church had been expressed in the traditions (plural) within the tradition (singular). While the Roman Church succeeded in combating the heretics with its various creeds and confessions, catholicity was lost when the church

---

5. Klein, et al., *Introduction to Biblical*, 136–38.
6. Klein, et al., add membership in the church as a necessary qualification of the interpreter. They said, "We need to recognize our membership in the Body of Christ, the Church." Ibid., 14.

ascertained the lines of bishops in "direct and uninterrupted succession" from the apostles, as if the apostles were the locus of authority in the early church. Apostolocity was not defined by the successions of bishops but by the teachings of the apostles according to the Scripture. The authority of the apostles was not in their office as apostles, but in their teachings of Christ and the Scriptures. This is why Paul rebuked Peter when Paul saw Peter was acting contrary to the Scripture (see Gal 2:11). The early church had never placed authority on the apostles but on the Scriptures. The early church had demonstrated not "sole or single" leadership, but shared leadership. Theologically, the dogmas of the church were expressed both in the fixated tradition (the creeds) and the task of "traditioning," that is, the ongoing interpretations of the Scriptures in the light of the evolving church and the society. The Creeds though were gradual and progressive, had in them the spirit of growing stability and maturity toward becoming part of the formed and fixed tradition of the church. The first four "Creeds" of the undivided church had the fixed character of the tradition of the church. Since the Reformation and onwards, the church had engaged in the task of "traditioning," although with little contributions to the tradition of the Roman Church. However, the church after the Reformation had paved the way to the "traditions within the tradition." The Reformation did not end in the formation of the Lutheran Church as the Church to replace the Roman Church—that would have been the mother of all cults or sects. Fortunately, the Reformers never had the illusion of thinking that Lutheran or others such as the Anglican and the Reformed were the "true" church. But the Reformers gave birth to the catholic church not in the cult of uniformity but in the spirit of diversity—many yet one. As a result, the "traditioning" of the church had led to various "traditions"—the Lutheran, the Anglican, the Anabaptist, the Eastern Orthodox, the Methodist, and the Reformed.

Christianity almost collapsed itself into a dogmatic religion. The development of theology and its use of philosophy had turned the Christian faith into dogmatism. Protestant churches secured themselves in the dogmas created by the experts, the theologians. So, many Christians viewed the dogmas of the church as a form of cold orthodoxy. Some thought that the church had lost its practical connection to life and the society. There arose the various movements that put emphasis on the practical expressions of Christianity and its spirituality. In the Roman Church there were the monks; in the Protestant churches there were the Puritans, the Moravians, and later the Methodists. They were all known for their pietism; hence, they were called the "pietists." They called the church to a more personal and reflective study of the Bible and to prayer and meditation of the Christian life and service. Along with their personal pietism were their social actions that demonstrated their love for their neighbors. With their influence, catholicity became more than orthodoxy. The church had regained its "holy" mark—as such the church was viewed as both holy and catholic.

Church and Culture

Moreover, the catholic spirit of the church embraces both the church and culture (the world). The church as catholic is unique. It is local and yet is also universal; it is human but it is also divine. It is out of the world, and it lives in the world; it is not of this world, yet it exists for this world. H. Richard Niebhur's book on *Christ and Culture* is insightful for our purposes.[7] Perhaps Niebhur's thesis can be applied to the relationship between the church and culture. The church neither exists on its own nor for itself. The church was instituted by Christ and constituted by the Spirit to serve as a witness to and for the world. The church is Christ to the world.

Catholicity does not eclipse culture. Christ came to redeem cultures and to bring them before the kingdom of God to become part of the great fellowship of nations. The great commission orders the church to make disciples of all nations, not to destroy nations and the cultures therein. Admittedly cultures, like humans, have been corrupted, and therefore, in need of redemption and restoration. Sadly mission has been influenced by secular imperialism, e.g., during the Greco-Roman world, where Christianity became the dominant religion of the empire, the church had acted in the spirit of the empire and its power destroying cultures and enforcing an imperialistic culture. Unlike in the early church where nations were not asked to follow the Judeo-Christian culture, the Roman church had envisioned a one world Christendom under the authority of bishops leading to the Roman Church. It was the Reformation that gave nations not only Scriptural faith but also freedom to exercise Christianity in their own contexts. As a result, the church and culture had gone hand in hand in developing and shaping the church as catholic—one but many.

---

7. See Richard Niebhur, *Christ*.

The Catholic Spirit and Hope

The prayer of Jesus in John 17 makes catholicity a hope for the church of Jesus Christ. The author of the book of Hebrews writes, "Now faith is being sure of what we hope for and certain of what we do not see" (1:1). Faith does not stand alone. The essence of faith is not only in what it confesses but in what it hopes for. Hope is an integral part of the Christian faith. The gospel of Christ does not only offer the atoning sacrifice of Jesus Christ in and through his death but it also offers the hope of the resurrection of Christ: "That if you confess with your mouth, 'Jesus is Lord,' and believe in your heart that God raised him from the dead, you will be saved" (Rom 3:9). The catholic spirit holds the message of hope in the context of the dynamic kingdom of God which embraces both the future and the present. The hope of the Kingdom is an already but not yet reality, which is perfectly demonstrated in the life and mission of the church as catholic. The catholic church ushers people of all nations into the kingdom of God by bringing everybody in the fellowship of Christ, where God reigns here on earth as it is in heaven. What Christ established in and through his life and mission has been made realized in and through the life and mission of the catholic church. As such in and through the church, the kingdom has already come. But this is only possible in the context of the church as catholic. The kingdom is neither limited to the local community of faith nor to the universal fellowship of churches. The church through its life and mission brings the kingdom of God to the world with its message of reconciliation of all mankind and restoration or renewal of creation. This is the catholic spirit; this is the catholic hope.

Empirical and Ideal

And so the catholic spirit puts a balance between the empirical and the ideal of the message of hope. The ideal aspect of the gospel of Christ has taken prevalence over the empirical due to the church's understanding of the gospel in terms of an eschatological hope. While announcing the good news to the world, the church is often pessimistic on the empirical effects or impact of the gospel. The gospel is viewed not as power that would transform the world, but more in terms of personal and spiritual transformation that prepares men and women to the coming kingdom of God which will be consummated on the Second Coming of Christ. There is little hope

Conclusion

for the empirical world. Emphasis on an earthly hope has been suspected as a distortion of the gospel. Sadly, the eschatological hope has been the emphasis taken by the majority of the evangelicals. But for the evangelical churches to be truly catholic, they must embrace the catholic hope in terms of both empirical and ideal.

Theologically, the catholic church has to embrace theologians like Karl Barth and Rudolf Bultmann, and to bring their theological emphases towards the development of a more catholic theology that defines hope both as an encounter and existential. While the church cannot be identified with individual theologians (that would be detrimental to the catholic church, if we do so), the faith reflections and Scriptural thoughts of theologians, like Barth and Bultmann, can bring the Word and the world together in the life and mission of the church as catholic. The church of Jesus Christ is called to stand in the gap. The catholic church and its catholic faith have benefited from the theological works of Christians who were faithful to the Scripture and the Christian faith and their implications to the life of the people they served. Theological works have given faith a firm assurance to what the church hope for and a certainty of what it does not see indeed. Catholic theology has given hope flesh and blood. Our confidence in the promises of God in the Scripture is made stronger. We have been given reasons to live the ideals of the Christian faith in the empirical reality of life in the world. We live faithfully today because of the assurance of our faith anchored in the promises of God. This leads us to the ministry of the church in terms of hope in the language of action and compassion.

Action and Compassion

The catholic hope is neither a dream nor an ambition people need to achieve or work on for the rest of their lives. In hope, we live (action); in hope, we serve (compassion). The missional aspect of the ecumenical movement partly demonstrates hope in action. The Christian faith is not an abstract theological construction, but one that is practical and applicable to life. The Christian faith touches the lives of the oppressed, the poor, the marginalized, the outcasts of the society, "the sin-against" (or victims) of the nations, and others. It was faith that turned the five loaves of bread and the two fish into meals for five thousand men (not including women and children). It was faith that opened the eyes of the two blind men who came to Jesus. It was faith that healed the woman bleeding for twelve years, and so many others that demonstrated faith and hope in action and compassion.

We act because we have hope. We make this hope something that people can see with their eyes, hear with their ears, and touch with their hands (1 John 1:1–5). The pietists' emphasis on compassion challenges the church to turn our hope into action. The catholic church must indeed be a church of action and compassion. Through our action we offer the world hope of freedom, hope of joy, hope of justice, hope of love, hope of peace, and many others that express the Christian hope in action. This hope, however, is not defined in the language of liberation theology; its goal is not humanization. It is an action anchored in God's work of redemption. It is an action that is deeply rooted in what Augustine calls *"charitas"*—a genuine compassion to our neighbors in the name of *"agapē."*

John Wesley calls this "social holiness." He strongly warned the Methodists and of course the same applies to the rest of the Christendom of making holiness a matter of pure spirituality without social impact. If it is not social then it is not holiness. The gospel of holiness is for Wesley the catholic hope, but it is no hope if it lacks action and compassion. Sadly, modern Methodism, influenced by the liberals and liberation theology, has abandoned John Wesley and his message of holiness with their gospel version inclined to humanization rather than in the context of God's work of redemption—justification and sanctification.

Present and Future

Hope in terms of the Kingdom of God presents to us not only the future consummation of the kingship of God on the Second Coming of Christ, but also the in-breaking of the reign of God here on earth as it is in heaven in and through the victory of Christ. In Christ the kingdom of God has come. It, in fact, has already begun with the life and ministry of Christ. This is the Christian hope. And the work of the church is to proclaim the arrival of the kingdom to all the nations—to offer hope to all men and women. The book of Acts presents to us how the early church had demonstrated through their mission to all the nations the presence and power of the kingdom through signs and wonders that accompanied their preaching indicating indeed the present reality of the kingdom of God here on earth. Zweigle writes,

> You can't read the book of Acts without noticing that the witness of the early Christian church goes hand in hand with signs and

wonders, including physical healing, deliverance from the demonic, restoration of damaged and broken lives, and the spread of new communities throughout the Greco-Roman world that are filled with wonder, love, and praise.[8]

The dynamic life and growth of the church today is attributed to the present reality of the kingdom of God. The gospel offers hope that transforms not only men and women but also culture and society. The Western world, for example, would not be what it is today had it not for the influence of Christianity and the gospel it preaches.

But the truth still remains that the ultimate hope of the Christian faith lies not on what men and women can do, but on what God would do on behalf of the world for whom Christ died. History, as part of the old age, will have its own end. The tension between good and evil will soon come to an end. While we work toward the betterment and development of both life and the society here on earth, we are also aware of the sinfulness of men and women that affects the quality of life, and the sovereignty of God over history—the world and its evil desires have been subjected to destruction and will one day pass away (cf. 1 John 2:17). This is the eschatological hope. The catholic spirit puts a balance, indeed, between the present and future aspects of the Christian hope. The catholic church cannot give up its hope. It is hope that allows the church to live by faith.

The Catholic Spirit and Love

The catholic spirit boils down to the catholic love. There is no catholic spirit without love. Love is the power of catholicity. All theological constructions and confessions must come to their final expression in love. The fullness of life is experienced in the fullness of love. God himself loved the world (John 3:16) so that everyone who chooses to respond in faith will live. Barth notes that love is what the church shares to the world, "What shines for it, and illumines it when it is given to it to see it, is the love (John 3:16) with which God has loved the world to such a degree and in such a way that He has

---

8. Zweigle, *Worship*, 51. The author offers a renewed or in his term *reimaged* paradigm of evangelism patterned after the Kingdom of God model presented to us by scholars like N. T. Wright, Scot McKnight, and others who challenge the church to redefine the gospel in the light of the King Jesus and his message of the in-breaking of the gospel centered on the Kingdom of God as a present and earthly reality or good news. See McKnight, *King Jesus*.

given His only Son for it. If it is to share this love, where can it find itself set, or try to set itself, but at the side and indeed in the midst of this world which God has so loved?"[9] God's love is an offer of life to the world. There can be no life without love. The very being of God is defined in terms of love: "God is love" (I John 4:8, 16). And those who live in God must live in love. The catholic life is summed up in love—love God and love others. Jesus said that love is the defining character of his disciples: "Love one another. As I have loved you, so you must love one another. By this all men and women will know that you are my disciples, if you love one another" (John 13:34–35).

Having realized the differences that exist among Christians, John Wesley cried out,

> But although a difference of opinions or modes of worship may prevent on entire external union, yet need it prevent our union in affection? Though we can't think alike, may we not love alike? May we not be of one heart, though we are not of one opinion? Without all doubt we may. Herein all the children of God may unite, notwithstanding these smaller differences. These remaining as they are, they may forward one another in love and in good works.[10]

To the very least the catholic spirit calls all of us to be one in love. Love, indeed, does not depend on our opinions or ways; it embraces everyone who believes in Christ, in Spirit and in truth, as brothers and sisters in the Lord—whether this relation is real or potential: "If your heart is right, as my heart is with my heart? . . . if it be, give me your hand" (2 Kgs 190:15).

By exercising the catholic love, Christians must not fall into the trap of a different (*heteros*) catholic spirit. John Wesley strongly warned Christians of misapprehension and misapplication of the catholic spirit in the name of love. The enemies of faith can use "love" to perpetuate their words, their works, and their world—to these we must be aware of false spirit of catholicity. Here I borrowed heavily from John Wesley's three guides to the catholic spirit vis-à-vis the spirit of latitudinarianism.

---

9. Barth, *Community*, 507.
10. Wesley, *Catholic Spirit*, 300.

Conclusion

Catholic Spirit and Speculative Latitudinarianism

The catholic spirit does not disregard the truth. Truth matters. Love operates in the spirit of the truth. Love and truth go together. As such, Christians must establish themselves in the truth. We cannot afford to loosen our grip of the truth. Among the Christendom, for examples, there are absolute truths that we cannot compromise in the name of the catholic spirit. Speculative latitudinarianism, to Wesley, "is the spawn of hell, not the offspring of heaven." He said further, "This unsettledness of thought, this being 'driven to and fro, and tossed about with every wink of doctrine,' is a great curse, not a blessing; an irreconcilable enemy, not a friend, to true Catholicism."[11] The catholic spirit is well grounded on the truth of Christ and that of the Holy Scriptures. Catholicity offers the church fixed and firm foundations for its faith. The catholic church, as it stands in the truth of the Scriptures, is neither open to falsehood nor distortion. It is "fixed as the sun in *its* judgment concerning the main branches of Christian doctrine."[12]

Though there is diversity in the body of Christ, catholicity does not promote plurality of "faiths." The original ecumenical movement was organized to bring Christian churches together in the spirit of cooperation toward the evangelization of the world through joint efforts in mission. Ecumenicity in the catholic sense is a unity in diversity, not a unity in plurality. Mission cooperation in fact must be based on the truth. The evangelical apprehension toward the growing "ecumenical" spirit today is caused primarily by a difference in the movement's theology of mission. This is the spirit of what John Wesley said, "Go first and learn the first elements of the gospel of Christ, and then shall you learn to be of a truly catholic spirit."[13] The catholic spirit goes with the catholic gospel or the catholic faith. The two cannot be divorced.

Catholic Spirit and Practical Latitudinarianism

Practical latitudinarianism is a spirit of pragmatic philosophy, which when misapprehended and misapplied could destroy the catholic spirit rather than build and promote it. Again John Wesley said, "It is not indifference as to public worship or as to the outward manner of performing it." Praxis

---

11. Ibid., 307.
12. Ibid. The italic is used in reference to the church.
13. Ibid., 308.

without theology is equally erroneous with theology without relation to practice. Catholicity does not hold an either/or principle but a both/and one. Theology without practice is dogmatism; practice without theology is paganism/humanism. Neither of the two is Christian or catholic.

The man or woman of a catholic spirit is firm in what he or she does. According to John Wesley, "The man of a truly catholic spirit, having weighed all things in balance of the sanctuary, has no doubt, no scruple at all concerning that particular mode of worship wherein he joins. He is clearly convinced that his manner of worshipping God is both scriptural and rational." The catholic spirit has its firm foundations for Christian ministries.

Catholic Spirit and Congregational Latitudinarianism

The catholic spirit does not take liberty in being loosely tied with a congregation. This is another sort of latitudinarianism, which for Wesley is absurd and unscriptural than the above two. The catholic church is grounded in the local congregation. Every member of the body of Christ is formally tied to his/her congregation. "He *or she* is united to it, not only in spirit, but by all the outward ties of Christian fellowship."[14] If he or she is not, then, he or she is far from being a man or woman of a truly catholic spirit. John Wesley said,

> There he *or she* partakes of all the ordinances of God. There he receives the Supper of the Lord. There he *or she* pours out his soul in public prayer, and joins in public praise and thanksgiving. There he *or she* rejoices to hear the word of reconciliation, the gospel of the grace of God. With these his *or her* nearest, his *or her* best beloved brethren, on solemn occasions he *or she* seeks God by fasting. These particularly he *or she* watches over in love, as they do over his *or her* soul, admonishing, exhorting, comforting, reproving, and every way building up each other in the faith. These he *or she* regards as his *or her* own household, and therefore according to the ability God has given him *or her* naturally cares for them, and provides that they may have all the things that are needful for life and godliness.[15]

---

14. Ibid. Italic is mine.
15. Ibid. Italics are mine.

Conclusion

There is no catholicity in latitudinarianism. The catholic spirit is deeply rooted in its faith, in its practice, and in its membership, which are grounded in the local church—for where the local church is, there is the catholic church indeed. Disassociation with the local and the universal does not represent the catholic spirit. Catholicity is a unity in the body of Christ in terms of both local and universal. Wesley beautifully summed it up in the following words,

> But while he *or she* is steadily fixed in his *or her* religious principles, in what he *or she* believes to be the truth as it is in Jesus; while he *or she* firmly adheres to that worship of God which he *or she* judges to be most acceptable in his *or her* sight; and while he *or she* is united by the tenderest and closes ties to one particular congregation; his *or her* heart is enlarged toward all mankind, those he *or she* knows and those he *or she* does not; he *or she* embraces with strong and cordial affection neighbors and strangers, friends and enemies. This is catholic or universal love.[16]

There is no faith where there is no love; there is no hope where there is no love. Faith and hope are both tied into one catholic spirit—the catholic love. As God is love so the church must be—love. This is what catholic, catholicity, and catholicization are all about. And this is who we are and what we are—we are catholic!

---

16. Ibid., 308–9. Italics are mine.

Bibliography

Adewuya, J. Ayo. *Holiness and Community in 2 Corinthians 6:14—17:1—A Study of Paul's View of Communal Holiness in the Corinthian Correspondence.* New York: Peter Lang, 2001.

Anderson, Bernhard W. *Understanding the Old Testament.* Fourth edition. Quezon City, Philippines: Claritan, 1986.

Anderson, Ray S., ed. *Theological Foundations for Ministry: Selected Readings for a Theology of the Church in Ministry.* Edinburgh: T. & T. Clark; Grand Rapids, Michigan: Wm. B. Eerdmans, 1979.

———. *The Shape of Practical Theology: Empowering Ministry with Theological Praxis.* Downers Grove: InterVarsity, 2001.

Anglican. "Articles of Religion." Htpp://anglicanonline.org/basics/thirty-nine_articles.html.

Arnold, G. E. "Centers of Christianity." In *DLNTD.* Edited by Ralph P. Martin and Peter H. Davids. Downers Grove, Illinois: InterVarsity, 1992.

Barrois, Georges A. "Marks of the Church." In *New 20th-Century Encyclopedia of Religious Knowledge.* Edited by J. D. Douglas. Grand Rapids, Michigan: Baker, 1991.

Barth, Karl. *CD, vol. 1: The Doctrine of the Word of God, Part 2.* Edited by G. W. Bromiley and T. F. Torrance. Peabody, Massachusetts: Hendrickson, 2010.

———. "The Community for the World." In *Theological Foundations for Ministry.* Edited by Ray S. Anderson. Grand Rapids, Michigan: William B. Eerdmans, 1979.

———. "The Place of Theology." In *Theological Foundations for Ministry.* Edited by Ray S. Anderson. Grand Rapids, Michigan: William B. Eerdmans, 1979.

Bernard, J. H. *A Critical and Exegetical Commentary on the Gospel According to John.* ICT. Edinburg: T. & T. Clark,1976.

Beyerhaus, Peter. *Missions—Which Way? Humanization or Redemption.* Grand Rapids, Michigan: Zondervan, 1971.

Bevans, Stephen B. *Models of Contextual Theology.* Manila: Logos, 2003.

Bloesch, Donald G. *The Church: Sacraments, Worship, Ministry, Mission.* Downers Grove, Illinois: InterVarsity, 2002.

Boadt, Lawrence. *Reading the Old Testament: An Introduction.* New York: Paulist, 1984.

Brewin, Kester. *Signs of Emergence: A Vision for Church that is Organic/Networked/Decentralized/Bottom-up/Flexible/Always Evolving.* Grand Rapids, Michigan: Baker, 2007.

BIBLIOGRAPHY

Brown, Colin. "Historical Jesus, Quest of." In *DJG*. Edited by Joel B. Green and Scot McKnight. Downers Grove, Illinois: InterVarsity, 1992.

———. *Jesus in European Protestant Thought: 1778–1860*. Grand Rapids, Michigan: Baker, 1985.

Brueggemann, Walter. *Biblical Perspectives on Evangelism: Living in a Three-Storied Universe*. Nashville: Abingdon, 1993.

Bruner, Frederick Dale. *Matthew: A Commentary, vol. 1: The Christbook, Matthew 1–12*. Paperback edition. Grand Rapids, Michigan: William B. Eerdmans, 2007.

Cairns, Earle E. *Christianity Through the Centuries: A History of the Christian Church*. Third Edition. Grand Rapids, Michigan: Zondervan, 1996.

Calvin, John. *Institutes of the Christian Religion*. Translated by Henry Beveridge. London: James Clarke and Co., 1949.

Caragounis, C. C. "Kingdom of God/Kingdom of Heaven." In *DJG*. Downers Grove, Illinois: InterVarsity, 1992.

Childs, Brevard S. *The Book of Exodus: A Critical Theological Commentary*. Philadelphia: The Westminster, n.d.

Clowney, Edmund P. *The Church: Contours of Christian Theology*. Downers Grove, Illinois: InterVarsity, 1995.

Cole, R. Alan. *The Gospel According to Mark*. TNTC 2. Grand Rapids, Michigan: William B. Eerdmans, 1989.

Coleman, Robert. "Evangelism." In *EDWM*. Edited by A. Scott Moreau. Grand Rapids, Michigan: Baker, 2000.

Collins, Kenneth J. *The Evangelical Moment: The Promise of an American Religion*. Grand Rapids, Michigan: Baker Academic, 2005.

Congar, Yves. *Diversity and Communion*. Mystic, Connecticut: Twenty-Third, 1985.

CRTA. "Westminster Shorter Catechism." http://www.reformed.org/documents/WCS/index.html.

Cullmann, Oscar. *Peter: Disciple-Apostle-Martyr*. London: SCM, 1962.

Culpepper, R. Alan. *Anatomy of the Fourth Gospel: A Study in Literary Design*. Philadelphia: Fortress, 1987.

Danker, F. W. et al. *A Greek-English Lexicon of the New Testament and other Early Christian Literature*. Chicago and London: The University of the Chicago Press, 2000.

Darr, John A. *On Character Building: The Reader and the Rhetoric of Characterization in Luke-Acts*. Louisville, Kentucky: Westminster/John Knox, 1998.

David, P. H. "Rich and Poor." In *DJG*. Illinois, Downers Grove: InterVarsity, 1992.

Dieter, Melvin Easterday. *The Holiness Revival of the Nineteenth Century*. London: The Scarecrow, 1980.

Dulles, Avery. *Models of the Church*. Expanded edition. New York: Double Day, 1987.

———. *The Catholicity of the Church*. Oxford: Clarendon, 1985.

———. *The Craft of Theology: From Symbols to System*. New York: Crossroad, 1995.

Dunning, H. Ray. *Grace, Faith, and Holiness: A Wesleyan Systematic Theology*. Kansas City, Missouri: Beacon Hill, 1988.

Dyrness, William A. *Let the Earth Rejoice: A Biblical Theology of Holistic Mission*. Eugene, Oregon: Wipf and Stock, 1991.

E. A. *Dr. Martin Luther's Saemmtliche Werke*. Erlangen, 1826ff.

Ellison, H. L. "Tradition." In *BDT*. Edited by Everett F. Harrison. Grand Rapids, Michigan: Baker, 1960.

Bibliography

Eugenio, Dick. "Christ-centered Preaching for Postmodern Audiences." In *The Lordship of Jesus Christ in the 21st Century*. ACTS, Seoul Korea: ATA Theological Consultation, 2014.

Fee, Gordon D. *The First Epistle to the Corinthians*. NICNT. Reprint. Grand Rapids, Michigan: William B. Eerdmans, 1993.

Ferguson, Everett. *Church History, vol. One: From Christ to Pre-Reformation*. Grand Rapids, Michigan: Zondervan, 2005.

Flemming, Dean. *Contextualization in the New Testament: Patterns for Theology and Mission*. Illinois: InterVarsity, 2005.

Foster, Richard J. *Celebration of Discipline: The Path to Spiritual Growth*. Rev. Ed. New York: HarperCollins, 1988.

France, R. T. *The Gospel According to Matthew*. TNTC 1. Reprinted. Grand Rapids, Michigan: William B. Eerdmans, 1990.

Gener, Timoteo G. "Revisioning Local Theology: An integral Dialogue with Practical Theology, A Filipino Evangelical Perspective." *JAM*, 6:2 (2004) 133–66.

Gill, Jerry H. *Faith in Dialogue: A Christian Apologetic*. USA: Jarrell, 1985.

Green, Joel B. *The Gospel of Luke*. NICNT. Grand Rapids, Michigan: William B. Eerdmans, 1997.

Green, Michael. *New Testament Evangelism: Lessons for Today*. Manila: OMF, 1982.

———. *Evangelism in the Early Church*. Updated. Eagle, Guildford, 1995.

Grudem, Wayne. *Systematic Theology: An Introduction to Biblical Doctrine*. Reprinted. Leicester, England: InterVaristy, 2005.

Hallig, Jason V. "Contextualization of the Life and Ministry of Jesus in the Four Gospels, and its Significance in Proclaiming the Gospel to Asian Cultures in the 21st Century." In *The Lordship of Jesus Christ in the 21st Century*. ACTS, Seoul Korea: ATA Theological Consultation, 2014.

———. "The Eating Motif in the Third Gospel and Luke's Characterization of Jesus as the Son of Man." *BSac* 173 (2016): 206-21.

———. "Luther's Understanding of Sola Scriptura." A paper submitted to Dr. Won, Jung Chun as part of the requirements for the class "Reformation" at AIGS, Seoul Korea (2004).

———. "The Spirit and Suffering in Acts: A Lukan Juxtaposition in Relation to the Life and Mission of the Early Church." PhD diss., AIGS, 2005.

Han, Sang-Hwa. "Currents in Christological Debates." In *The Lordship of Jesus Christ in the 21st Century*. ACTS, Seoul Korea: ATA Theological Consultation, 2014.

Harrison, Everett F. "Catholic." In *BDT*. Edited by Everett F. Harrison. Grand Rapids, Michigan: Baker, 1960.

Harvey, Van A. *A Handbook of Theological Terms*. New York: McMillan, 1964.

Howell, Kenneth J. "A Culture Divided, A Church United," (2014) <http://chnetwork.org/2014/10/culture-divided-church-united> Accessed 20 October 2014.

Hur, Ju. *A Dynamic Reading of the Holy Spirit in Luke-Acts*. New York/London: T & T Clark, 2004.

Johnston, Arthur. *The Battle for World Evangelism*. Wheaton, IL: Tyndale, 1978.

Jenson, Robert W. "The Church as *Communio*." In *The Catholicity of the Reformation*. Edited by Carl E. Braaten and Robert W. Jenson. Grand Rapids, Michigan: William B. Eerdmans, 1996.

Karkkainen, Veli-Matti. *An Introduction to Ecclesiology*. Downers Grove, Illinois: InterVarsity, 2002.

Bibliography

Kaulfuss-Diesch, Karl, ed. *Das Buch der Reformation, Geschreiben von Mitle-benden*. 2nd ed. Liepzig, 1919.
Kik, J. Marcellus. *Ecumenism and The Evangelical*. Grand Rapids, Michigan: Baker, 1957.
Kingsbury, J. D. *Conflict in Luke: Jesus, Authorities, Disciples*. Minneapolis: Fortress, 1991.
Kittelson, James M. *Luther, the Reformer: The Story of the Man and His Career*. Minneapolis: Augsburg, 1986.
Klein, William W., et al. *Introduction to Biblical Interpretation*. Revised. Nashville: Thomas Nelson, 2004.
Koch, Klaus. *The Prophets: The Assyrian Period*, vol. 1. Philadelphia: Fortress, 1984.
———. *The Prophets, vol. 2: The Babylonian and Persian Period*. Philadelphia: Fortress, 1984.
Kunene, Musa Victor Mdabuleni. *Communal Holiness in the Gospel of John: The Vine Metaphor as a Test Case with Lessons from African Hospitality and Trinitarian Theology*. PhD Dissertation, University of Manchester, 2012.
Küng, Hans. *The Church*. Trans. R. and R. Ockenden. New York: Sheed & Ward, 1968; London: Search, 1969.
Kurz, William. *Reading Luke-Acts: Dynamics of Biblical Narrative*. Kentucky: John Knox, 1993.
Ladd, G. E. *A Theology of the New Testament*. Revised. Grand Rapids, Michigan: W. B. Eerdmans, 1993.
Land, Darin. *The Diffusion of Ecclesiastical Authority: Sociological Dimensions of Leadership in the Book of Acts*. Eugene, Oregon: Pickwick, 2008.
Lane, William L. *The Gospel According to Mark*. NICNT. Grand Rapids, Michigan: William B. Eerdmans, 1974.
Laroya, Joven. "Liberatory Pedagogical Mode for MultiNational Evangelical Graduate Theological Seminaries in Luzon." PhD Dissertation, Saint Louis University, 2004.
LaSor, William Sanfor, et al. *Old Testament Survey: the Message, Form, and Background of the Old Testament*. Grand Rapids, Michigan: William B. Eerdmans, 1982.
Lattoureth, Kenneth Scott. *A History of Christianity, vol. I, Beginnings to 1500*. Paper edition. New York: Harper and Row, 1975.
Leupp, Roderick T. *Knowing the Name of God: A Trinitarian Tapestry of Grace, Faith, and Community*. Downers Grove, Illinois: InterVarsity, 1996.
———. *The Renewal of Trinitarian Theology: Themes, Patterns & Explorations*. Downers Grove, Illinois: IVP, 2008.
Liao, Yuan-Wei. "The Significance of the Chalcedon Creed and the Reformation Confessions for the Life in the Asian Churches in the 21st Century." In *The Lordship of Jesus Christ in the 21st Century*. ACTS, Seoul Korea: ATA Theological Consultation, 2014.
———. "The Significance of the Chalcedon Creed and the Reformation Confessions for the Life in the Asian Churches in the 21st Century." *JAET* 19:1 (2015) 5–19.
Lohue, Bernard. *Martin Luther's Theology: Its Historical Systematic Development*. Minneapolis: Fortress, 1999.
Macquarrie, John. *Christian Unity and Christian Diversity*. Philadelphia: The Westminster, 1975.
Maslow, A. *The Farther Reaches of Human Nature*. New York: The Viking, 1971.
———. *Motivation and Personality*. New York: Harper, 1954.
McCrcken, R. J. "Let the Preacher Preach the Word." *ThT*, 2 (1945) 77–90.

BIBLIOGRAPHY

Marshall, I Howard. *The Acts of the Apostles: An Introduction and Commentary in TNTC.* Grand Rapids, Michigan: William B. Eerdmans, 1980.

McKim, Donald K. ed. *How Karl Barth Changed My Mind.* Grand Rapids, Michigan: William B. Eerdmans, 1986.

McKnight, Scot. *The King Jesus Gospel: The Original Good News Revisited.* Grand Rapids, MI: Zondervan, 2011.

Minear, Paul. *Images of the Church in the New Testament.* Philadelphia: Westminster, 1960.

Moreau, A. Sott. "Mission and Missions." In *EDWM.* Edited by A. Scott Moreau. Grand Rapids, Michigan: Baker, 2000.

Morris, Leon. *The Epistle to the Romans.* Reprint. Grand Rapids, Michigan: William B. Eerdmans, 1988.

———. *The Gospel According to John.* NICNT. Grand Rapids, Michigan: W. B. Eerdmans, 1971.

Niebuhr, H. Richard. *Christ and Culture.* New York: Harper and Row, 1975.

Noble, T. A. *Holy Trinity: Holy People: The Theology of Christian Perfecting.* Eugene, Oregon: Cascade, 2013.

Oberman, Heiko A. *The Reformation: Roots and Ramification,* translated by Andrew Colin Gow. Grand Rapids, Michigan: William B. Eerdmans, 1994.

Oden, Thomas C. *Pastoral Theology: Essentials of Ministry.* New York: Harper San Francisco, 1983.

Otto, Rudolf. *The Idea of the Holy: An Inquiry into the non-rational factor in the idea of the divine and its relation to the rational.* Reprint. Translated by John W. Harvey. New York: Oxford University Press, 1973.

Oxenham, John. "In Christ There Is No East or West." In *Sing To the Lord Hymnal.* Ed. Ken Bible. Kansas City, MO: Lillenas, 1993.

Pelikan, Jaroslav. *The Christian Tradition: A History of the Development of Doctrine: 1 The Emergence of the Catholic Tradition (100–600).* Paperback edition. Chicago and London: The University of Chicago Press, 1975.

Phillips, Timothy. "Neo-Orthodox Theology." In *EDWM.* Edited by A. Scott Moreau. Grand Rapids, Michigan: Baker, 2000.

Pierson, Paul E. "Ecumenical Movement." In *EDWM.* Edited by A. Scott Moreau. Grand Rapids, Michigan: Baker, 2000.

Piper, John. *The Future of Justification: A Response to N. T. Wright.* Wheaton, Illinois: Crossway, 2007.

Platt, Daryl. "Unity." In *EDWM.* Edited by A. Scott Moreau. Grand Rapids, Michigan: Baker, 2000.

Powell, Paul W. *The Church Today.* Dallas, Texas: Annuity Board of the Southern Baptist Convention, 1997.

Rahner, Karl. "Scripture and Tradition." *ThI* 6 (1969) 98–112.

———. "Scripture and Tradition." In *Encyclopedia of Theology.* New York: Seabury/Crossroad, 1975.

Rees, Paul. "Holiness, Holy." In *BDT.* Edited by Everett F. Harrison. Grand Rapids, Michigan: Baker, 1960.

Retzinger, Joseph Cardinal. *Principles of Catholic Theology: Building Stones for a Fundamental Theology.* San Francisco: Ignatius, 1987.

Richardson, Kurt Anders. *Reading Karl Barth: New Direction for North American Theology.* Grand Rapids, Michigan: Baker, 2004.

Bibliography

Roloff, J. "ekklesia." In *EDNT*. Edited by Horst Balz and Gerhard Schneider. Grand Rapids, Michigan: William B. Eerdmans, 1990.

Schweibert, E. G. *Luther and His Time: The Reformation from a New Perspective*. St. Louis: Concordia, 1950.

Smith, David L. "Ecclesiology." In *A Contemporary Wesleyan Theology: Biblical, Systematic, and Practical*. Edited by Charles W. Carter. Grand Rapids, Michigan: Francis Asbury, [n.d.].

Spitz, Lewis W. *The Renaissance and the Reformation Movements*, vol. 2. St. Louis, [n.d.].

Stott, John. *Evangelical Truth: A Personal Plea for Unity*. Downers Grove: Inter-Varsity, 1999.

Tannehill, Robert C. *Luke*. Nashville: Abingdon, 1996.

Taylor, V. *The Name of Jesus* New York: McMillan, 1953.

Thomas, W. H. Griffith. *Christianity in Christ*. Grand Rapids, Michigan: Zondervan, [n.d.].

Tuell, Jack M. *The Organization of the United Methodist Church*. Nashville: Abingdon, 1985.

Vanlaningham, Michael G. "An Evaluation of N. T. Wright's View of Israel in Romans 11." *BSac* 170 (2013) 179–93.

Walker, Williston, et al. *A History of the Christian Church*. Fourth edition. New York: Charles Scribner's Sons, 1985.

Wesley, John. "The Catholic Spirit." In *John Wesley's Sermons: An Anthology*, edited by Albert C. Outler and Richard P. Heitzenrater. Nashville: Abingdon, 1991.

Wright, Christopher J. H. *The Mission of God's People: A Biblical Theology of the Church's Mission*. Grand Rapids, Michigan: Zondervan, 2010.

Wright, N. T. *How God Became King: The Forgotten Story of the Gospels*. New York: HarperOne, 2012.

Zahn, T. "Regula Fidei," (2009) <http://www.ccel.org/s/schaff/encyc/encyc09/htm/iv.vii.cxix.htm> [Accessed on 17 November 2014]

Zweigle, Grant. *Worship, Wonder, and Way: Reimagining Evangelism as Missional Practice*. Kansas City: Beacon Hill, 2015.

Name Index

A
Albrecht of Brandenburg, 74
Albrecht of Mainz, 75
Ambrose, 19
Aquainas, Thomas, 19, 22, 75–76
Athanasius, St., 19
Augustine, St., 17, 19, 77, 146, 162
Astruc, Jean, 28

B
Barth, Karl, 82–84, 106, 161
Bernard, J. H., 8
Beyerhaus, Peter, xii, 30
Bloesch, Donald G., 135
Bultmann, Rudolf, 151, 161
Baur, Ferdinand C., 28

C
Calvin, John, 25–26, 77
Caragounis, C. C., 151
Cole, R. Allan, 48
Congar, Yvez, 123
Constantine, 66, 94
Crisostome, 19
Culpepper, R. Alan, 53
Cyprian, 19

D
Darwin, Charles, 82
Deasley, Alex R. G., 11
Dulles, Avery, 8, 88, 92, 95, 102, 104

E
Ellison, H. L., 58
Eusebius, 16

F
Fee, Gordon, 155
Ferguson, Everett, 95
Flemming, Dean, 46, 50
France, R. T., 45, 47, 128

G
Graf, Karl H., 25
Green Michael, 143
Grudem, Wayne, 129

H
Hegel, W. F., 28
Howell, Kenneth, 118, 126
Hur, Ju, 49
Hus, John, 22

I
Ignatius, 3, 15, 17, 87, 89
Irenaeus, 19, 100

J
Jerome, 19
Jerome of Brandenburg, 75

Name Index

K
Kelly, N. D., 12
Koch, Klaus, 63
Küng, Hans, 88, 94, 100, 135

L
Ladd, G. Eldon, 53, 59, 60–61, 64, 106–07
Lane, William, 47
Latourette, Kenneth, 18, 20, 66
Leo I, 20
Leo X, 74
Leo XIII, 22
Lessing, Gotthold, 25
Leupp, Roderick T., 125
Lodensteyn, Jacob von, 79
Luther, Martin, 22–26, 75–76, 80, 120, 150, 151

M
Martyr, Justin, 15–17
Maslow, Alfred, 137
Morris, Leon, 110

N
Noble, T. A., 99, 117, 133, 150–51

O
Origen, 16–17
Otto, Rudolf, 15
Oxenham, John 131

P
Pelikan, Jaroslav, 10, 96
Pius, Antoninus, 16

R
Reimarus, Hermann S., 28
Ritscl, Albretch, 28

S
Schleiermacher, Frederick D. E., 28
Spener, Philip Jacob, 19
Strauss, David F., 28
Stott, John, 111

T
Teelinck, Willem, 79
Tertullian, 19
Tetzel, Johann, 74–75
Thomas, Griffith, 96
Torrance, Thomas F., 61
Tuell, Jack M., 132

V
Valentinian, 20
Vincent of Lerins, 18, 73
Voet, Gisbert, 79

W
Welhausen, Julius, 28
Wenham, David, 59
Wesley, Charles, 80
Wesley, John, 80, 81, 164–67
Wright, N. T., 101–02, 107, 152
Wycliffe, John , 22

Z
Zinzendorf, Nikolaus Ludwig von, 28, 80, 137

Subject Index

A

anthropocentric, 15–16
anti-catholicity, 98
anti-semitism, 98
apologetic/s, 93, 147–49
apologist/s, 15, 66, 148
Apostles, ix, 6, 14, 17, 20, 25, 27, 31. 59, 62–63, 67–69, 77, 83, 89–91, 95, 98–99, 103, 106, 116, 121, 125–26, 134, 139, 147–49, 154, 158.
apostolic, ix–x, 18, 20–21, 26, 65, 68, 74–77, 81–82, 86, 92, 95, 98, 114, 117, 127, 149, 153
apostolicity, 5, 95, 116, 153
application/s, 85, 114, 118, 128–29, 153
authority, 9, 12, 18, 20–23, 25, 27, 32–33, 47, 55, 63, 65, 73–76, 84, 93, 100–02, 105, 120–21, 132, 140–42, 150–51, 156, 158–59

B

baptism, baptismal, pre-baptism, 27, 60, 67–69, 90, 118, 123, 140–42
belief/s, 17, 24, 63, 79, 88, 109, 148–49
believe, ix, 6–7, 12–13, 15–18, 22, 24–25, 27, 31–32, 38, 40, 48, 50, 52–54, 59, 61–69, 72–83, 87, 90, 92–95, 98, 101, 103–04, 106, 109, 111–14, 117, 120, 124, 130–32, 134–38, 140, 142, 144–45, 149, 155–56, 160, 64, 167

Bible, xii, 19, 22, 24, 27–28, 32, 36, 76–77, 79, 80, 82–83, 88, 95, 120–22, 129, 139, 150, 159
biblical, biblically, ix, 3–5, 15, 27–28, 30, 32, 34–35, 52, 56, 59, 69–70, 73, 77, 82, 86, 90, 94–95, 102, 111–12, 115, 120–22, 126, 129, 136, 138, 142, 147, 149–50, 153, 157
Body of Christ, ix, x, 7, 16, 20, 33, 58, 64, 67, 69, 85, 88, 90, 93, 104, 114, 119, 130–31, 133, 135, 140, 142, 144–45, 150–51, 157, 165–67

C

call, called, calling, x, 1–4,7–10, 12, 14–15, 19–26, 30, 33, 36–38, 40–41, 43, 46–48, 51–52, 56, 60–61, 64, 66–67, 76, 78–81, 83, 85–92, 98, 102–03, 105–08, 110–11, 114, 116, 120, 125, 127, 130–32, 135–37, 139, 143–45, 147, 149–51, 154, 156, 159, 161–62, 164
canon, 5, 12, 15, 60, 63, 74, 85, 93, 122,140, 156
canonization, 61
caritas, 144
catechism, 139, 145
catholic, ix-xiii, 1–22, 26–31, 34–45, 47–49, 54, 56–59, 64, 67–71, 73–74, 77–78, 81–109, 112, 114–24, 126–40, 142–67

Subject Index

catholicity, ix–x, 1–13, 15–18, 20–21, 23, 25–29, 31, 33–34, 40, 44, 73, 85, 87–90, 93–98, 102, 105–06, 108–09, 112, 116–17, 121, 123, 128–29, 133, 136–37, 143, 147, 153–60, 163–67
catholicization, 1–2, 6–7, 110–17, 120–21, 124, 126–27, 129, 183
Chalcedon, chalcedonian, Chalcedon Definition, 20, 70, 95–96, 114, 121–22
character/s, 39, 43, 49, 53, 121n31, 128, 136n13, 144, 148–49, 154, 158, 164
characterization, 50-51, 53, 54
Christian, x–xi, 2, 10, 13, 14n14, 15-16, 18–21, 27–29, 30n47, 31n51, 32, 45–46, 48–49, 58–59, 61, 63–67, 69, 71, 73, 75–76, 79, 80–84, 86–90, 96n18, 98n23, 100n27, 102n31, 110n3, 111, 112n6, 113n9, 114, 116–22, 125–27, 129–30, 133, 135–37, 139–40, 142–51, 153–66
Christianity, 5, 10, 15n15, 17n17, 18–19, 21,
42n38, 65–67, 75, 76n32, 77n35, 78–82, 96–97, 125, 137, 147, 158–59, 163
Christ and Culture, 159
christlike, 154
christlikeness, 154
christocentric, 14, 15, 96, 119
christocentricity, 119
church fathers, 4, 13–14, 17–18, 25, 33, 75, 77, 87–88, 95, 104, 118, 126, 150
commitment/s, x– xi, 5, 23, 30–32, 91, 101–02, 118, 145, 150
commission, 3–4, 9, 11, 33, 47, 49, 74, 105, 135–36, 159
communion, 3, 29, 37, 68, 92–93, 95, 102, 104, 109, 131
communism, 81
community, xi, 3-4, 8–13, 26, 37–38, 41, 45–48, 54–56, 60–61, 67, 85, 90, 92, 94, 98, 101, 104–06, 108–09, 114–16, 122–24, 130, 132, 134–36, 139, 143–44, 146–47, 152, 160, 164n9
concupiscentia, 144
cupiditas, 144

congregation, xi, 14–16, 75, 79, 88, 91, 118, 131–32, 137, 139, 141, 166–67
confession/s, x, 5, 7, 10, 13–5, 17, 19, 31–32, 41, 62–66, 69–70, 73, 77, 82–83, 87, 91, 96, 102, 114, 117, 122–24, 128–30, 139, 143, 149, 157, 163
conflict/s, 23–24, 33, 45, 69, 73, 96, 115, 121n31
connection/s, 6, 15, 17, 25, 44, 634, 91, 132, 158
context/s, x, 3–4, 16, 35–36, 39, 40n9, 42–45, 52, 55, 59, 64, 69, 80, 83–84, 87, 95, 98, 108, 111, 113, 115, 117, 119, 121, 123, 128, 132, 134–35, 143–44, 146, 148, 155, 159, 160, 162
contextual, 5, 113–15, 127
contextualization, 45n14, 46n16, 50n22, 112–16, 119, 127, 152
council/s, 20–21, 23, 30, 34, 58, 73–75, 89, 95, 120, 141–42
covenant, 5, 11, 36–44, 47–48, 55–56, 79, 90, 97, 99, 129–30
creed/s, ix, 13–14, 17, 20, 27, 29, 57, 64–65, 67–70, 73, 75, 86, 95–96, 101, 114, 116, 118, 121–24, 126, 139–41, 149, 157–58, 172
criticism/s, 28, 45, 51, 87, 107, 121
culture, xii, 45, 57, 78, 112–16, 119, 121, 125–27, 152, 159, 163
custodian, 107

D

demythologize, demythologized, demythologizing, 15, 83, 151–5 2
deviate, 61, 156
deviation/s, 4–5, 21–22, 26, 69, 75, 120, 132, 147
denomination/s, 3, 27-28, 30, 109, 111–13, 117, 127, 132, 145
denominational
unity, 111
cooperation, 111
distinctive, 140
emphasis, 150
unique identities, 153

Subject Index

denominational/ism, 79, 83, 85, 108, 157
dialogue/s, x–xi, 32, 52, 106, 113, 148, 149n28
disciple/s, x–xii, 1–5, 8–13, 28, 47, 49, 53–55, 60–62, 64, 86, 92, 98–99, 105, 110–112, 125, 128–30, 135–36, 139, 144, 159, 164
discipleship, 8, 9, 35n1, 148
distinctive/s, 11, 12, 21, 85, 108, 117, 140, 150
diversity, 6, 27, 29, 31–33, 81, 85, 92–94, 112, 123n34, 158, 165
divine, 5, 9, 14, 21–22, 26–27, 33, 37n4, 43, 50, 59, 85, 88, 94, 96–97, 102, 127, 133–34, 136, 138, 143, 149, 159
division/s, x, 21–22, 28, 87, 91–92, 103, 117, 125, 135
doctrine, ix, 16–19, 21–22, 25, 27, 32, 58, 63, 69, 73–75, 77–80, 95–97, 102, 111–12, 117–20, 122–24, 128–29, 133–34, 140, 142–43, 147, 149–51, 156, 165
doctrinal, 18, 26–27, 31, 69, 77, 85, 129, 139–40, 147, 150, 156
dogmatic, 26-27, 79, 96, 123, 137, 156, 158
dogmatism, 27–28, 31, 158, 166
dynamic, 3–6, 28, 33, 49, 50n21, 54, 58, 60, 62, 79, 80, 83–84, 86, 91, 92n12, 94, 105n41, 106, 109, 130–31, 151–53, 160, 163
dynamism, 94

E

early catholicism, 55
early church, 4, 10–13, 33, 44, 54–55, 60n8, 62, 64, 69, 77, 88, 95, 116, 118, 123, 147, 152, 158–59, 162
eccentric, 69, 112, 147
ecclēsia, 40, 79–80, 94, 104, 145
ecclesiastical, 21–22, 26, 29, 33–34, 55, 58, 69, 73–74, 77, 91, 93, 112, 117, 137, 149, 155–56
ecclesiasticism, 17, 19
ecclēsiolae, 79, 80
ecclesiology, ix, 103, 104n38, 118

ecumenical, xii, 6–7, 20, 27–31, 33–34, 84–85, 111, 134, 136–37, 161, 165
ecumenicity, 29, 85, 165
emerging church, 8, 110, 133
encounter, 14, 39, 82–83, 161
eschatological, 6, 56, 108, 151, 160–61, 163
eschatology, 108
essence, 23, 28, 113, 138, 144–45, 152, 156, 160
eternal/eternal Life, 37, 52, 71, 82, 102, 120, 141, 151–52
ethnocentric, 39, 47, 56
ethnocentricity, 39
ethnocentricism, 43
evangelical/s, ix, xii, 13, 24–25, 29–35, 63, 76, 80–84, 87, 97, 101–02, 104, 108, 111–13, 115, 121, 126, 139, 148, 150, 161, 165
euangelion, 101
evangelism, 29, 31–32n21, 112–13, 136–38, 143–44, 148, 163n8
evangelist, 11, 31, 44–45, 47, 52, 64, 83, 102, 112
evangelistic, 89, 116, 125, 138
evolution, 5, 27, 33, 69, 82, 86–88, 92, 109
exclusive, x, 12–13, 18, 43–45, 50, 52, 55, 83, 97, 111, 115, 118, 120–21
existence, 8, 21, 23, 31, 43, 48, 54, 119, 155
existential, 13, 83, 129–30, 133, 144, 150–51, 161
expansion, 48–50, 54–55, 61, 105, 116
experience, xii, 12–16, 23–25, 29, 32, 43, 47–48, 54, 64, 66, 80, 82, 85, 90–91, 94, 111, 113n11, 118n24, 121n30, 123–27, 133–34, 139, 152, 156–57, 163

F

factions, 91, 135
faith, x–xii, 7, 11, 13, 16–21, 23–49, 50–53, 57–61, 63–67, 69, 73, 75–85, 89–96, 98, 100–03, 106–08, 110–15, 118–24, 126–28, 130–32, 134, 136–40, 144–67
foundations, 7, 82, 165, 166

Subject Index

fulfilled, 3–5, 24, 35–36, 40, 44–45, 50, 56, 59–61, 92, 99, 129, 135–36
fulfillment, 3–6, 12, 16, 38, 42, 45–48, 56, 61, 107–08, 112, 136, 151, 168
function, 3, 33, 43, 73, 87, 91, 93, 102, 106, 108, 114n11, 117, 123, 127, 130, 133, 135, 156
function/s, Functional, 3, 33, 43, 73, 87, 91, 93, 102, 106, 108, 114, 117, 123, 127, 130, 133, 135, 156

G

gentile, x, 12–16, 45–50, 52, 65, 91, 98, 101, 106, 108, 115–16, 135, 152
geographical, 11, 17, 49–50, 54, 87, 105, 116
geography, 88, 109, 132
gift, 3, 6, 12, 33–34, 38–39, 54, 59, 75, 93, 98, 100–01, 110, 119, 126, 135, 143, 155
gospel/s, x, 1–2, 8–14, 19–20, 23, 25, 28, 30–31, 33–34, 36n2, 44–55, 60–64, 76, 82–85, 89, 98, 101–03, 106–08, 110n2, 112–13, 115–16, 118, 121, 125–28n1, 152n7, 136, 139–40, 148, 150, 152–53, 160–63, 165–66
grace, 12n12, 15, 24-25, 32, 37n6, 38, 41, 51, 62n12, 63, 70n25, 73n27, 75–77n34, 80–81, 89n8, 90, 97, 100–01, 104, 106n42, 107–08, 110––11, 117n18, 118n24, 119, 126–30, 133, 166

H

hermeneutics, 121, 157
herald, 92, 102, 106
heresies, 67, 85–87, 94, 104, 119, 121–22, 147
heresy, 94, 96
heretics, 5, 7, 18, 20, 22–23, 60, 73, 87, 94, 109, 120, 147–48, 157
heritage, 46, 112, 126, 138–39
hierarchy, 19, 76, 137, 153
history, 3–5, 8, 14, 18n24, 22n31, 26, 28, 30, 33, 35–37, 39–46, 49, 52, 54, 57, 59, 61, 65, 66n18, 67n20, 75n30, 77n34, 78n37, 79n39, 83–84, 99, 107–09, 111, 121, 131–32, 134, 139, 163
holiness, 5, 14, 78, 80–81, 98, 116n18, 142, 146–47, 149–51, 153, 162
human, humanity, 2, 5, 9, 14, 16, 30–34, 37, 42–43, 49–50, 57, 63, 72, 82, 84–85, 89n8, 91, 96, 99, 119, 122, 126–27, 129, 133, 138, 149, 159, 162, 166

I

identity, 2–4, 6–7, 9–10, 13–14, 16–18, 39, 41, 45, 48, 52–56, 58, 64, 73, 87–88, 94, 115, 124–25, 128, 132–33
illumination, 58, 74
image/s, 35–36, 56, 88, 93, 97, 104, 106, 118, 130, 163
incipient, 4, 11, 12
incarnate, 14, 53, 68, 120
inclusive, x, 4, 11–12, 14, 44, 46–47, 50, 52, 55, 87–89, 98, 103, 109, 116, 120, 138, 145
independent, 14, 16, 33–34, 40, 44, 88–89, 94, 109, 112, 133, 139, 140
individualism, 124, 147
indulgence, 74, 75, 79
indulgentia, 22, 75, 76, 79
inspiration, x–xi, 62, 65, 67, 74
institutes, x, 77, 92, 159
institution/s, 17, 30, 33, 37, 78, 80, 92–93, 100, 121, 135, 138, 155
insufficient, 58, 74, 84
intellectual, intellectualism, 14, 19, 26, 73, 78–79, 125, 153
interdependence, 88, 89
international, internationalization, xi–xii, 30n46, 116, 121
Israel, 4, 9, 10–12, 35–52, 54, 56, 59–61, 83, 97, 108n47, 115, 145, 151
interpretation, 16–17, 23, 26, 57–58, 60, 69, 73–74, 76, 78, 81, 83–85, 95, 109, 111, 114, 121, 129, 140, 142, 147, 151, 157–58
institution/s, institutional, institutionalized, 17, 30, 33, 37n4, 78, 80, 92–93, 100, 121, 135, 138, 155

Subject Index

J

Jews, x, 10–13, 16, 45–47, 49–50, 52–53, 65, 91, 97–98, 101, 115–16, 121–22, 135, 152

just, justice, justification, 23–25, 27, 32, 73, 75, 77, 80, 98, 101–02, 104, 107–08, 141, 149–53, 162

K

king, 10, 21, 46, 47, 53, 163

kingdom, 1–2, 5–6, 9–10, 21, 30, 36, 40, 42, 45–46, 47, 56, 59–63, 65, 67–68, 70, 76, 85, 94, 96–97, 101, 106–108, 115, 132–33, 143–44, 146, 151–53, 159–60, 162–63

kingship, 36n2, 46, 162

koinonia, 90

kosmos, 9

L

language, 17, 36, 54, 57, 91, 93, 131, 150, 161-62

latitudinarianism, 164–67

leader/s, leadership, xi–xii, 5, 12, 19–20, 25, 28, 51, 55, 74, 79–80, 89, 95, 100, 105, 116, 135, 145, 158

liberal, liberalism, 26, 28, 30n47, 31, 81–82, 114, 119, 162

liberation, 28, 30, 41, 50, 81–82, 113, 162

liberty, 64, 166

literary approach, 121

liturgy, 62, 124, 145–46

lord, lordship, x–xi, xiii, 2, 9–10, 14n14, 15, 23, 32, 34, 42, 50, 60, 62–66, 68, 70–72, 88, 90–92, 95, 97, 100, 103, 105, 110, 115, 118–19, 126, 130–32, 140, 142, 151, 160, 164, 166

love, x–xi, 4, 7, 13–14, 24, 36, 52, 59, 67, 78, 81, 94, 102, 106, 111, 125, 130–31, 135, 138, 143–44, 147, 154–55, 159, 162–67

M

mark/s, 4–6, 10, 13, 18, 31, 40, 73, 86–88, 98, 100, 106n43, 108–09, 116–17, 128, 130, 159

magisterium, 108

mediator, 31, 32, 105

mediatorial, 97

messiah, 10–11, 42–43, 46–47, 52–53, 59, 61, 63–65

Methodist/s, 29, 80, 132, 158, 162

militant, 63, 84, 95, 103, 104

ministry, x, xii, 1–2, 5, 9, 17, 34–35, 44–45, 47–48, 50–55, 59–61, 64, 77, 86, 89, 90, 109, 111–12, 114–15, 127, 135, 139, 142, 148, 157, 161–62

model/s, 8n3, 9n5, 10n10, 92–93, 97, 102, 104, 113n9, 124n37, 163n8

mystery/s, 88, 92, 94, 97

mystical, 92, 104

myth, mythology, 82–83, 127

N

Narrative Criticism, 45, 121

nation/s, x, 2–4, 9–12, 33, 37–49, 51–52, 54–56, 61–62, 65, 90, 92, 99, 103, 105, 108, 114–16, 120, 129, 135–36, 140, 145, 159–62

Nicene Creed, ix, 20, 27, 68–69, 86, 121

O

objective, objectively, x, 13, 14, 36, 38–39, 58, 60–61, 84, 91, 111, 119, 126, 133–34, 136, 156

office/s, 74, 93, 102n34, 121, 149, 158

offspring/s, 37–38, 44, 46–48, 56, 99, 129–30, 165

one, ix–xiii, 2–3, 5–10, 12–20, 22, 25–29, 31–34, 36–40, 42, 46, 48, 50–53, 55–56, 59, 61–62, 64–65, 67–74, 77–80, 83, 86–94, 96–99, 103–05, 108–11, 113, 116–18, 122–36, 138, 140, 142–46, 148–50, 153–55, 157–59, 161, 163–64, 166–67

ontology, 127

Subject Index

ontological, 7, 102, 106, 117, 130
organic, 58, 69, 110, 129, 133
orthodox, orthodoxy, x, 18, 22–23, 25–28, 32, 78–79, 82–83, 89, 94–95, 108, 125, 129, 158–59

P

paradoxical, 127
participation, 3, 29, 31, 41–43, 90, 109, 111, 134–36
Patriarch/s, 38–40, 42, 172
Pentecost, 9, 11–12, 54, 98–100
Pentecostal, 31–32, 98, 108, 142–43
people/s, 4, 9–12, 14n14, 15–16, 35, 38, 40–54, 56–57, 59–61, 65, 79, 82, 86, 88–91, 94, 96, 98, 106–07, 109, 113, 115–16, 120, 124n35, 128–129, 131–37, 141, 143, 148–49, 151, 155, 160–62
pietism, 31, 78–79, 80, 136, 147, 158, 159
pietist/s, 28, 79–80, 137, 147, 149, 159, 162
plot, 36, 45–46, 49, 50, 53, 115
plurality, 94, 165
poor, x, 49–51, 80, 161
Pope/s, 20–23, 74, 93, 102, 120
postmodernism, 114, 115n14
practice/s, 22–23, 25, 31, 66–67, 73, 75–77, 84, 88, 93–94, 106, 112, 115, 117, 120, 122, 124, 126, 129, 140, 156–57, 166–67
practical, 19–20, 22, 27, 77–79, 113–14, 127–30, 134, 137, 150, 153, 156, 158, 161, 165
praxis, 59, 110, 113, 120, 124, 127, 129, 165
prayer, x–xi, 6–7, 9, 23, 29, 79–80, 91, 101, 109–19, 117, 123, 125, 134–36, 138–39, 144, 146, 157, 159–60, 166
preaching, 23, 49, 59–60, 62, 66, 83, 101–02, 139, 143, 162
presence, 1, 12, 14–15, 21, 48, 61, 89, 92, 119, 143, 151, 155, 162
promise/s, 3–5, 10–13, 37–47, 52, 54, 56, 98, 100, 107, 151, 161

promotion, 134, 136
prophecy, 11n11, 48, 61
Prophet/s, 19, 42–43, 62, 68, 70, 83, 86, 107, 111, 134, 140, 154, 156
prophetic, 3, 62, 139
protestant/s, ix, 19, 22, 26–31, 33n53, 63, 75, 77–78, 80, 82–83, 87, 89, 97, 100, 109, 112, 117, 120, 123, 126, 135, 139, 151, 153, 158

R

rational, 14, 78, 134, 149, 166
rationalism, 27–28, 78, 81
reason, 2–4, 7, 22, 66, 87, 92n12, 97–98, 121n30, 133, 137, 147–49, 156, 161
reconciliation, 30n47, 36, 43, 143, 155, 160, 166
reconstruction, 157
redemption, 2, 10, 30, 34, 36–37, 40, 56, 61, 92n12, 98–99, 106, 146, 159, 162
redemptive, 3, 5, 28, 35–37, 39–40, 42–46, 49–50, 52, 54, 56, 59–61, 85, 106–08, 129, 151–52, 156
reformed, 22, 26, 32, 77, 78, 115, 139, 143, 150, 158
reformation, x, 4–5, 7, 19, 21–27, 31, 33, 57, 73–80, 93, 102n31, 109, 112, 114, 117, 121n29, 150, 153, 156, 158–59
religion, 5, 27–28, 43, 66–67, 71, 78, 93–94, 96, 114, 124, 129, 137–38, 140, 147, 149, 155, 158–59
repentance, 50–51, 91, 98
responsibility, 2, 6, 9, 11, 55, 89, 92, 110–11, 133–35, 140, 142, 145
revival/s, 4, 28–29, 80–82, 109, 118
righteous, Righteousness, 23–25, 36, 38, 51, 101, 120, 151–52
rituals, 165
ritualistic, 79
Roman (Roman Catholic), x, 4, 13–14, 17–27, 29, 32–33, 48, 58, 65–66, 75, 77, 78n36, 82–83, 87, 89n7, 93, 97, 100–01, 102n34, 109, 112, 116n18, 117, 123–24, 139, 150, 157–59, 163

Subject Index

S

sacrament/s, 17, 32, 62, 76, 79, 92, 101, 117, 141
sacred, 18, 27, 124
salvation, 2, 14, 17–18, 30, 31n51, 32, 37, 43n13, 45–46, 50–51, 60–61, 68, 70, 72, 75–76, 80, 85, 89, 99–101, 103, 105, 107, 116, 140–41, 152
sanctification, 14, 80, 98, 150–51, 162
save, 25, 46, 48, 62, 70, 72–73, 105–07, 109, 160
savior, xiii, 9, 32, 34, 46, 50–51, 84, 131
scholasticism, 26, 78–79, 93
secular, 27, 82, 124, 125, 159
secularism, 27, 29, 125
secularization, 78, 81, 125–26
servant, xii, 62–63, 92, 100–01, 106, 129
socio-economic, 152
socio-political, 82, 152
Scripture, x, 5, 12, 14n14, 16, 22–23, 25–27, 31–32, 36, 58–59 61–62, 64–65, 68–69, 73–79, 81–85, 113n11, 117, 120–23, 126, 129–30, 134, 140–42, 147–48, 150, 156–58, 161, 165
secularization, 78, 81, 125–26
sect, sectarian, sectarianism, x, 11, 89–90, 139, 140, 150, 158
sola scriptura, 22–23, 25, 75–78, 82–83, 120, 123, 156
source, 7, 22, 31, 58, 74, 76–77, 82–84, 118, 120–21, 124, 133–34, 140, 150, 156
statistics, 109
story, 8–11, 13, 14n14, 15, 17, 19, 21, 23, 25, 27, 29, 31, 33, 36–46, 48, 53, 54, 56, 81
subjective, x, 13n14, 14n14, 36, 38–39, 58, 62, 79, 85, 91, 98, 111, 119, 121, 126, 130, 133–34, 144, 156–57
subordinationism, 69
sufficiency, 141, 156
supplementary, 121, 156
systematic, 16, 26–27, 73, 79, 86n1, 127, 129

T

theological, ix, xii, 3–7, 12–15, 17, 19–22, 25–27, 31–33, 35, 37, 39, 44, 47, 52–54, 57–59, 64, 69, 73–84, 87–90, 92–97, 102, 104–06, 109–13, 118–24, 126–29, 139–40, 147, 151, 156–58, 161, 179
theology, xi–xii, 12–13, 19, 21–23, 26–28, 30–31, 35, 38, 45, 53n28, 55, 59–60, 64n15, 67, 73, 75–79, 81–84, 86, 89, 94–96, 100n26, 104, 107n44, 108n47, 11, 113–15, 117–18, 120–21, 124n36, 125, 127, 129–30, 136n13, 139, 146, 152–53, 156–58, 161–62, 165–66
totalitarianism, 81
tradition/s, 4–6, 10, 13, 17, 19–23, 26, 32–33, 41, 50, 53, 57–63, 65, 69, 73–85, 88, 95, 96n18, 100n27, 104, 109, 115, 120, 121n30, 123, 139–40, 142–43, 150, 151, 157, 158
traditional, 30, 87, 101, 109, 142, 151,
traditionalism, 75,
traditioning, 85, 158
Trinity, 13, 14n14, 19, 27, 69–70, 72–73, 90, 95, 98, 99n25, 109, 117–20, 122, 134n9, 140, 144, 146, 151n31
trinitarian, 32, 69, 118–119, 122
tritheism, 69
triumphant, 63, 84, 95, 103–04, 108, 123
triune, xi, 32–33, 117–18, 120, 124, 126, 155
true, 10, 13–134, 17–18, 21, 30–31, 40, 45, 52, 58, 60, 73, 75, 78, 86–87, 90, 93, 96–97, 99–100, 105, 106, 112, 114, 117, 131, 145, 156, 158, 165
truth, 14n14, 16, 23, 25, 31n50, 32–33, 37, 45, 47, 63, 76, 82, 85, 90, 96–99, 102, 104–08, 112, 114, 116, 119–20, 122, 123n33, 126, 129–30, 133–36, 142, 149, 163–65, 167

U

union, 17, 70, 130–32, 143, 164
united, x, 26, 29, 33, 42, 85, 91, 96, 117, 127, 130–32, 137, 142, 144, 166–67

Subject Index

unity, ix, 5–7, 13–17, 19, 21, 27–34, 55, 58, 60n7, 64, 69–70, 72–73, 81, 84–86, 90–91, 93–94, 98, 109–27, 130–32, 134, 136–38, 143–46, 153, 156, 163, 167

universal, ix, 2, 6, 9, 12, 15, 17–19, 37–38, 40, 43–47, 58, 61, 73, 87–90, 92–95, 97–99, 101, 108, 117, 121, 132, 145, 151–52, 157, 159–60, 167

universality, 12, 18, 87–89, 96n19, 116n18

V

validity, 14, 63, 74
Vatican, 58, 78
vicissitude, 4–5, 38, 42, 134
victory, 18, 66–67, 104–105, 162

W

way, xi, xiii, 2, 6, 11–12, 14–15, 19, 30, 45–46, 55, 57, 73, 78, 83–84, 89, 96, 99, 101, 107, 114, 117, 122, 124, 126–28, 134, 143, 147–48, 150, 153, 155, 158, 163–64, 166

Wesleyan, 48, 81, 124, 142–43, 149, 150–51
west, 4, 18, 90, 112, 123, 131, 137, 147
western, 19, 39, 125, 145, 163
witness/es, x, 4, 7, 11, 31, 34, 43, 49, 54–55, 58–59, 61–62, 66, 83, 91, 94, 101, 103, 107, 114, 118, 123, 125, 128–29, 131, 134, 136–40, 118, 123, 128, 129, 131, 134, 136–37, 137–40, 143–46, 153, 156

word, x, xii–xiii, 1–15, 17, 21, 24, 27, 29–31, 33, 36, 41–42, 49–50, 52–55, 59–60, 64–69, 72, 78, 81, 83–84, 89–91, 94, 96, 99, 101, 104–09, 111, 113, 125–29, 131–32, 136–40, 143–44, 148–49, 151–53, 155, 159–65

worship, 8, 14, 18, 41, 57, 68–73, 79, 93, 118, 123–24, 128, 130–31, 146–47, 155, 163n8, 164–67

Y

yardstick, 18, 122
YHWH, 9, 64

www.ingramcontent.com/pod-product-compliance
Lightning Source LLC
Chambersburg PA
CBHW062041220426
43662CB00010B/1603